The Body in Everyday Life

We all have a body, but how does it impact upon our day-to-day life? How we experience our bodies is at once both intensely personal and extremely public. This book sets out to explore how ordinary women, men and children talk about their bodies and how they experience them in a variety of situations. The material is approached through four main themes: physical and emotional bodies; illness and disability; gender; and ageing.

The Body in Everyday Life is the first coherent collection of empirical research on this subject and a welcome complement to important theoretical and philosophical developments in this field. The volume brings together a number of leading authors and researchers culminating in a new and fresh approach to the study of the body. This book will be of particular interest to students of sociology, health studies and cultural studies.

Sarah Nettleton is Lecturer in Social Policy in the Department of Social Policy and Social Work, University of York.

Jonathan Watson is Director of Research and Evaluation at the Health Education Board for Scotland in Edinburgh.

The Body in
Everyday Life

Edited by
Sarah Nettleton
and Jonathan Watson

London and New York

First published 1998 by Routledge
11 New Fetter Lane, London EC4P 4EE

Simultaneously published in the USA and Canada
by Routledge
29 West 35th Street, New York, NY 10001

Typeset in Bembo by Florencetype Ltd, Stoodleigh, Devon
Printed and bound in Great Britain by T.J. International Ltd, Padstow, Cornwall

British Library Cataloguing in Publication Data
A catalogue record for this book is available from the British Library

Library of Congress Cataloguing in Publication Data
The body in everyday life / Sarah Nettleton and Jonathan Watson.
  p. - cm.
Includes bibliographical references and index.
1. Body, Human–Social aspects. 2. Mind and body.
3. Social medecine. I. Nettleton, Sarah, 1960–
HM110.B6   1998
306.4–dc21   97–44695
                                                  CIP

ISBN 0–415–16200–9 (hbk)
ISBN 0–415–16201–7 (pbk)

Contents

PART II
Health and illness

101

PART III
Gender

161

PART IV
Ageing

241

Figures

Contributors

Kathryn Backett-Milburn, Senior Research Fellow at the Research Unit in Health and Behavioural Change, University of Edinburgh.

Julie H. Barlow, Director of the Psychosocial Rheumatology Research Centre in the School of Health and Social Sciences at Coventry University.

Gillian A. Bendelow, Lecturer in Applied Social Studies at the University of Warwick.

Michael Bloor, Senior Lecturer and Director of the Social Research Unit at the University of Wales, Cardiff.

Cathryn Britton, Midwifery Tutor in the Department of Health Studies at the University of York.

Bill Bytheway, Researcher at the Department of Sociology and Anthropology at the University of Wales, Swansea.

Sarah Cunningham-Burley, Senior Lecturer in Medical Sociology, Department of Public Health Sciences at the University of Edinburgh.

Rebecca E. Dobash, Professor of Social Policy in the Department of Social Policy at the University of Manchester.

Russell P. Dobash, Professor of Social Policy in the Department of Social Policy at the University of Manchester.

Eileen Fairhurst, Course Leader of the BA in Health Studies at Manchester Metropolitan University.

Mike Featherstone, Research Professor of Sociology and Communication at Nottingham Trent University.

Mike Hepworth, Reader in Sociology, Department of Sociology, University of Aberdeen.

Paul Higate, doctoral student in the Social Policy and Social Work Department at the University of York.

Alexandra Howson, Lecturer in Sociology, Department of Sociology, University of Aberdeen.

Julia Johnson, Lecturer in Health and Social Welfare at the Open University.

Deborah Lupton, Associate Professor in Cultural Studies at the School of Social Sciences and Liberal Studies, Charles Stuart University, Australia.

Emily Martin, Professor of Anthropology at Princeton University, New Jersey.

Lee Monaghan, Research Associate at the University of Wales, Cardiff.

Sarah Nettleton, Lecturer in Social Policy, Department of Social Policy and Social Work, University of York.

Jonathan Watson, Director of Research and Evaluation at the Health Education Board for Scotland, Edinburgh.

Bethan Williams, Research Assistant at the Psychosocial Rheumatology Research Centre in the School of Health and Social Sciences at Coventry University.

Simon J. Williams, Research Fellow at the University of Warwick.

Acknowledgements

We are very grateful to Heather Gibson and Fiona Bailey at Routledge for their support and help during the production of this book. We are also grateful to Roger Burrows for his helpful suggestions and comments. Thanks are due to Suzanne Manclark at the Health Education Board for Scotland for her word processing and technical support.

Chapter 1

The body in everyday life

An introduction

Sarah Nettleton and Jonathan Watson

If one thing is certain, it is that we all have a body. Everything we do we do with our bodies – when we think, speak, listen, eat, sleep, walk, relax, work and play we 'use' our bodies. Every aspect of our lives is therefore embodied. Sometimes we may be more aware of our bodies than others but from the moment we wake, we are to a greater or lesser extent, consciously or sub-consciously relying on our body. When we wake up in the morning we may automatically leave our beds and go to the bathroom and carry out our morning 'bodily' routines. Some of us, however, may do this less instinctively, and find that our body is cradled so comfortably within its 'nest' that extricating it from the bed becomes something of a challenge. This may be compounded by the fact that during the previous evening we poured large quantities of alcohol into our bodies and are then, in the morning, struck by the fact that our head is 'pounding', that we have a 'raging' thirst and a 'rasping' throat. For some 'bodies', perhaps those who are babies, or have certain forms of disability, getting out of bed might be something which requires the help of other 'bodies', be they those of parents, carers or partners, or perhaps other technical aids. Once we are 'up' we then prepare our body for public display, we probably groom it and select some clothes which might be appropriate for whatever we are doing on that particular day. We may look at our body in the mirror and notice bodily changes: yet another grey hair, the size of our stomach, a spot that has just appeared on our chin. Even the most minor bodily changes may, for some of us, impact upon how we feel about facing the day and all the social interactions that it may comprise. It may be that the spot on the chin occurred on the day of an interview, a wedding or an eighteenth birthday party.

The extent to which we are conscious of our bodies and how we feel about them will vary throughout our lives and within different social contexts. During our teenage years for example, we are likely to become especially sensitive to the biological changes which our bodies endure and our altered appearance. Such changes can impact upon our social relationships. Our body–image, how we perceive our body, may in turn affect our ability to relate to others and will influence how others respond to us. The physical changes associated with ageing must also figure prominently in how we feel about ourselves, and are tangible reminders of our mortality. A sprained back, the loss of hair, a trip to the optician only to discover that one can no longer read *all* the letters on the optician's eye-test chart, may be an incident which triggers off reflection about the trajectory of one's life.

Everyday life is therefore fundamentally about the production and reproduction of bodies. Given the centrality of the body to everyday life, and the fact that it is something that all humans share, it is perhaps surprising that there has been so little empirical investigation into the body as it is experienced by human beings, who both *have* and *are* bodies. In particular, there has been little research which involves engaging ordinary men and women in talk about their personal bodily experiences. There is however a whole industry of research and scholarship on the body. During the 1990s books have been published on the body (e.g. Gatens 1996; Turner 1996, 1992; Falk 1994; Grosz 1994; Shilling 1993; Featherstone *et al.* 1991; Leder 1990); conferences have chosen the body as their theme; new journals such as *Body and Society* have been launched; and students of sociology and cultural studies are offered courses on 'the body'.

Ironically, whilst only in the late 1980s, sociologists were lamenting the absence of the body from sociology, the sociology of the body has, by and large, ignored the voices that emanate from bodies themselves. This is mainly because this sphere of study tends to suffer from theoreticisim, a condition which implies that attention is limited to theory, which in turn is not grounded in the empirical domain.[1] Perhaps this is to some extent understandable because the study of the body does raise a whole series of philosophical and theological issues. However the lack of empirical data on the body as it is experienced is in marked contrast to a number of related areas of study, prime amongst which is the sociology of chronic illness and disability. Clearly the work in this field offers important insights into our understanding of the body, it has been dominated by research into the *experience* of chronic illness and disability, and as such has yielded rich empirical data (see for example Anderson and Bury 1988; Charmaz 1983).

The aim of this volume is to bring together a range of empirical studies which have examined how people experience their bodies from the perspectives of the people themselves. As such it 'fills a gap' in the literature on the sociology of the body. Just as investigations which have empirically explored the experience of the illness have generated valuable data which help to develop our sociological appreciation of concepts such as the relationship between the body, self and identity, we hope that the empirical material presented in this collection may be used by sociologists to reflect upon the recent debates within the sociology of the body. In this respect our aim is a modest one. We do not aspire to transform our sociological appreciation of the body, rather we try to inject the contemporary debates with some more grounded material. Approaching the literature in this field of study for the first time can be a rather alienating experience for the student or scholar, again this is rather ironic as the body is something that we all have in common. This is a view neatly captured by Wacquant (1995) who did in fact undertake an ethnographic study of boxers:

> One of the paradoxical features of recent social studies of the body is how rarely one encounters in them actual living bodies of flesh and blood. The books that have appeared in recent years on the topic . . . typically offer precious few insights into the actual practices and representations that constitute the human body as an 'ongoing practical achievement', to borrow an expression from Garfinkel. . . . [T]he newer sociology of the body has paid surprisingly little focused attention to the diverse ways in which specific social worlds invest, shape, and deploy human bodies and to the concrete incorporating practices whereby their social structures are effectively embodied by the agents who partake of them.
>
> (Wacquant 1995: 65)

What all the chapters in this volume have in common is that their analyses of the body derive from the point of view of 'the agents who partake of them'. All the studies take an embodied perspective, that is they assume that action and lived experience may be grasped from the vantage point of the actor who is invariably *embodied*.

Whilst the aim is to counter the overly theoretical trend within the sociology of the body we do not want to lapse into overt empiricism. In particular there are certain wider social transformations which have both given rise to sociology's recent interest in the body, and which shape how we currently experience our bodies. A central thrust of contemporary studies of the body is, after Foucault (1979), that the body itself has a history and so it is possible to write the history of the body (for a fascinating example see Duden 1991). Any analysis of empirical data must be placed in a broader context. It is for this reason that we briefly review the social transformations which have precipitated the current interest in the body. Analyses of empirical data are also shaped by or draw upon (albeit implicitly or explicitly) certain theoretical perspectives on the body. The various dominant perspectives on the body have been extensively reviewed elsewhere (see Nettleton 1995; Shilling 1993; Turner 1992) and so there is no need to re-rehearse them in any great depth here. However, some attention will be devoted to the more phenomenological approaches which do appear to be particularly pertinent to the study of the body as it is experienced. When we examine the body in everyday life, we might therefore more accurately speak of a *sociology of embodiment* rather than a *sociology of the body*. Having set this context we will then delineate some of the themes which have emerged from this collection. We have organised these under the following headings: the 'taken-for-grantedness' of the body; bodily controls, body-image and gender.

Social change and the body

There is a consensus in the literature that the growing salience of the body is related to a number of factors (Turner 1996, 1992; Nettleton 1995; Shilling 1993). First, there has been something of a *politisation of the body*. It was the work of feminist writers and activities which has been of importance here in that they revealed the political status of the body and demonstrated how it was a medium through which women have been exploited by men. An example of this is the way in which women have attempted to reclaim control over their own bodies from a male dominated medical profession. Writers and activists who are concerned with disability provide another illustration of the political status of the body (Oliver 1990). Turner (1992: 12–13) has argued that the body has come to form a central field of political and cultural activity, in that the major concerns for governments revolve around the regulation of bodies. To capture this he describes contemporary society as a 'somatic society'.

Second, *demographic factors* such as the 'greying of populations' have highlighted the changing nature of bodies. The processes associated with ageing now form a substantial field of study some of which are explored in this volume. Such changes raise moral and ethical debates on issues such as euthanasia, and again draw attention to tricky questions which pertain to the 'ownership' of bodies.

Another not unrelated transformation is the *changing nature of the disease burden*. Whilst people are living longer, they are not necessarily healthier as there has been a concurrent rise in people who suffer from long-standing limiting illnesses (Dunnell 1995). As we have already mentioned, chronic illness, like ageing, affords a substantial area of research, which is especially salient to our appreciation of embodiment (see for example Williams 1996; Helman 1990; Kleinman 1988; Murphy 1987). From this literature we have learned how biophysical changes have significant social consequences. The experience of chronic illness can impact upon the sufferers' daily living, their social relationships, their identity and their sense of self. Responses to chronic illness are not therefore simply determined by either the nature of biophysical symptoms or individual motivations, but rather are shaped and imbued by the social, cultural and ideological context of a person's biography. These insights have been developed predominantly by sociologists working within interpretative paradigms.

A third social change is one which is associated with modern industrial societies and that is the rise of the *consumer culture*. Featherstone (1991) and Glassner (1989) have pointed to the proliferation of commercial goods and services which are consumed by those who want to keep fit, retain their youthful appearance or simply 'maintain' their bodies. Appearance, Featherstone (1991: 186) argues, within this context becomes central to a person's social acceptability. This in turn, he maintains, has important implications for ageing.

A fourth way in which wider societal developments may precipitate interest in the body, and indeed impact upon how bodies are experienced, is the advent of *new technologies* (Williams 1997;

Featherstone and Burrows 1995). The boundaries between our physical and technological bodies are shifting more rapidly. In this merger of biological and technological technologies of corporeality 'the body is reconceptualized not as a fixed part of nature, but as a boundary concept' subject to 'an ideological tug-of-war between competing systems of meaning' (Balsamo 1995: 215). This is apparent, for example, in relation to differences between biomedical and feminist interpretations of the meaning of the menopause, and specifically hormone replacement therapy. In this context Wei Leng (1996) drawing on Haraway's cyborg myth (1991) comments that 'against the heritage of metaphysical thought-systems, there is only room for the powerfully heretical; there is only room for the cyborg' (Leng 1996: 49), a hybrid of machine and organism. This in turn may make us more uncertain about what our body is, where it begins and where it ends. Indeed, there is a degree of irony here, as Shilling (1993) has pointed out; the more we know about bodies, the more we are able to control, intervene and alter them, the more uncertain we become as to what the body actually is.

A further factor is the broader social transformations which are associated with the move from modernity to *late* or *high modernity*. The theme of uncertainty is central to the work of Giddens and a number of other commentators such as Beck (1992) and Douglas (1986) who have argued that a key feature of contemporary societies is *risk*. Doubt, Giddens (1991) argues, is a pervasive feature which permeates into everyday life 'and forms a general existential dimension of the contemporary social world'. Within post-traditional societies, our identities and our sense of self are not givens. That is, we can no longer hang on to, or derive our identity from our traditional place in society – be it class, family, gender, or locality. Rather our self and identity becomes 'a reflexively organised endeavour'. Less and less can we rely on continuous biographical narratives but these tend to be flexible and continually revised (see also Featherstone and Hepworth 1991). The reflexive self is one which relies on a vast array of advice and information provided in a myriad of sources. As Giddens points out, the self is of course embodied and so the regularised control of the body is a fundamental means whereby a biography of self-identity is maintained.

> The body used to be one aspect of nature, governed in a
> fundamental way by processes only marginally subject to

human intervention. The body was a 'given', the often incon-
venient and inadequate seat of the self. With the increasing
invasion of the body by abstract systems all this becomes
altered. The body, like the self, becomes a site of interaction,
appropriation and reappropriation, linking reflexively organised processes and systematically ordered expert knowledge.
. . . Once thought to be the locus of the soul . . . the body
has become fully available to be 'worked upon' by the influences of high modernity'. . . . In the conceptual space between
these, we find more and more guidebooks and practical
manuals to do with health, diet, appearance, exercise, love-
making and many other things.

(Giddens 1991: 218)

According to this thesis we are more uncertain about our bodies,
we perceive them to be more pliable and are actively seeking to
alter, improve and refine them. This of course, empirically, remains
to be seen.

Shilling (1993) also sees the *body as a project*. He argues that the
body might best be conceptualised as an unfinished biological and
social phenomenon, which is transformed, within limits, as a result
of its participation in society. For example, styles of walking, talking
and gestures are influenced by our upbringing. The body is therefore in a continual state of 'unfinishedness' the body is 'seen as an
entity which is in the process of becoming; a project which should
be worked at and accomplished as part of an individual's self
identity' (Shilling 1993: 5).

The idea that contemporary societies are characterised by change
and adaptability has also been postulated by Emily Martin (1994),
in her book *Flexible Bodies*. In contrast to the work of Giddens,
Beck and others, her thesis is based on an extensive empirical study
of American culture. By way of data collected via interviews,
analyses of documents, participant observation and informal
exchanges she has found that 'flexibility is an object of desire for
nearly everyone's personality, body and organisation' (Martin 1994:
xvii). Flexibility is associated with the notion of the immune system
which now underpins our thinking about the body, organisations,
machines, politics and so on. In her interviews with ordinary men
and women the idea of developing a strong immune system
appeared to be in common currency (see Martin, Chapter 3 in
this volume). To be effective, that is to protect the body against

the threats of disease and illness, the immune system must be able to change and constantly adapt. This work not only provides a valuable analysis of late modernity but also reveals how our accounts and interpretations of our bodies are historically and socially contingent, and that they are not 'immune' from broader social transformations. How we experience our bodies is invariably social.

Approaches to the study of the body

Within the theoretical debates on the body, tension revolves around the ontological status of the body, between the foundationalists, who assume that the biological basis of the body is a universal given and impinges on our experience of the body, and the anti-foundationalists who maintain that the body is simply an effect of discursive processes or contexts. This is mirrored by the debate between the social contructionists and the anti-constructionists. The former argue that the body is socially created. The body from this perspective is contingent on the social and discursive context in which it resides. The anti-constructionists on the other hand argue that the body exists independently of its social context, and like the foundationalists see it as a universal physical entity (for a fuller overview see Turner 1992). In practice, within the literature on the sociology of the body, much of the debate has focused on the *extent* to which the body is socially constructed. Most writers (Connell 1995; Scott and Morgan 1993; Shilling 1993; Turner 1992) argue that we ought to accept that the body has a material, biological base, and that this is altered and modified within different social contexts. As such they maintain that the body *is* socially constructed, but they may disagree about the mechanisms and processes which contribute to its social variability. In sum, they argue for a synthesis between these two perspectives. This debate need not concern us here because it is not central to the aims of the volume, suffice to say it is valuable to appreciate the socially contingent nature of the body, and how it is experienced will vary according to how, where and when it is located and the nature of the social relations which prevail.

What we are concerned with here is the salience of bodies to the creation and recreation of everyday life. How do people think about their bodies? Do people think about their bodies? How do people describe their bodies? How do people 'use' their bodies?

To what extent do the biological processes associated with people's bodies impact upon their daily routines and how they think about themselves? These are the sorts of questions that we are concerned to address within this collection. Given that our aim is to explore how the body is experienced in everyday life the theoretical insights gained from those working within the more phenomenological frameworks are likely to be useful.

Phenomenology: the 'lived body' and 'embodiment'

Attempts to integrate some of the approaches noted above have argued that a useful way out of this theoretical impasse is to develop the phenomenological approach to the study of the body (see for example Bendelow and Williams 1995; Csordas 1994; Leder 1992, 1990; Turner 1992). We see this not so much as a solution as an *alternative* approach which certainly offers a more appropriate starting point for our themes in the present volume. A basis for all sound research is using theories, methodologies and research techniques which are appropriate to the research problem, or issue in hand. Our concern is to examine how people experience their bodies and in particular how they articulate their experiences. Given this, we consider that the phenomenological and, more generally, interpretative approaches are the most appropriate paradigms to work within. This is what Turner refers to as 'methodological pragmatism', that is: 'the epistemological stand-point, theoretical orientation and methodological technique which a social scientist adopts, should at least in part be determined by the nature of the problem and by the level of explanation which is required' (1992: 57).

The phenomenological perspective focuses on the 'lived body', the idea that human beings and their consciousness is invariably embedded within the body. The human being is an embodied social agent. The work of Merleau-Ponty, in particular his text, *The Phenomenology of Perception* (1962), has been revisited, and it is regarded by many as critical to our appreciation of embodiment (see for example Crossley 1995; Csordas 1994). Essentially he argued that all human perception is embodied, we cannot perceive anything and our senses cannot function independently of our bodies. This does not imply that they are somehow 'glued' together, as the Cartesian notion of the body might suggest, but rather there is something of an oscillation between the two. This idea forms the basis of the notion of 'embodiment'. As Merleau-Ponty (1962) writes:

> Men [*sic*] taken as a concrete being is not a psyche joined to an organism, but movement to and from of existence which at one time allows itself to take corporeal form and at others moves towards personal acts. . . . It is never a question of the incomprehensive meeting of two casualties, nor of a collision between the order of causes and that of ends. But by an imperceptible twist an organic process issues into human behaviour, an instinctive act changes direction and becomes a sentiment, or conversely a human act becomes torpid and is continued absent-mindedly in the form of a reflex.
>
> (Merleau-Ponty 1962: 88 cited by Turner 1992: 56)

Thus while the notion that embodied consciousness is central here, it is also highlighted that we are not always conscious or aware of our bodily actions, we do not routinely tell our body to put one leg in front of the other if we want to walk, or to breath in through our nose if we want to smell a rose. The body in this sense is 'taken-for-granted', or as Leder puts it, the body is 'absent':

> While in one sense the body is the most abiding and inescapable presence in our lives, it is also essentially characterised by absence. That is, one's own body is rarely the thematic object of experience. When reading a book or lost in thought, my own bodily state may be the farthest thing from my awareness . . . the body, as a ground of experience . . . tends to recede from direct experience.
>
> (Leder 1990: 1)

If the body is so taken-for-granted, other than in certain bodily states such as disease, pain and death (when Leder points out it tends to *dys*-appear, that is we become conscious of the body because it is in a *dys*-functional state), then this will have implications for the study of the lived experience of the body when it is functioning normally. How can we ask people to talk about something of which they are not aware? If we do encourage people to talk about their bodies will this necessarily be artificial? (We return to this point below.)

The lived body is presumed therefore to both construct and be constructed by the lifeworld. The lived body is an intentional entity which gives rise to this world:

> in a significant sense, the lived body helps to constitute this world as experienced. We cannot understand the meaning and form of objects without reference to bodily powers through which we engage them – our senses, motility, language, desires. The lived body is not just one thing *in* the world but a way in which the world comes to be.
>
> (Leder 1992: 25)

We can see therefore that it is analytically possible to make a distinction between *having* a body, *doing* a body and *being* a body. Turner (1992) and others have found the German distinction between *Leib* and *Korper* to be instructive here. The former refers to the experiential, animated or living body (the body-for-itself), the latter refers to the objective, instrumental, exterior body (the body-in-itself).

The main point of briefly outlining this approach is to highlight that the concepts of the 'lived body' and the notion of 'embodiment' remind us that the self and the body are not separate and that experience is invariably, whether consciously or not, embodied. As Csordas (1990) has argued the body is the 'existential ground of culture and self', and therefore he prefers the notion of 'embodiment' to 'the body' as the former implies something more than a material entity, it is rather a 'methodological field defined by perceptual experience and mode of presence and engagement in the world' (Csordas 1994: 10). This idea that the self is embodied is also taken up by Giddens (1991: 56–7) who also emphasises the notion of day-to-day *praxis*. The body is not an external entity but is experienced in practical ways when coping with external events and situations. How we handle our bodies in social situations is of course crucial to our self and identity and has been empirically and extensively explored by Goffman (1969, 1971), symbolic interactionists, Garfinkel (1967) and other ethnomethodologists. Indeed, the study of the *management* of bodies in everyday life, and how this serves to structure the self and social relations, has a long and important history within sociology. It highlights the preciousness of the body as well as humans' remarkable ability to sustain bodily control through day-to-day situations. What remains absent, however, is the voices emanating from the bodies themselves. We want now therefore to reflect upon how ordinary men and women *articulate* their bodily experiences.

The 'taken-for-grantedness' of the body

A number of writers have emphasised that in our day-to-day lives our bodies are 'absent' (Leder 1990) or are taken-for-granted. We become aware of them only when they are in pain or suffer from disease or illness – when they are *dys*-functional. Simon Williams (1996) has illustrated this by drawing on the findings of research into chronic illness. He demonstrates how the experience of chronic illness involves a move from an 'initial' state of embodiment (a state in which the body is taken-for-granted in the course of everyday life) to an oscillation between states of '*dys*-embodiment' (embodiment in a dysfunctional state) and 're-embodiment'. He shows that attempts to move from a dys-embodied state to a re-embodied state requires a considerable amount of 'biographical work' or what Gareth Williams (1984) terms 'narrative reconstruction'. This theme is also demonstrated by Seymour (1998) in her empirical study of twenty-four men and women who experienced profound and permanent body paralysis. As the title of her book, *Remaking the Body*, suggests she reveals how these men and women go about remaking their bodies and accordingly, in doing so, remake their worlds.

Such analyses have provided valuable insights into the nature of embodiment; however, the focus on chronic illness and profound bodily paralysis might reinforce the idea that it is only in circumstances of altered bodily states such as pain, the onset of disability, or suffering, that we become aware of our bodies. Whilst it is quite obviously the case that most of us do, to a significant extent, take our bodies for granted whilst going about our daily routines, one of the salient themes that emerges from reading the chapters in this volume is just how evident the body is in the mainstream of everyday life. How, when people are either interviewed or observed, they appear to be aware of their bodies. Cunningham-Burley and Backett-Milburn (Chapter 8) demonstrate that the body is central to understanding health and change in the middle years, suggesting that their research identifies some of the ways and means in which 'we attend to and objectify our bodies'. Perhaps bodies are not quite so 'taken-for-granted' as has often been supposed by contemporary theoreticians.

Lupton's (Chapter 5) investigation into the dominant discourses of emotions as they were articulated by men and women during interview found that feelings and emotions were articulated as having physical effects. Emotions could manifest themselves by making one feel tired or energetic, failure to express emotion was cited as a possible cause of disease. On reading this chapter it becomes evident that people become aware of their bodies in a whole range of circumstances, for example if one is nervous one's stomach might churn, or the hands may become sweaty. If people have to speak in public they may be conscious that the body may let them down – 'Perhaps I might fall over', 'What if I drop my papers?' The bodily presentation of the self, and what Goffman calls the 'easy control' of the body enters the consciousness.

Awareness of physicality is also apparent in the chapters on ageing. As Bytheway and Johnson (Chapter 13) point out: 'The visual signs of age, like the weather, is a universal topic of everyday conversation between adults'. Certainly the impact of ageing is something which is evident throughout the life course; adolescents for example, may be acutely 'aware' of bodily transformations. This also appears to be the case during the 'midlife' years (Hepworth and Featherstone, Chapter 15). Elsewhere, Featherstone and Hepworth (1991) have argued how the process of ageing in contemporary society encourages individuals to devise 'flexible biographical' narratives to contribute to the construction and main-tenance of the new identities which accompany biological ageing. The 'modernisation of ageing', they argue, 'involves a distancing from deep old age – a distancing which is achieved through flex-ible adjustments to the gradually blurring boundaries of adult life' (1991: 385). Thus ageing may involve an awareness of the phys-ical body and associated attempts to construct narratives about ones new social world. The world has to be constantly 're-made' as one's body alters within it. The men and women interviewed by Fairhurst (Chapter 14) articulate the importance of altering one's dress, behaviour and presentation of one's self, even if this is at odds with what they feel; it seems that it is morally preferable to act one's chronological age even if one does not feel it.[2] This requirement is confirmed in day-to-day social relations. Fairhurst provides in some detail an account by one woman who found that she was ignored by a shop assistant and assumed that this was because she was visibly 'older' than her companion. We may there-fore be reminded of our bodies in a wide range of social situations.

Bodily controls

Maintaining control of the body is crucial for the presentation of the self in everyday life. This has been demonstrated by some symbolic interactionists and it has also been a key finding in the literature on the experience of chronic illness and disability. The ability to be perceived and accepted as a competent social actor requires a certain level of competencies. A further aspect of the awareness of the body articulated by many of the men and women in the studies presented in this collection was the salience of keeping control over one's body. Again this is evident in discussions on ageing and is at its most extreme when there is the fear of bodily dependence. There is also the concern that the body will not be able to support the type of activities that people may hope to participate in, in later life (see Fairhurst, Chapter 14). The idea of loss of control was also apparent in the accounts of emotions in Lupton's Chapter 5, where people used terms such as to 'lose your temper' 'lose control', and 'lose it'. Unacceptable feelings might be unleashed from the body.

Higate (Chapter 10) in his autobiographical study of life in the Royal Air Force demonstrates how bodily control was used both intentionally and unintentionally to subvert the regulated bodily movements required within a military context. For example, a senior officer falling onto a desk in front of subordinates as a result of a 'liquid lunch' demonstrates an unwitting lack of bodily control which potentially undermines accepted hierarchical relations. The more junior men intentionally betrayed bodily controls through acts such as suddenly collapsing to the floor or perusing the 'ritual' of the 'simulated falling backwards'. These represent embodied actions which serve to subvert social relations and undermine the prevailing social order.

Similarly in Bloor et al.'s Chapter 2 on bodybuilding and steroid use the informants in the study provided atrocity stories of those steroid 'abusers' (who were never actually the informants themselves) who were not able, knowledgeable or sensible enough to control, regulate and monitor their steroid use. Indeed, the absence of control was equated with abuse. The ability to effectively control one's body was therefore critical to maintaining one's social status and would result in a physical manifestation of this status.

By contrast, Watson (Chapter 9) shows how, for the men in his study, the acquisition of social status can lead to a perceived loss of control over one's body. Marriage is seen as a time when men 'settle down' and 'let themselves go' whilst the advent of children brings with it responsibilities and the social valuing of present, 'hands on' fathering. The physical experience of the 'dance all night', 'play hard' and 'hungover body' of the bachelor gives way to a body more functionally adapted to deal with crowded daily routines and the jostling of various socially ascribed roles. This is a time when some reflect that 'there is nothing happening to my body'.

The loss of bodily control can be associated with a loss of social acceptability. Featherstone and Hepworth (1991) have used the notion of *bodily betrayal* to capture this idea. In a discussion on ageing they write:

> Loss of bodily controls carries similar penalties of stigmatisation and ultimately physical exclusion. . . . Degrees of loss impair the capacity to be counted as a competent adult. Indeed, the failure of bodily controls can point to a more general loss of self image; to be ascribed the status of a competent adult person depends upon the capacity to control urine and faeces.
>
> (Featherstone and Hepworth 1991: 376)

This thesis does appear to accord with some of the empirical data presented in the chapters within this volume on ageing and the emotions. A further illustration of this is in Britton's Chapter 4 on breastfeeding. Here we see that women were taken aback by the involuntary loss of milk, which is a function of the interrelation between emotional, social and physiological factors. Fluid exuding from bodily boundaries can be experienced as a source of embarrassment and exclusion, and this was articulated by a number of the women in her study. The transcending of bodily boundaries is according to Douglas's accounts of the representational body, the quintessential metaphor of social disorder and chaos (Douglas 1970).

Douglas's (1966) thesis that the social body constrains how the physical body is perceived is the starting point for Williams and Bendelow's (Chapter 6) analysis of children's perceptions of health, risk and cancer. The body as a social representation appears to structure the thoughts and beliefs of young children in that their beliefs about cancerous bodies are found to reflect and reinforce age old metaphors and dominant beliefs in western society.

Centuries of accumulated cultural baggage are evident. What is also striking is the diversity of knowledge, ideas and beliefs which are drawn upon by these 9 and 10 year olds when they articulate and depict bodies. They clearly draw upon a range of sources of information, the most evident of which appeared to be the television. But this is a feature of high modernity; there is a proliferation and diversification of knowledge, of advice and of information from which people are able to draw and make choices about their bodily regimes and practices (Giddens 1991). They form part of the body as a reflexive project.

This said, as Bloor and his colleagues (Chapter 2) point out: 'Bodybuilders would eschew any analysis which portrayed their activities as driven by a late-modern crisis', so, we suspect, might many of the other informants and participants of the other research projects within this collection. Nevertheless it does appear to form an empirical illustration of the body as a reflexive project. As Bloor *et al.* write: 'Ethnopharmacological knowledge emphasises the importance of individualised knowledge, of flexibility, change and personalised planning'. It is precisely this 'project-like character' of bodybuilding activities which serves to differentiate steroid use from other forms of drug use.

Bodily controls and their impact upon the self and identity are both internally and externally rooted. Social controls and internal controls of the body and the self are inherently interrelated and mutually reinforcing. Much has been made in the literature on the sociology of the body, of the concept of surveillance, and in particular those practices which routinely monitor and assess bodies. Howson (Chapter 12) taking the example of screening for cervical cancer illustrates the shortcomings of the Foucauldian notion of surveillance. Taking an embodied perspective, and listening attentively to the women who have actually taken part in these screening programmes, she finds that they participate out of a positive sense of obligation. It forms a dimension of their desire to act as responsible citizens. This she captures in the neat term 'embodied obligation'. This is not a docile body which adheres to a government initiated exercise but an expression of self governance, whereby the women actively negotiate and express a sense of moral urgency and 'embodied engagement with the process of screening'.

Body-image

The image we hold of our bodies will to a greater or lesser extent impact upon how we experience our bodies in everyday life. It may impact upon our sense of self, our degree of confidence in social situations and the nature of our social relationships. The concept of 'body-image' has been developed and much theorised by psychoanalysts, neurologists, surgeons, psychologists, anthropologists and sociologists throughout the twentieth century. It is now a term that is in common currency and was indeed used by some of the participants in the studies presented in this collection. Our body-image is shaped not just by what we perceive our body to look like, but what we see and how we interpret our vision of our body is mediated by our social and cultural context (see for example studies on anorexia: Probyn 1988; Cooper 1987; Lawrence 1984). The act of perception is a socially constructed process. Sault (1994), an anthropologist, captures this integrated nature of 'body-image' when she writes about the 'body-image system' which 'is dynamic, interactive, and so closely integrated that neither the body-image nor social relations has a priority or precedence over the other'. She draws attention to the fact that the body-image system involves both the 'experience of bodily changes' and their 'social perception' (1994: 18). In other words our body-image and our social relations impact upon each other.

The idea that our image of our own body is socially mediated and impacts upon not only how we feel about ourselves but also our social relations is evident in a number of the studies in this collection. Perhaps most conspicuously amongst the men and women who suffer from arthritis in Williams and Barlow's Chapter 7. The men and women interviewed for this study articulated how their physical constraints made them uncomfortable in certain social settings, and how they feared that their altered bodies might undermine how significant others felt about them. Nevertheless, this was not invariably a passive acceptance, a number of people noted how they made particular efforts to improve on their appearance – to try and bring their perceived body-image more in line with ideal images. For example, men and women described how they would make an effort to exercise or, in the case of one woman go on 'binge shopping' for clothes and make-up, 'to present an image which looks good.[3] These comments reflect those expressed by the men and women who were interviewed by Fairhurst (Chapter

14) in that they described how they made careful attempts to modify their appearance in ways that were not out of kilter with their 'ageing' bodies. This might relate to the clothes that they wear, the colour of their hair, cosmetics used and so on. To appear inappropriately 'old' or to be 'mutton dressed as lamb' in our contemporary society appears to be a source of tension. It can also be associated with loss of status. For example, one woman who was in her twenties, cited in Williams and Barlow's study (Chapter 7), suggested that she felt that she had been 'robbed' of twenty or more years of her life because she said that she 'looked' as though she was in her forties or fifties. A number of theorists have suggested that within a consumer society a youthful body forms the dominant ideal. Indeed it is said to contribute to the body's 'physical capital' (Bourdeiu 1984).

What constitutes the image of old age forms one of the key strands of Bytheway and Johnson's Chapter 13. Having gathered popular media representations of 'old people' they identify three strategies which are used to depict people as old. First, physical appearance, for example wrinkles or gait. Second, relationships in that the 'older' person is presented as being dependent on a younger person. Third, the use of appendages – a popular example being a zimmer frame. Material objects, Schilder (1935) has argued, can themselves be incorporated into the body-image, and once they have been associated with the body retain something of the quality of that body-image. Indeed, material objects can serve to both enhance and undermine ones 'image'.

Gender

A striking feature of this collection is the extent to which lay accounts of embodiment open up masculine experiences to a richer and subtler assessment. 'True masculinity' has almost always been thought to proceed from men's bodies (Connell 1995: 45) but, as Watson (Chapter 9) has noted, the male body has, in this respect, suffered from 'a narrow and partial existence'. The accounts of ordinary men accessed in various ways throughout this volume open up some of the spaces, silences and tensions of male embodiment which themselves are entwined with broader social changes that shape our knowledge of the body. In relation to gender this is clearly seen in Hepworth and Featherstone's study of the male menopause (Chapter 15). They argue that lay accounts of the male menopause have evolved and been legitimised in the context of 'broader changes in gender relations and the social status of men, and the influence of these changes on what it means to be a man, and in particular, an ageing man, in contemporary western society'.

Similarly, the gendered obligations of fatherhood related by Watson (Chapter 9) open up the possibility of new forms of embodied (emotional) interaction with their children. This seems to challenge orthodox accounts of the development of a separated gendered male identity (solid, aggressive, watchful, isolated) which suggests limits to the extent to which men can care for children. For example, Chodorow says that 'boys come to define themselves as more separate and distinct, with a greater sense of rigid ego boundaries and differentiation . . . the basic masculine sense of self is separate' (1978: 169). This view is echoed in Fasteau's (1974) depiction of the American male as a 'male machine' which by its own separateness confronts the world in which it exists (see also Johnson 1992). Yet again, the separateness of male identity is challenged by Higate (Chapter 10) who notes in regard to a group of male clerks in the military that they had 'a particular bodily group identity – a repertoire of bodily actions that symbolised their difference from mainstream military value systems'.

By contrast, Bendelow and Williams (Chapter 11) in exploring lay beliefs about the nature of pain found that 'the attribution to men and women of differential capacities for experiencing, expressing, understanding and responding to pain' was predominantly grounded in 'gender-differentiated processes of socialisation and emotion management'. In that sense, women's sense of identity is not undermined by admission of being in pain compared to men, for whom it may amount to an admission of vulnerability.

A final word about this book

When approaching this book we had presumed that the empirical study of the body in everyday life would yield a particularly vexing methodological problem. This is because we had assumed the body to be so absent that it would be difficult to access any data on people's experience of it. This may be in part because, with some notable exceptions (e.g. Martin 1989) there have been few attempts to allow people to speak about their bodies. Furthermore as Zola (1991) has pointed out, people need to be allowed, or even empowered to speak about their bodies because of the 'socially structured barriers to hearing and speaking with the voice of personal bodily experience' (1991: 3). Although referring here to people with physical disabilities he also notes that 'it must be equally difficult for the proverbial man and woman on the street when they try to write or speak about their bodies' (1991: 4). Perhaps this is because hitherto they have not been asked.

In this respect it has been noted elsewhere that a key methodological challenge for sociology of embodiment is the need to start developing the 'conceptual tools that would enable the articulation of lay ideas about and experiences of the body that have previously been treated as unexpressible' (Watson *et al.* 1995). At the same time we had fears about the extent to which one could legitimately approach that experience, in settings and circumstances in which a concern with embodiment may be felt to have little obvious validity. The various chapters in this volume demonstrate that accessing lay accounts of the body is possible and offer diverse ways of doing so including: semi-structured and in-depth interviews, focus groups, visual prompts, draw and write techniques, media representations and autobiography. Most of the chapters give some detail on the use of these various approaches to 'bringing the body back in'.

The bottom line is that we have set out to address the everyday realities of what Connell has called 'the body as used or the body-I-am (1987: 83) and in doing so we have taken as our starting point, the embodied experience of individuals within their everyday worlds. What we hope this volume demonstrates is that in many ways, it is from the contradictions and tensions that are present in the interplay between 'biological and physical necessities' (Geertz 1973: 30) and external economic, political and social realities of individual embodiment that provides the terrain for empirical study.

Notes

1   There are however some notable exceptions e.g. Leder (1992) and Scott and Morgan (1993). There is also a considerable amount of work on the anthropology of the body, much of which is based on empirical research e.g. Blacking (1977), Csordas (1994) and Sault (1994).

2   This notion of changing identity is one that has previously been examined by Berger and Luckman (1967) who have argued that 'identity is a phenomenon that emerges from the dialectic between individuals

and society' (1967: 195), and that identity itself is meshed with an individual's 'biological substratum' (ibid.: 201). However, Fairhurst is suggesting that this dynamic has a moral dimension, one that mediates 'bodily activities and experiences' (Blacking 1977: 23; see also Backett 1992).

3 For a useful, but more theoretical overview of the value of the concept of 'body-image' for the study of chronic illness see Williams (1996).

References

Anderson, R. and Bury, M. (eds) (1988) *Living with Chronic Illness: the experience of patients and their families*, London: Unwin Hyman.

Backett, K. (1992) 'Taboos and excesses: lay health moralities in middle class families', *Sociology of Health and Illness* **14**, 2, 255–74.

Balsamo, A. (1995) Forms of technological embodiment: reading the body in contemporary culture, *Body and Society* **1**, 3–4, 215–37.

Beck, U. (1992) *Risk Society: towards a new modernity*, London: Sage.

Bendelow, G. and Williams, S. (1995) 'Pain and the mind–body dualism: a sociological approach', *Body and Society* **1**, 2, 83–104.

Berger, P.L. and Luckman, T. (1967) *The Social Construction of Reality*, London: Allen Lane.

Blacking, J. (1977) *The Anthropology of the Body*, London: Academic Press.

Bourdieu, P. (1984) *Distinction: a social critique of judgement and taste*, London: Routledge.

Charmaz, K. (1983) 'Loss of self: a fundamental for suffering in the chronically ill', *Sociology of Health and Illness* **5**, 168–95.

Chodorow, N. (1978) *The Reproduction of Mothering: psychoanalysis and the sociology of gender*, London: University of California Press.

Connell, R. (1987) *Gender and Power*, Cambridge: Polity Press.

Connell, R. (1995) *Masculinities*, Cambridge: Polity Press.

Cooper, T. (1987) 'Anorexia and bulimia: the political and the personal', in Lawrence, M. (ed.) *Fed Up and Hungry: women, oppression and food*, London: The Women's Press.

Crossley, N. (1995) 'Merleau-Ponty, the elusive body and carnal sociology', *Body and Society* **1**, 1, 43–64.

Csordas, T.J. (1990) 'Embodiment as a paradigm for anthropology', *Ethos* **18**, 1, 5–47.

Csordas, T.J. (1994) *Embodiment and Experience: the existential ground of culture and self*, Cambridge: Cambridge University Press.

Douglas, M. (1966) *Purity and Danger: an analysis of the concepts of pollution and taboo*, London: Routledge and Kegan Paul.

Douglas, M. (1970) *Natural Symbols: explorations in cosmology*, London: Barrie and Rockliff, the Cresset Press.

Douglas, M. (1986) *Risk Acceptability According to the Social Sciences*, London: Routledge and Kegan Paul.

Duden, B. (1991) *The Woman Beneath the Skin: a doctor's patients in eighteenth-century Germany*, Cambridge, MA: Harvard University Press.

Dunnell, K. (1995) 'Are we healthier?' *Population Trends* **82**, 12–18.

Falk, P. (1994) *The Consuming Body*, London: Sage.

Fasteau, M.F. (1974) *The Male Machine*, New York: McGraw-Hill.

Featherstone, M. (1991) 'The body in consumer culture', in Featherstone, M., Hepworth, M., Turner, B.S. (eds) *The Body: social processes and cultural theory*, London: Sage.

Featherstone, M. and Burrows, R. (1995) 'Cultures of technological embodiment: an introduction', *Body and Society* **1**, 3–4, 1–20.

Featherstone, M. and Hepworth, M. (1991) 'The mask of ageing and the postmodern lifecourse', in Featherstone, M., Hepworth, M., Turner, B.S. (eds) *The Body: social processes and cultural theory*, London: Sage.

Featherstone, M., Hepworth, M., Turner, B.S. (eds) (1991) *The Body: social processes and cultural theory*, London: Sage.

Foucault, M. (1979) *Discipline and Punish: the birth of the prison*, Harmondsworth: Penguin.

Garfinkel, H. (1967) *Studies in Ethnomethodology*, Englewood Cliffs, NJ: Prentice Hall.

Gatens, M. (1996) *Imaginary Bodies: ethics, power and corporeality*, London: Routledge.

Geertz, C. (1973) *The Interpretation of Cultures*, London: Fontana Press.

Giddens, A. (1991) *Modernity and Self-Identity: self and society in the late modern age*, Cambridge: Polity Press.

Glassner, B. (1989) 'Fitness and the postmodern self', *Journal of Health and Social Behaviour* **30**, 180–91.

Goffman, E. (1969) *The Presentation of Self in Everyday Life*, Harmondsworth: Penguin.

Goffman, E. (1971) *Relations in Public: microstudies of the Public Order*, Harmondsworth: Penguin.

Grosz, E. (1994) *Volatile Bodies*, Bloomington, IN: Indiana University Press.

Haraway, D. (1991) 'A cyborg manifesto: science, technology, and socialist-feminism in the late twentieth century', in her *Simians, Cyborgs, and Women: the reinvention of nature*, New York: Routledge.

Helman, C. (1990) *Culture, Health and Illness*, London: Wright.

Johnson, D.H. (1992) 'The loneliness of the male body', in Thompson, K. (ed.) *Views from the Male World*, London: Aquarian Press.

Kleinman, A. (1988) *The Illness Narratives: suffering, healing and the human condition*, New York: Basic Books.

Lawrence, M. (1984) *The Anorexic Experience*, London: The Women's Press.

Leder, D. (1990) *The Absent Body*, Chicago: Chicago University Press.

Leder, D. (1992) 'Introduction', in Leder (ed.) *The Body in Medical Thought and Practice*, London: Kluwer Academic.

Leng, K.W. (1996) 'On menopause and cyborgs: or, towards a feminist cyborg politics of menopause', *Body and Society* **2**, 3, 33–52.

Martin, E. (1989) *The Woman in the Body*, Milton Keynes: Open University Press.

Martin, E. (1994) *Flexible Bodies: the role of immunity in American culture from the days of polio to the age of Aids*, Boston, MA: Beacon Press.

Merleau-Ponty, M. (1962) *Phenomology of Perception*, trans. C. Smith, London: Routledge and Kegan Paul.

Murphy, R.F. (1987) *The Body Silent*, New York: Henry Holt.

Nettleton, S. (1995) *The Sociology of Health and Illness*, Cambrdige: Polity Press.

Oliver, M. (1990) *The Politics of Disablement*, London: Macmillan.

Probyn, E. (1988) 'The anorexic body', in Kroker, A. and Kroker, M. (eds) *Body Invaders: sexuality and the postmodern condition*, London: Macmillan.

Sault, N. (ed.) (1994) *Many Mirrors: body-image and social relations*, New Brunswick, NJ: Rutgers University Press.

Schilder, P. (1935) *The Image and Appearance of the Human Body*, New York: International Universities Press.

Scott, S. and Morgan, D. (eds) (1993) *Body Matters: essays on the sociology of the body*, London: Falmer Press.

Seymour, W. (1998) *Remaking the Body*, London: Routledge.

Shilling, C. (1993) *The Body and Social Theory*, London: Sage.

Turner, B.S. (1992) *Regulating Bodies: essays in medical sociology*, London: Routledge.

Turner, B.S. (1996) *The Body and Society*, 2nd edn. London: Sage.

Wacquant, L.J.D. (1995) 'Pugs at work: bodily capital and bodily labour among professional boxers', *Body and Society* **1**, 1, 65–94.

Watson, J., Cunningham-Burley, S., Watson, N. (1995) 'Lay theorising about the body and health', paper presented to British Sociological Association (BSA) Medical Sociology Group Conference, York, September.

Williams, G. (1984) 'The genesis of chronic illness: narrative reconstruction', *Sociology of Health and Illness* **6**, 175–200.

Williams, S. (1996) 'The vicisstudes of embodiment across the chronic illness trajectory', *Body and Society* **2**, 2, 23–47.

Williams, S. (1997) 'Modern medicine and the "uncertain" body: from corporeality to hyperreality?' *Social Science and Medicine* **45**, 7, 1041–9.

Zola, I.K. (1991) 'Bringing our bodies and ourselves back in: reflections on a past, present and future "medical sociology"', *Journal of Health and Social Behaviour* **32**, 1–16.

Part 1

Physical and emotional bodies

Chapter 2

The body as a chemistry experiment

Steroid use among South Wales bodybuilders

Michael Bloor, Lee Monaghan,
Russell P. Dobash and Rebecca E. Dobash

The bodybuilding scene, with its studios and sub-culture, has been described as one aspect of the so-called 'body-boom' experienced in many western cultures (Weis 1985: 287). Characterised by the lifting of weights and adherence to special dietary regimens, bodybuilding is a growing participation sport which involves development of the physique for aesthetic effect (ZviFuchs and Zaichkowsky 1983; Thirer and Greer 1978). Whether individual bodybuilders aspire to sculpt their body simply for personal satisfaction, competitive endeavour, or both, drug-taking has also been described as an important aspect of this sporting lifestyle (Gaines 1974: 73; Klein 1986: 122–4; Klein 1993: 147–52; Monaghan 1995: 34–5). The issue of drug-taking in bodybuilding is the topic addressed in this chapter.

One important dimension of drug use among bodybuilders is that of systematic personal experimentation in types, courses and dosages of drugs taken. Consider, for example, the remarks of this experienced competition bodybuilder, interviewed by Lee Monaghan, about the twenty-odd courses (or 'cycles') of steroids taken over his bodybuilding career:

> my cycles were my own cycles. They're not standard cycles, like I wouldn't take a six-week [course]. I would possibly, like, do six months on steroids and at least do two months of *this* and do two months *that*. And the last two months I'd do *this*. I would see what would work better. I would experiment on myself.

> (Interview 046: 2147–2158)

It will be argued that many bodybuilders view their drug use as a tool, a means for self-realisation and self-expression. Their drug use is carefully planned, monitored and adjusted. Drawn from their own accumulated experimentation and experience, from conversations with fellow-users, and from the study of magazine articles and underground handbooks, many bodybuilders' knowledge of drug regimens, effects and side-effects qualifies them as 'ethnopharmacologists'. That is, lay persons with a detailed sub-cultural understanding of the pharmacological properties of particular compounds, similar to that knowledge of native remedies and native taxonomies of disease studied by anthropologists among non-western peoples (e.g. Frake 1980). This ethnopharmacological knowledge is not necessarily consonant with that of scientific pharmacology (it may be partly opposed to, and critical of, clinical knowledge), nor is it necessarily clear and distinct: it is very much individualised knowledge about which particular drugs, combinations of drugs, courses and dosages are likely to be most effective for a particular individual in building the body to which that individual aspires: building your very own body through your very own chemistry experiment.

Ethnopharmacological knowledge by bodybuilders can be conceived as a parallel phenomenon to other areas of lay expertise on health matters. For example, there are parallels with the expertise which many patients with chronic or recurrent conditions develop about the individual manifestations of the condition in their own particular case (see, for example, Macintyre and Oldman (1977) on the expertise of migraine sufferers). Nor are steroid-users unique among drug-users in their interest in the effects of drug-taking: an absorbing interest in the effects of drug-taking is a feature of most drug-using sub-cultures. Where steroid-users differ from users of other drugs is the extensiveness of their ethnopharmacological knowledge and in the purpose of their drug use: steroid use, for the most part, is an instrumental activity undertaken with the aim of developing the user's body.

However, not all steroid-using bodybuilders are thought by bodybuilders themselves to view steroids in this instrumental and experimental light. Many bodybuilders will draw a distinction between steroid *use* and steroid *abuse*. Steroid-users will distance themselves from the reported *abuse* of steroids through excessive or indiscriminate steroid-taking, or steroid-taking in the absence of a proper training regime. This abuse of steroids is seen in a similar light to the taking of opiates or amphetamines and provides a contrast to the ennobling and self-realising project of the dedicated, steroid-using bodybuilder. A parallel can be drawn with the contrast found between LSD-using 'heads' and Methedrine-using 'freaks' in 1960s San Francisco, where the older, higher status 'heads' would emphasise the self-realising objective of their acid use and distance themselves from the hedonistic speed 'freaks' (Davis and Munoz 1968).

In this chapter we will review the experimental, instrumental, ethnopharmacological orientation to steroid use of many bodybuilders and analyse narratives (atrocity stories or cautionary tales) bodybuilders would tell about steroid *abuse*, showing how this contrast between use and abuse serves to distance the narrators from unwelcome associations with other drug-users ('junkies') and legitimise, in their eyes, their drug-taking activities. First, we offer a brief account of the study methodology.

Methods

Data collection methods embraced both ethnographic work and depth interviews. Ethnographic pilot work was undertaken at a range of possible fieldwork sites in twelve cities and towns across South Wales (fifteen gyms, twelve leisure centres, two needle exchanges, one clinic and three bodybuilding competitions). On the basis of this pilot work, a small number of gymnasia (all of them commercial properties open to any member of the public) were selected for detailed ethnographic study. In order to minimise bias in fieldwork contacts, the main ethnographic study was conducted on a time-sampling basis. Additional data were collected at a local needle exchange and at a Well Steroid Users Clinic. Despite the sensitive nature of the research topic, productive fieldwork was conducted in these various interactional settings. Whilst other drugs researchers have encountered difficulties in accessing the views of steroid-using bodybuilders in South Wales (see Pates and Barry 1996), overt ethnopharmacologic research was facilitated in this male-dominated subculture given the ethnographer's age, gender and other aspects of self. Lee Monaghan (male, mid-twenties and a keen sportsman) reported little difficulty obtaining 'the native's point of view' whilst conducting participant observation.

Sixty-seven depth interviews were conducted with both steroid-using and non-using bodybuilders, both men and women. While most of the interviewees were recruited through ethnographic contacts, deliberate efforts were made to recruit some of the sample by other means, including a group of interviewees interviewed at a local prison. All the interviews were transcribed and the transcripts and ethnographic fieldnotes were indexed using Ethnograph – a computer software package. Indexing of the fieldnotes and transcripts has allowed a systematic approach to data analysis, developing analytical propositions which apply to the entire universe of data carrying particular indexed codes; this approach is variously termed 'analytic induction' or 'deviant case analysis' (Bloor 1978).

Ethnopharmacology: 'You've got to be like a scientist'

Many bodybuilders describe their drug use as a planned and carefully monitored activity, formulated and conducted in the light of evolving experience and detailed study:

> I've not used em now for almost nine months. Really, if you're concerned about your health, you don't want to be on them all the time, maybe two cycles a year is best – on for two months, off for four months, then back on again for two months. Last year though I took five cycles. That's why I've laid off them for a while. I've been buying a supply for myself though, been stocking up for my next cycle. I plan to use my head a bit more this time though. Like, I read that the receptor sites in your muscles don't recognise the same steroid after three weeks use. So the best thing is to change the steroid after that amount of time. I'm planning on using Dianabol, then Sustanon, then some Deca.
>
> (Fieldnotes: 4362–4382)

And:

> *Interviewer: Okay. Right, how many cycles have you completed? Roughly.*
> S07: Um, 12 to 14 I would say.
> *Int: 12 to 14. And how frequent are they? Is there a sort of pattern or . . . ?*
> S07: Before I started competing I would like do 3 months on, 3 months off, but since I've started competing I've tried to

get 10 weeks off between the cycles. But the cycles may last, like this one is a 21 week cycle, this one is. But I've had 10 weeks off before I've started it. . . . I pre-plan everything and I make a note of most things . . . .

Int: So how do you take them?

S07: Injections and orals. . . . But I've tended to stay off the orals lately because they seem to suppress my appetite. But I will take them. I mean, saying that it's the bulkers that seem to suppress my appetite more than the cutting orals, because I suppose the cutting orals need to suppress your appetite a bit. But I've had a bit of trouble with the bulking ones suppressing my appetite. . . .

Int: Okay, now can you describe to me the current cycle?

S07: Right. At the moment now I'm doing a 9-week bulking cycle. Do you want to know what I'm taking? *(Yes please)* Deca for 3 weeks, Heptylate for three weeks, Testoviron for 3 weeks. And then the last 4 weeks – then I'll stack them [i.e. combine them] with Pronabol. . . . Weeks 1 to 3 is just Deca on its own. Weeks 4 to 6 will be Heptylate. But on week 6 I'll start the Pronabol as well. *(Right)* Yeah. And then weeks 7, 8 and 9 will be Testoviron and the Pronabol. *(Right. Fine)* Do you want the amounts or . . .? *(Yes please)* With the Deca, it's about 300mg a week, which would be three 100mg injections. The Heptylate would be about 750mg a week. The same with the Testoviron. And the Pronabol will be, um, week 6 will be six 5mg tablets a day which is 210mg. And then weeks 7, 8 and 9 will be 270mg.

(Interview S07: 2333–2651)

The multiple use of drugs within a particular cycle (known as 'stacking' or 'pyramid stacking') is typical. In Korkia and Stimson's (1993) national survey of steroid use, the mean number of drugs taken within the respondent's last cycle was 3.2 for men and 2.2 for women. Steroid use is only one aspect of a planning project that also involves a carefully regulated and modulated training programme and dietary regime, complete with various nutritional supplements and perhaps other non-steroid drugs such as Human Chorionic Gonadotrophin (HCG), diuretics, and growth hormones:

S43: I try to alter my diet every few months. . . . Because I don't just rely on the steroids. I rely on everything I've got:

my vitamins, my food, my training, everything. Because I change everything all the time. . . . When I do come off them I take HCG to turn my own hormones back on, which people don't know a lot about, things like that. It's like I say, I don't like people they do 3, 6 months on the stuff. I don't do that: I'll be like 6 to 8 weeks. Full stop. And I'm off. On and off. And then I leave it 3 weeks before the HCG has gone right through my system. So I use them because I honestly believe that I'm using them correctly . . . you can't use the same steroid all the time because it's like any drug, your body will build a resilience up to it and get used to it. So what you want to be doing, just like I said with your workouts, you swap them round . . . you've got to be like a scientist as well.

(S43: 127–2850)

This ethnopharmacological knowledge is a shared knowledge communicated not only through handbooks and dealers' instructions, but also through countless casual conversations like that reported in this fieldnote:

Aneurin: Theoretically, Dianabol shouldn't work, as it's a very crude form of testosterone. It does work though, practically for everyone, as it binds itself easily to the receptor sites. As I say though, Dianabol is so crude, it shouldn't work.
Tegwin: Cyp [Testosterone Cypionate] puts the mass on. That really works.
Aneurin: You're likely to lose it afterwards though.
Tegwin: Yeah. The only reason why I think I kept it is because I went on the Deca [Nandroline Decanoate] after the Cyp.

(Fieldnote: 2742–2757)

Names have a considerable symbolic value in any ethnopharmacological knowledge system. It is possible to construct a taxonomy of different steroids used by local bodybuilders together with their slang diminutives ('Cyp'), their supposed properties, dosages and administration routes. Another aspect of ethnopharmacological knowledge related to steroid taxonomies is the extensive argot ('stacking', 'pyramid stacking', 'hardeners', 'cutters', 'bulkers', etc.). However, the aspect of steroid-users' ethnopharmacological knowledge which deserves particular attention here is that of the highly complex 'cycling theories'.

Cycling theories concern the lengths of courses, variations in dosages within courses, combinations of different courses both sequentially and interactively, combinations of different courses with other dietary and training regimes, and spacings between different courses. Most steroids are taken in cycles: in a national UK survey of steroid use, 88 per cent of the ninety-seven respondents reported that they took their drugs in cycles (Korkia and Stimson 1993: 83). Cycling theories also embrace lay theorising about how steroids work: many research subjects discussed at length the role of 'receptor sites', for example. It is, of course, the cycling theories which link ethnopharmacological knowledge with the planned and instrumental character of much steroid use. While novice steroid-users may follow a cycle suggested by a dealer or an experienced acquaintance (a 'gym doctor', in the argot), more-practised users quickly begin to plan their own cycles. Some novices when first using steroids may fail to complete a cycle for fear of side-effects or detection:

> S039: I had a few tablets and I gave myself one jab. And I thought, 'Oh, I can't feel right, doing this.' Like the guilt, because I felt, you know, like a drug addict, you know. So that's what really put me off. I thought, I was thinking, 'Oh God. If my mother walked into my bedroom and caught me sticking a needle in my arse.' I'd just, it would just be the shame of it. So.

And, as we shall see below, it is the failure to complete a cycle which marks out, according to many respondents, the abuser. Failure to use steroids within a cycle betokens a lack of discipline and the absence of a planned goal.

It should be clear here that this ethnopharmacological knowledge is not equivalent to the pharmacological knowledge of the scientific specialist. It is not simply that this ethnopharmacological knowledge is not clear and distinct. There are certainly confusions in our steroid-users' knowledge: while one respondent (S03) confidently described Winstrol as 'liver toxic', another (S44) stated equally confidently that 'Winstrol is non-toxic to the body'. However, as Schutz (1970, 1962; Schutz and Luckmann 1974) has pointed out in his work on the social distribution of knowledge, there are many elements of common-sense thinking in scientific thinking and indistinctness in scientific thinking too. What distinguishes steroid-users' ethnopharmacological knowledge most clearly from pharmacological knowledge is its focus on the particular rather than the general, its focus on the particular bodily experience of the individual user. This individualised knowledge is explained by users partly in terms of differences in genetic make-up and susceptibility to different regimens, but mainly in terms of the need continually to alter cycles in order to overcome increased toleration of the drugs in the present cycle:

> *Int: How come you sort of changed from them and tried different things? I mean did you just start experimenting or what? What were you doing?*
> S35: No. What . . . what it is, as soon as I started taking em I wanted to find out a bit more about em. Because, like you know, I didn't want to just take something where I didn't even know what the effect was, what it does, or nothing. So I thought I'd have read up on it. Other people talk to you about it, people who know about it, like. And they said that if you do stay on the same thing for. . . . After about six weeks, it's not going to work for you anyway, no matter what is. Cos your body gets used to it. Your receptors won't accept it any more. So after it's about six weeks, you're better off changing to. . . . Still using an anabolic, but using a different anabolic, so your body is having something different, so it won't get too used to it. So that way then your body [is] still going to keep growing, whereas if you do stay on the same thing for six months you're just going to have no effect at all. Like, so you're just wasting money that way. So that's the only reason why I just keep changing.

Ethnopharmacological knowledge emphasises the importance of individualised knowledge, of flexibility, change and personalised planning. It emphasises the importance of the careful monitoring of drugs administration and of effects; it encourages and legitimises an experimental approach to drug-taking.

Use and abuse: 'It's about control'

While ethnographies of other groups of drug-users have also noted the consuming interest that all drug-users have in matters connected with drug use – strengths, purities and effects, for example – the extent and specificity of many steroid-users' ethnopharmacological knowledge is clearly exceptional. Indeed, steroid-users distinguish themselves sharply from other drug-users. When a South Wales needle-exchange began to provide injecting equipment suitable for steroid-users (who, because they normally inject into muscle tissue, require larger needles than intravenous injectors), exchange staff were asked by steroid-using clients if staff would schedule separate sessions for steroid-users, as the bodybuilders did not like mixing with the exchange's other 'junkie' clientele.

The self-differentiation of one group of drug-users from another has been noted before in the literature. Davis and Munoz (1968) described the self-differentiation of LSD-taking 'heads' from Methedrine-taking 'freaks' in 1960s San Francisco. There were obviously differences in patterns of drug use, with acid being taken by 'heads' perhaps once a week, while Methedrine ('speed') was being taken by injection by 'freaks', often very much more frequently. But a critical heads/freaks distinction made by the heads themselves related to the purpose of drug use: a freak uses drugs as an end itself, but 'a head . . . uses drugs for purposes of mind expansion, insight and the enhancement of personality attributes, . . . as means for self-realisation or self-fulfilment' (ibid.: 160). Davis and Munoz noted that heads were older, higher status persons (artists, shop-owners, etc.), in contrast to the transient, quasi-criminal freaks. Playfully, and controversially at a time when the American counter-culture sought to stress a complete disjunction between itself and the culture of earlier generations of Americans, Davis and Munoz equated the instrumental/expressive, head/freak distinction with wider distinctions between American classes: 'put crudely, LSD equals self-exploration/self-improvement equals middle class, while Methedrine equals body stimulation/release of aggressive impulses equals working class' (ibid.: 161).

There is an obvious parallel here between 1960s 'heads', dropping acid as an instrument of mental and spiritual development, and that of 1990s bodybuilders injecting themselves with steroids as an instrument of bodily development. The parallel can also be taken somewhat further, since Davis and Munoz point out that by no means all acid-takers are 'heads', with 'heads' deprecating those who would trip acid at music venues and the like, just for expressive reasons, just for the hell of it, without realising the supposed higher meditative and religious potential of the drug.

Similarly, all our steroid-using bodybuilders were able to draw a distinction, not only between steroid use and the use of drugs such as amphetamines and opiates, but also between steroid *use* and steroid *abuse*. Some respondents would equate abuse simply with over-use or indiscriminate use. But there was also a view that abuse of steroids connoted the improper and unplanned taking of steroids, taking steroids without cycling plans. Indeed, over-use might be operationally defined as exceeding planned dosages, an absence of control:

> S39: there's safe limits to take [on] which to make steady gains. Or there's . . . you can make gains by taking a real. . . . If you take a large amount you are abusing it, but if you take an adequate amount, then it's nothing. Well, you know, it's safe.
> (S39: 2695–2703)

And:

> S47: Abusing is overdosing on them, taking way over the top every day, and not having breaks, and just keeping on taking them. And using is using what you are supposed to use, just taking a bit training and taking it in the right dosages.
> (S47: 1745–1751)

And:

> *Int: would you say steroid users then are similar or dissimilar to other drug users, drug abusers, like users of heroin, cocaine, or . . .?*
> S38: Um, I would say they're different.
> *Int: So could you explain?*
> S38: Different in the sense that, when they're used properly, they're done in a cycle. You come on for so long and do your cycle and then you come off. Then you're, say, off it then for a couple of months. Er, someone who's on heroin, they're on it on a daily basis, year in year out. And there's no control, there's no control on the quantities that they take
> (S38: 2717–2730)

There was a widespread recognition that steroids could be psychologically addictive, in the sense that some bodybuilders found themselves unable to cope with the inevitable weight-loss between cycles and so would attempt to combat this by continual steroid-taking. Again, such absence of control is indicative of the steroid-abuser; an individual who fails to take steroids 'correctly' and who thus increases the likelihood of potential side-effects without necessarily enhancing drug effectiveness:

> S36: it is hard to control yourself, you know, when you are losing weight, because you do get a drastic weight loss. But you learn to cope with it over the years and stop it depressing you. Like a mate of mine who is working with me now, he had a weight loss and his trousers were falling down. And he had to go back on them. This was what I was saying: he can't control it in his head, this weight loss. He had to go back on them, you know. And I lose a lot of weight. It does bother me in a way, but I know I have to come off them and I have to stay off them. This is the best way to do it and go on them when the time is right. . . . It's about control.
>
> (S36: 3342–3367)

The uncontrolled, unplanned abuse of steroids was frequently illustrated by the use of 'cautionary tales' – the term is Goffman's (1968) – like that of the friend with the falling trousers (above). These narratives nearly always relate to third parties:

> There's Meredydd who comes here [gym]. He didn't have a clue. He took a jab of Sustanon 250 and after three days took another because he thought the first jab wasn't working. Then when he didn't see any change he took another at the end of the week. F*****g hell, it takes three weeks for it to work anyway . . . Meiron said this lad doesn't train seriously.
>
> (Fieldnotes: 3559–3571)

> I know someone who took em three months before starting training as he thought they'd get him ready. F*****g prat! He just got fat – big belly hanging out here.
>
> (Fieldnotes: 3465–3471)

> S39: this person down the gym, the night before, um, he done the 'Wales' show, he literally, he literally. . . . They had, him

and a friend had a bag full of 'gear' [drugs]. He tipped it all out the bag. And he was jabbing up all night. And he took everything. And he watched his body in the mirror change . . . his head grew, his cheekbone grew. I mean he almost died actually on the stage. And he didn't know if he was coming or going. And that's bloody steroid abuse isn't it? I mean he was sticking needles in his leg, in his arse and in his back. *Int: Was he taking that Esiclene? It sort of makes the muscles swell up temporarily.* S39: Oh you put it straight into the muscles don't you? *(Yeah)* Oh I think he was taking everything. He was taking 'growth' [growth hormone]. You know, just handfuls of tablets. And, you know, just devastated: he didn't know he was on the stage . . . he didn't know where he was.

(S39: 2710–2745)

Respondents are always users, not abusers. Abusers are always third parties, except in a few instances where the currently responsible user/narrator may admit to previous abuse, when a novice:

P1: The first time I used steroids was years ago . . . I had a jab off a friend who had been training for three or four years and I'd seen him go from eleven stone to around. . . . So that's the first jab I took. In the leg as well – f*****g killed [me]. F*****g hell, that's I think down to stupidity like: I didn't even know whether . . . I could have been injecting into a main artery, like, for all I knew. I didn't know nothing, that was the first time. Eight years ago. That was the first time I ever took any steroid, injected steroid. *Int: You weren't even training then were you?* P1: No. *Int: Did you know you had to train as well for the steroids to work?* P1: No I didn't have no knowledge whatsoever about training and all that. I thought: bang at it and away you go, like.

(P1: 2256–2308)

These narratives, like story-telling in other cultures, serve to define a normative order, distinguishing proper steroid use from improper steroid abuse for all collectivity members (Coffey and Atkinson 1996). Further, delineation of boundaries is reinforced in various media of communication; for instance, broad-ranging parameters for effective and safe usage are identifiable in steroid handbooks (e.g. Phillips 1991; Duchaine 1989). However, since steroid-users' cycling theory promotes and demands *experimentation* in courses and dosages, it is not possible for narrators to specify normative 'cycles' which are universally applicable. Certainly, it would be wrong to assume cynically that improper use is simply a higher dosage or a longer course than that currently being prac-tised by the narrator, though extremely high dosages are universally condemned:

> Angharad had the *Sunday Express* and it had an article about women using anabolic steroids. There was something [in it] about the female bodybuilder featured on *The Cook Report* [television programme]. Angarad said: 'She's in a right state now. Even her teeth are supposed to have fallen out. It's her own f*****g fault though. She's a f*****g stupid cow: she took way too much.
>
> (Fieldnotes: 3811–3821)

And some drugs may also be universally condemned by story-tellers at all levels of use, for example, Nubain, an opiate-based painkiller that was briefly popular among some bodybuilders in South Wales, but led to addictive use (see the case studies reported by McBride *et al.* 1996) and is shunned by story-tellers; a ques-tionnaire study of 176 steroid-users in Cardiff reported only two instances of Nubain use (Pates and Barry 1996). Narrators also condemn steroid use unaccompanied by proper dietary regimes and training regimes, although (again) what constitutes 'proper' training may not be normatively established:

> Angharad . . . told me about Meredydd's diet: 'He said he'd made a real effort to eat before training. I asked him what he'd had that day and he said: Cake. F*****g cake! Can you believe it! He's a f*****g idiot. I asked him what sort of cake – maybe I'd got it wrong and he'd had a rice cake. No, it was a marzipan cake!
>
> (Fieldnote: 593–613)

There's some dickheads out there, there are people like that. Some of them are kids, but most aren't: they're in their twenties a lot of them. I used to train in Valleytown and they're mad there: they'll take anything, they don't care. These lads come up to me and say: 'Can you get us any gear then?' And I'd say: 'Well, you've got to be training hard for em to work.' These lads weren't: they'd only just started training really. But they'd go: 'Oh, we're training hard. Now, what can you get us?' So I'd say: 'Well, there's Dianabol'. They'd not know what it is, but they'd go, 'Dianabol, yeah, great! Get us some of that then.' I wouldn't bother, but they'd come up to me again after a week and ask: 'Where's the Dianabol then?' I'd say: 'Well you know it's twenty-five pounds' I could get it at the time for twelve pounds, but I'd say a ridiculous price, as they didn't know anything about it. I'd get it for them. Then they'd say: 'Oh my mate wants some.' So I'd be getting their mates some and here I was getting one hundred and fifty pounds a week for practically nothing. And, you know, they weren't training or eating right and after a few weeks you'd look at them and they don't look any different on it.

(Fieldnote: 3943–3978)

Clearly, to the above respondent, small-scale dealing to novice users is less opprobrious than improper steroid use. From the extracts provided, normative rules on proper and improper use may not be very specific about the content of regimens, but they nevertheless carry great force in defining the collectivity and those outside it. In short, 'outsiders', 'the fringe' and other 'marginal members' are regarded by narrators to be completely lacking in knowledge of drug-taking for bodybuilding purposes. However, it is also recognised that expertise is easily acquired by those who socialise with 'hardcore' (i.e. dedicated and committed) body-builders and who are therefore made aware of the existence of steroid handbooks and other relevant sources of information.

Conclusion

The body may itself be viewed as a reflexive project, according to Giddens (1991): the body is a possible locale (there are others) wherein the denizens of late modernity can construct for them-selves identities which are no longer their automatic birthrights. Bodybuilders would eschew any analysis which portrayed their activities as driven by a late-modern identity crisis, but their identities are crucially shaped by their physical appearance: Cooley's 'looking glass self' (1983) is no longer a mere metaphor. In this instance, identity-building takes a peculiarly physical form. Those bodybuilders who are steroid-users are engaging in chemical, not just social, constructions.

It is this project-like character of bodybuilding activities which serves to differentiate (for our respondents) steroid use from other forms of drug use and to differentiate steroid use from steroid abuse: like 1960s 'heads', bodybuilders take steroids for instrumental, rather than expressive reasons; the end of steroid-taking is not the experience itself, but the body beautiful, or the body powerful, or even the body health-full, achieved through a complex and plotted interaction of training, diet and chemical regimens. This distinction between steroid use on the one hand, and abuse (and other forms of drug use) on the other, is part of a normative order, illustrated and enforced through narratives of addiction, sloth and failure. What marks the subjects of these narratives as outcasts of the bodybuilding world, or mere apprentices not yet fit for admittance, is either over-indulgence or the lack of any planned character to their steroid use. And even over-indulgence may have connotations of a lack of planning.

Central to the planned and instrumental character of steroid use is 'cycling theory', the individual and flexible tailoring of dosages, of course-lengths, of course-combinations, of other drug combinations, of training programmes and of diets in order to maximise individual 'gains' and minimise potential side-effects in the face of different genetic susceptibilities and changing patterns of drug tolerance. Cycling theory both requires detailed ethnopharmacological knowledge and self-monitoring and encourages a degree of individual freedom in self-experimentation. The bodybuilder scans the mirror, not just in gratification, but also as a scientific scrutineer: the adage 'your body is a temple' is being replaced with 'your body is a laboratory' (*Muscle-Media 2000* 1996). This self-experimentation has no final and triumphal end. There is no Holy Grail at the end of The Cycling Quest, no ultimate and perfect cycle: cycling theory demands constant and progressive change to confound drug tolerances.

Concern has been expressed about the health risks associated with steroid use (e.g. Klein 1995). Steroid use has been linked (although not perhaps directly or conclusively) with increased propensities to violence ('roid rage'), with acne, gynaecomastia, changes in libido and appetite, with blood-borne diseases, lesions and trauma associated with harmful injecting practices, with infertility (Lloyd *et al.* 1996) and with long-term physiological damage – particularly damage to the liver, kidneys and the cardiovascular system (see, for example, the review by Kashkin (1992) and the self-reported side-effects of steroid use in Korkia and Stimson's (1993) national survey of steroid-users). Not all the necessary laboratory work has been concluded, but it seems plausible that physiological damage to the liver and kidneys is likely to be associated with medium-to-long-term steroid use, often at high and increasing dosages. Following this line of argument through, cycling theory, with both its careful self-regulation of use and its legitimisation of continuing and progressive self-experimentation, becomes both a guard against, and a spur towards, such self-damage. Indeed, bodybuilders themselves may concede that some chemistry experiments are best conducted in the laboratory, rather than the home. However, citing limitations in the existing research base and medicine's longstanding reluctance to accept the performance-enhancing properties of steroids, bodybuilders are currently more likely to give primacy to their own shared ethnoscientific understandings of anabolic steroids over the warnings of clinicians and pharmacologists.

Acknowledgements

The research reported on here was supported by the Economic and Social Research Council (ESRC). An earlier version of this chapter was presented at the BSA Medical Sociology Group Conference. We gratefully acknowledge the help of our many anonymous research subjects, of numerous service-providers in South Wales (not least Dick Pates, Huw Perry and Andrew McBride) and of Sam Edwards, who assisted in some of the interviewing.

References

Bloor, M. (1978) 'On the analysis of observational data: a discussion of the worth and uses of inductive techniques and respondent validation', *Sociology* **12**, 542–52.
Coffey, A. and Atkinson, P. (1996) *Making Sense of Qualitative Data: complementary research strategies*, London: Sage.
Cooley, C. (1983 [1902]) *Human Nature and Social Order*, London: Transaction.

Davis, F. and Munoz, L. (1968) 'Heads and freaks: patterns and meanings of drug use among hippies', *Journal of Health and Social Behaviour* **9**, 156–65.

Duchaine, D. (1989) *Underground Steroid Handbook II*, USA: Daniel Duchaine.

Frake, C. (1980) 'The diagnosis of disease among the subanun of Mindanao', in *Language and Cultural Description*, Stanford, CA: Stanford University Press.

Gaines, C. (1974) *Pumping Iron: the art and sport of bodybuilding*, New York: Simon and Schuster.

Giddens, A. (1991) *Modernity and Self-Identity*, Oxford: Polity Press.

Goffman, E. (1968) *Asylums*, Harmondsworth: Penguin.

Kashkin, K. (1992) 'Anabolic steroids', in Lowinsohn, J. (ed.) *Substance Abuse*, Baltimore, MD: Williams and Wilkins.

Klein, A. (1986) 'Pumping irony: crisis and contradiction in bodybuilding', *Sociology of Sport Journal* **3**, 112–33.

Klein, A. (1993) *Little Big Men: bodybuilding subculture and gender construction*, Albany, NY: State University of New York Press.

Klein, A. (1995) 'Life's too short to die small', in Sabo, D. and Gordon, F. (eds) *Men's Health and Illness: gender, power, and the body*, London: Sage.

Korkia, P. and Stimson, G. (1993) *Anabolic Steroid Use in Great Britain: an exploratory investigation*, Final Report to the Departments of Health for England, Scotland and Wales, London: The Centre for Research on Drugs and Health Behaviour.

Lloyd, F., Powell, P., Murdoch, A. (1996) 'Anabolic steroid abuse by body builders and male subfertility', *British Medical Journal* **313**, 100–1.

McBride, A., Williamson, K., Peterson, T. (1996) 'Three cases of nalbuphine hydrochloride dependence associated with anabolic steroid use', *British Journal of Sports Medicine* **9**, 13–24.

Macintyre, S. and Oldman, D. (1977) 'The patient as expert: coping with migraine', in Davis, A. and Horobin, G. (eds) *Medical Encounters*, London: Croom Helm.

Monaghan, L. (1995) *Becoming a Steroid User: a "phenomenological" approach to the activity of steroid use amongst bodybuilders*, Salford Papers in Sociology no. 16, Salford: University of Salford.

Muscle Media 2000 (1996) 'Your body is a laboratory', October, 123.

Pates, R. and Barry, C. (1996) 'Steroid use in Cardiff: a problem for whom?' paper presented to the Seventh International Conference on Drug-Related Harm, Hobart, April.

Phillips, W. (1991) *The Anabolic Reference Guide*, issue no. 6, USA: Mile High Publishing.

Schutz, A. (1962) 'Commonsense and scientific interpretation of human action', in Natanson, M. (ed.) *A. Schutz Collected Papers Volume I*, The Hague: Martinus Nijhoff.

Schutz, A. (1970) *Reflections on the Problem of Relevance*, ed. R. Zaner. New Haven, CT: Yale University Press.

Schutz, A. and Luckmann, T. (1974) *The Structure of the Life World*, London: Heinemann.

Thirer, J. and Greer, D. (1978) 'Competitive bodybuilding: sport, art or exhibitionism?' *Journal of Sport Behaviour* **1**, 531–48.

Weis, K. (1985) Letter from the Editor, *International Review for the Sociology of Sport* **20**, 237–8.

ZviFuchs, C. and Zaichkowsky, C. (1983) 'Psychological characteristics of male and female bodybuilders: the iceberg profile', *Journal of Sport Behaviour* **6**, 136–46.

Chapter 3

Immunology on the street

How nonscientists see the immune system[1]

Emily Martin

> They knew about the digestive system 'cause they had to eat, and they knew about the circulatory system because sometimes they bleed, by accidentally cutting themselves or falling. But who on earth has ever thought about the immune system? Only the elite few, people with allergies, understood, you know? Only the elite few, and now everybody else has got to learn about this thing? The immune system that's everywhere in the body? And, oh my God, what is a thymus gland?
>
> (Jewell Franklin)

> I mean the whole purpose of your studies is a sort of immunology on the street.
>
> (Bruce Kleiner)

Does 'the immune' system live in the popular imagination? When I began this study, I was quite prepared to have this question answered negatively or at least indifferently. Although by the 1990s the immune system had a robust existence in the disciplines of science, and although it had made many dramatic appearances on the stage of print and video media, these developments did not necessarily mean that ordinary people without training in the sciences would have much to say on the subject.

As we began to have conversations and carry out extended interviews in several neighbourhoods, it quickly became apparent that people had a great deal to say about the immune system. The topic itself, set in the context of a general discussion about health and well-being, seemed to open up an imaginative field in which people readily explored their ideas about the body and society.

What became clear is that the media coverage of the immune system does not encompass very well the body-imagery with which people are in fact operating. The dominant message of the media, clothed in the accoutrements of warfare, accompanied by the trappings of the hierarchies of gender, race and class, would be very misleading if we were to take it as evidence of how people are thinking. Other, subordinate messages present in the media, not as vividly brought to the fore – depictions of complex, nonhierarchical systems embedded in environments composed of other complexly interacting systems – are what many people have already given a lively existence in their daily lives and commonsense conceptions. In a sense, the ground on which the old-style immune armies would march has already been seized by completely new forces, who have something other than war in mind.

The basic idea

In our interviews, the most fundamental, widespread agreement – across all social categories of age, gender, class and sexuality – about the immune system is that it is something inside our bodies that protects us from disease. John Marcellino explains the shift in his thinking from germs that 'just didn't come in' to 'something inside that fights these things'.

> *Suppose that you're with a person that has something that is contagious, say the flu. And you do not get the flu. What would you say is happening inside you at that point?*
> What's happening inside of you is that your body is somehow fighting off those germs. I saw a National Geographic video, they had this thing, I think it's in your white blood cells or something, and a germ would go into your body, and this thing would like surround it.
> *The white blood cell?*
> Yeah, and it would come around, and then it would eat it. And that's what happens . . . I would say probably before what I thought happened is that you were just lucky not to get it, it just didn't come in, you know, didn't get to you. But I understand now.
> *But you didn't analyse it farther?*
> No . . . I would say probably it's because you were taking care of yourself. You know, you're getting enough sleep at night,

you know what I mean, or you're eating good, or whatever. But not I understand that there's something inside your body that's fighting these things, and so these things come in, and they fight them off.

Echoes of the general idea that Marcellino expresses are exceedingly common in our interviews with people from every ethnic and socioeconomic background, every gender and generation. An African-American female teacher in her forties told us: 'Well, the immune system, I think, is that part of your body which fights off disease, and it's a very important part of your system. Without an immune system that's functioning properly, you're susceptible to pick up a lot of germs, diseases, etc.' (Julia Sarton). When we asked 'what the body does if you're around someone that's sick, and say you don't get sick', an elderly Euro-American male who was a retired seaman responded:

> Well, I figure, what do they call them, you got, your immune. Your body builds up immunity to certain things, and if you're around a person has a certain type of sickness, if you don't get it, fine . . .
> *So what's your understanding of how the immune system works?*
> It's something in your body. Something inside your body that blood builds up. And they got a lot of technical names I don't know, but they help you build up in your body immunity to these certain diseases.
>
> (Jack Morgan)

A Euro-American, male financial adviser in his twenties said:

> I just know vague, vague things . . . basically that if your immune system works, it keeps you from being ill. If it doesn't work, you're susceptible to all kinds of things, whether it's the common cold or something like cancer or AIDS. I couldn't tell you where it's located.
> *So can you sort of speculate on how the system actually works or what's involved in the function?*
> Well, I mean I know there are antibodies that fight intruding bacteria or virus. I don't know if those things pop off the cell, you know, and invade these viruses or what have you. And I know that they have something to do with the white cells, I think.

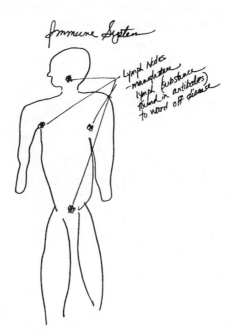

Figure 3.1 John Parker's drawing of the immune system

> *But do you know how all these things work together? What are the*
> *white blood cells doing, or, you mentioned antibodies?*
> Well, I think the white cells are killer cells, they kill off bacteria
> and unwanted particles that get into the blood stream, I guess.
> Red blood cells, I guess, keep you healthy otherwise. I don't
> know. I hated science.
>
> (John Parker)

In spite of his assertion that he did not know where the immune
system is located, this interviewee, John Parker, offered to draw a
picture of his idea of the immune system, which shows how widely
dispersed throughout the body he imagines it to be (Figure 3.1).

For most people, the system inside determines whether you are
going to get sick or stay well. As Sarah Christopher, a young
African-American fast-food worker, put it, in response to the question 'Well tell me, let's say you've been hanging around someone
who's sick, and by all rules of nature you should have gotten sick

too, but you don't catch it. What do you think's protecting you? I mean why is it that you don't have it?':

> I must have antibodies, a strong immune system, just fighting them off . . . my immune system must go to say, you know, you're not going to catch this, this is not for you to catch, and fight it off, those little germs in the air.

Katherine Johnson, a Euro-American midwife in her thirties, explained how she would tell her son why she caught a cold and he did not:

> One way of looking at that is that I got exposed to the bacteria and couldn't fight it and he could, and the other way of looking at that is that we both got exposed, but my system didn't hold up and his did. Or another way of looking at that is that we both always had that bacteria, but because of stress or whatever, it was able to take over in my system and not in his.

It seems to follow from a robust notion of an internal system of protection that the system exists to ward off continual threats. People focus their attention on the well-being of the system rather than on creating an environment that is free from threat. We have seen how the dominant model of disease prevention before 1970 focused on cleaning surfaces of the body and the house to keep them germ free. As we might expect, people in our interviews frequently express the notion that the environment surrounding our bodies contains many dangers that cannot ever be eliminated:

> *Why do you wipe the top of your soda can off?*
> Oh, because it's dirty, and it's germy, and I know even by wiping it, you noticed I used a wet cloth and then I dried it off? Even by wiping it, I'm still getting the germs, but at least I don't see that black dirt. I'm not putting my mouth up to it, but I know that it still gets dirty. I used to be really neurotic about certain things, like I wouldn't eat, I was just so, so fussy. If something dropped on the table, I wouldn't eat it cause it would, you know, probably get germs on it. Now I pick it up off the floor and eat it. I just know that I'm, you know, ingesting plenty of germs. I mean when you

see the kitchens of some restaurants and stuff and it just grosses you out.

(Gillian Lewis)

Nothing that I have said so far justifies my earlier claim that the warfare model so common in the media does not provide the dominant logic for these accounts of the immune system. In fact, there seems to be no dearth of military imagery used by the people we interviewed. For one man, an architect, the immune system is 'an incredible policing thing, a system-wide authority that works' (Eliot Green). For a midwife, it is 'a monitoring system and a defense system at the same time' (Katherine Johnson). For a special education teacher, the immune system is 'like our army. We have the army and then we have special forces . . . if one level of protection fails, the next step is taken. The body won't give up unless we give up' (Jewell Franklin). A reporter draws a picture (see Figure 3.2) to illustrate how it was 'fascinating there was this little war going on in your body; the good cells are fighting the bad cells' (Joel Robertson). Laura Peterson comments that 'the only thing modern medicine uses is this image of fighting, which is sort of a warlike image, so that's what I think I'll [draw]. I don't really know that that's accurate, but it's ingrained in my mind' (see Figure 3.3).

To put these uses of military metaphors in a more complicated context, we asked people to reflect specifically on their import. We did this while showing people media images of the body at

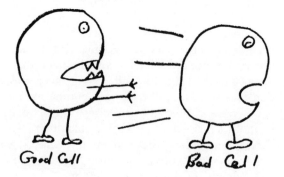

Good Cell   Bad Cell

Figure 3.2 Joel Robertson's drawing of the immune system

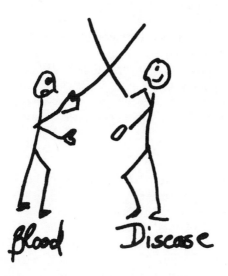

Figure 3.3 Laura Peterson's drawing of the immune system

war (covers of *Time* and *US News and World Report*). Given this opportunity, several people burst forth with statements about what they saw as the dire consequences of using militaristic imagery to picture what goes on inside the body. Peter Rodriguez, for example, thought that

> the military motif is an unhealthy way of constructing it because . . . it supports the military's kind of power structure and sexism of society . . . I think another effect of this military conception of the whole thing is it puts the conception into that of a foreign invasion, and there's this outsider that we don't like who's in our midst, and we want rid of them to get out, and we have to resort to violence against people to get rid of them. I think that only sparks violence against people. I think that only supports everyone's homophobia. I think it only supports everybody's xenophobia.

Although most people did not have such well-informed positions, many were able to produce a plethora of alternative images, such as eating (Brackette Thompson), dancing or playing (Sarah Christopher), or simply convincing it to go away (David Feldman):

The whole thing of war is not one that I take to very well. I mean, eating, this sounds, like, less threatening, because when you think of eating you're just like, 'oh, you need to eat'. But you think of war, what usually comes to mind is destruction and death and all of these things. When you really think about it, when you eat, like you're destroying stuff too, but ... food and eating is a necessary part of life, whereas war isn't. You don't need war. You need to eat to, you know, survive.

(Brackette Thompson)

See this Fred Astaire, and he's a white blood cell, and he's going to step on Ginger Roger's head, and it's the way, you know, he does it ... or make a game out of it. You're the white blood cell, and I'm the red blood cell. So, hey, that would be excellent, make a game out of it. You know, the white blood cell gets the red blood cell, and we would box or, you know, play a game of charades or something. So I guess there are a lot of different ways of looking at it.

(Sarah Christopher)

I've always thought of it as somehow eliminating it, rather than destroying it, and more subsuming it, depriving it of its power, more passive. Somehow less of a clash, more of a 'convince it to go way' kind of thing. Show it the door rather than ... somehow that seems more peaceful to me, that it takes it in and somehow digests the cell and then fits into the life cycle. Take the bad guys and use them for your own good rather than destroying them.

(David Feldham)

There are many possible reasons why people would frequently choose a militaristic image first but, when offered the chance, could come up with many different images. The omnipresence of military imagery in the media and the authority carried by information about a scientific topic are possible relevant factors. But the kind of society and world in which different people grow up may also be important. In our interviews, all manner of people could produce military images: young people, old people, and especially ageing baby boomers, who came of age during the Cold War era of the 1940s and 1950s, when imagery of the body as a fortress or a castle was most vibrant. But *all* the examples that struck me as the most elaborated, vivid departures from military imagery came from people in their late teens and early twenties, people coming of age at a time when Cold War assumptions are being drastically shaken and a new sensibility about how the body relates to the world may be arising.

In spite of my assertion that complex notions of the immune system occur throughout the interviews, there were a few cases in which someone had absolutely nothing to say on the subject. These instances include a teenage single mother who was unemployed, a couple in their seventies whose models of the body fit very well with the pre-1970 models and a social worker in her forties. I could understand the relative isolation of the young mother and the older couple, but the social worker's response remained a puzzle until she happened to mention that she was legally blind and so never read newspapers or magazines and never watched television. In a real sense these are exceptions that prove the rule. Being isolated from public culture – for whatever reason – may be the only way to escape acquiring, relating to, and worrying about an immune system.

Another way in which to see the complexity of people's thinking about health and their bodies is to look in some detail at how people have developed ways of looking at the immune system as a *complex system*. My goal here is simply to show how the basic elements of this idea permeate the accounts that people gave us of how their bodies work.[2]

Two accounts that include most of the main elements of the way in which the immune system is often thought to work are these:

> Basically, it's a real complicated series of things that ties everything together. And when something goes wrong in your body, signals go out, and cells go to attack it. I guess it's basically just a system of checks and balances, and most things the immune system in the body can deal with on its own. . . . For the most part, it just sort of keeps everything in line with the metabolic computer.
> *Metabolic computer – that's great! I love it!*
> I guess it says, 'You need some of this. You need some of this'. This constantly controlling your body. Keep the good things running correctly and get rid of the bad things.
>
> (Arthur Harrison)

What I learned was that the AIDS virus somehow hides in the body and the T cell doesn't know that it's there. And I thought, well, that makes sense. If we could find a way to expose it, then maybe the immune system, which is so complex and so intricate, beyond my wildest dreams, or a connecting network of things, could win. And I know my peers that have had AIDS, and I've spoken with them, they said, I would rather have been told I had cancer, 'cause at least they could have cut it out . . . AIDS seems so massive. We all learn quickly when we get it or if we come close to someone, that the immune system goes from your fingertips to the end of your hair. I mean, it's everywhere in your body; you cannot get away from it.

(Jewell Franklin)

Let us unpack the main elements of the way in which this system works. First, this system is not localised in particular places in the body. As Jewell Franklin says, 'it's everywhere'. Two men in their seventies (Jack Smith and John Braun) discussed *Time* magazine's illustration of the immune system as the white blood in a boxing match with the vicious virus. John Braun asserted that

the immune system is the whole body; it's not just the lungs or abdomen. . . . If I cut myself, doesn't my immune system start to work right away to prevent infection? So it's in your finger; I mean it's everywhere. So that would be my criticism to *Time* magazine.

This system is composed of a great many parts 'beyond our wildest dreams'. There *are* parts, and each has a job to do, but the point that interviewees stressed is that the parts work together in complex ways to make a whole: it is 'a complete network, a backup system' (Peter Black). Some of the most vivid descriptions of this feature of the system came when we showed people the media illustrations of the immune system:

What do you think of their [Time magazine's] representation of the immune system? Does it make a lot of sense to you or not? Would you make it different?
Yeah, I would, you know, 'cause it's like I said, I don't think of the immune system as being a one-being thing. You know,

I mean I would have a battle scene here, you know. Not just a fight, I would have a whole battle scene, kind of *Gone-with-the-Wind*-ish.

(Charles Kingsley).

Is there anything that compares itself to the immune system? I mean, putting platelets and blood aside, if you had to pick something else that it reminds you of?
Fish. You ever seen the little cartoon where the bigger fish eats the little fish?
Sure.
And then the bigger fish eats the medium fish. It's kind of like that. But sometimes, the only problem is if the disease is as big as the other fish, as your immune system, that's when you have problems.
OK, so this is Time magazine. This is how you imagine the immune system to be?
. . . Well, I think there's more than your white blood cells fighting. That's just totally too narrow. See, my fish was the whole system; it wouldn't just be the white blood cells. 'Cause you got all kinds of things.

(Charlene Kelsey)

This is from a Time magazine cover.
White cell wonder versus the virus, vicious virus. That could be a healthy person . . . I'd want my white blood cells to be that healthy. Kind of like it makes you wonder why he's just watching instead of helping.
The man in the picture?
Yeah, instead of doing more to help.
Like what kind of thing?
Maybe show him taking some medicine or eating something healthy or something like that. What gets the white blood cell to be healthy, healthy enough to fight off the virus?

(Tara Holcolm)

Charles imagines a panoramic view of a monumental battle scene in *Gone with the Wind*; Charlene imagines fish swallowing fish in an infinite regression to represent 'the whole thing'; Tara imagines the person's daily activities intrinsically related to what the cells inside the body are doing.

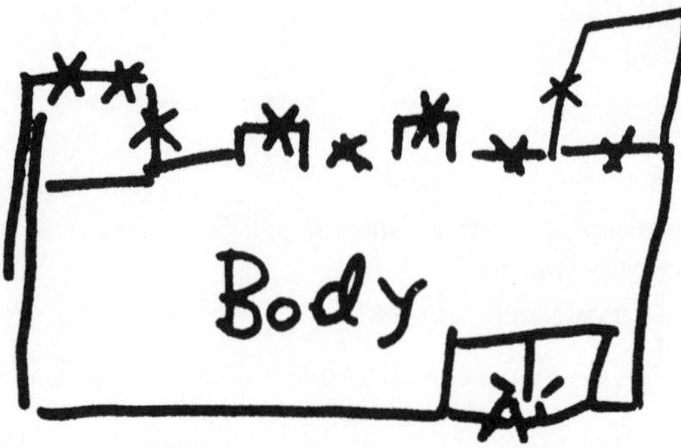

Figure 3.4 Barbara McGuire's drawing of the immune system

Even though the immune system is 'everywhere', it is clearly thought to interact with other complex systems in the body. Barbara McGuire develops a complex picture of how her uncle's cancer interfered with one system after another in his body. Finally it even entered the management system in his brain. She commented that, when one system succumbs to cancer, it is hard for the others to maintain themselves because they are interdependent. Later in the interview, she sketched in imagination, and in an actual drawing (see Figure 3.4), her conception of how the parts of the body's immune system work together:

> See, I think this is your body, and then you've got all these little critters that hang out in here, and they're guards. And when they see somebody trying to come in and hurt you, they'll go down, and they try to defend this. But, in order to have guards, these guys got to get fed someplace and get clothes. Your blood brings them stuff to make them like strong. ... They got to get some kind of nurture or something to take care of themselves so they can take care of something coming into the door that you don't want. They could have their own nice little sitting rooms. ... Let's say it's a normal house and you've got a leak in the roof. You know, mom and dad go to fix it. If you didn't feed mom or dad, put some clothes on them, they couldn't do that. These little guys, they've got a nice condo with a hot tub.
>
> (Barbara McGuire)

Even though she draws a picture of a fortress, stressing the older, pre-1970s vision of the body's separation from the outside, what is added here is the stress on the interdependence of its residents: the defending cells have to be cared for themselves in order to care for the body.

Vera Michaels objected to the *Time* cover because it depicts 'such violence going on in our bodies'. She insisted that such violence is 'not in there'. She claimed that her own representation would be 'less dramatic'.

> My visualisation would be much more like a piece of almost tides or something . . . the forces, you know, the ebbs and flows.
> *Could you draw anything like that?*
> I could. I don't think anybody would perceive it as a portrayal of the battle within.
> *What is it that ebbs and flows?*
> The two forces, I mean, the forces . . . imbalance and balance.

As she spoke, she drew an illustration (see Figure 3.5) labelling it *the waves*.

A case could be made that the women we interviewed were more likely than the men to elaborate non-military imagery for the immune system or to reject media images framed in those terms. In addition to the women I quote above, for example, Linda Rosen found 'the whole battle notion and the boxing gloves and all that stuff . . . alienating. I don't feel like that's what happens inside my body. And I feel like it's a real male image of how the immune system works.' But such a summary would not do justice to what we found. Not all women dislike military imagery, and some men reject it altogether. Among people we will meet later, a military veteran told us that his experiences fighting in Vietnam taught him that in war, as in the body's struggle for health, there

Figure 3.5 Vera Michaels's drawing of the immune system

is no way to know who the good guys are, and medical researchers have developed some astoundingly elaborate nonmilitary metaphors to describe the immune system. So there is no simple, linear, causal relation between one's identity as male or female and how one imagines the immune system. As we will see, this may have to do with some profound shifts that are taking place in the nature of identity itself.

In an article about the immune system, Donna Haraway asks 'Is there a way to turn the [military] discourse [of immunology] into an oppositional/alternative/liberatory approach? Is this postmodern body . . . *necessarily* an automated Star Wars battlefield in the now extra-terrestrial space of the late twentieth-century Western scientific body's intimate interior?' (Haraway 1991: 220–1). Amongst others, Vera Michaels, with her development of an image of ocean waves, tides ebbing and flowing in constant, turbulent change, begins to show us some possibilities.

So far, we have seen the immune system in popular imagination emerging as a complex, dispersed system intricately related to other complex systems. The relation between various systems is 'flat' in the sense that no one is obviously in charge; different systems may play the most important role at different times. Jewell Franklin put it particularly vividly, again in response to the *Time* magazine illustration of the boxing cells. We enter the interview as she begins to draw her rendition of the immune system (Figure 3.6).

> Well, this is my Neanderthal man.
> *OK.*
> OK? And we're going to make him happy because he doesn't have any diseases.
> *OK, great.*
> And one of the central points is in the chest bone. So I'm going to make that blue. It's going to happen right back here. And that's the thymus gland. And from that, this is where the T cells come. And there's this huge network that goes through the whole body. . . . And there's little glands over here, of course it's going to run into this person's brain, because the immune system is also, the endocrinology of the brain. . . . And there's this major network system that goes on. From that, though, you also have to consider the skeletal system. So now I want you to superimpose the skeletal system. And then of course we're going to have the bones, and this is going to

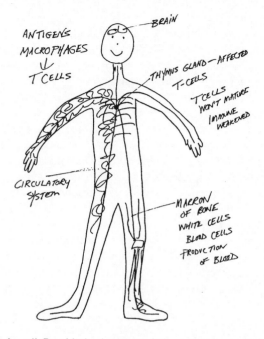

ANTIGENS
MACROPHAGES
↓
T CELLS

BRAIN

THYMUS GLAND — AFFECTED
T-CELLS

T CELLS
WON'T MATURE

IMMUNE
WEAKENED

CIRCULATORY
SYSTEM

MARROW
OF BONE
WHITE CELLS
BLOOD CELLS
PRODUCTION
OF BLOOD

Figure 3.6 Jewell Franklin's drawing of the immune system

> be the knee joint, to the amphibia, or whatever those bones
> are. Inside the marrow of the bone, white cells, blood cells,
> are produced. This is necessary for the production of blood.
> This is important because if the thymus gland is affected in
> any way, then the T cells don't mature. . . . And the immune
> system is weakened. Now that I involved the bones, where
> the production is, you also have to include the circulatory
> system because that's how everything travels.

In line with the shifting nature of the roles played by different
systems, the elements of the immune system are understood to
operate in a nonlinear fashion. That is to say that elements of the
system vary over time and their ideal stage at any one time may
not be their ideal state at another. This is completely unlike linear
variables such as strength or wealth, in which (perhaps) the more
you have, the better off you are. When it comes to the immune
system, many people think that the desirable amount of each

substance or activity depends entirely on the total context. Too much of something can be as bad as too little.

This feature of the immune system was often stressed in our interviews in the many remarks people made about health problems that they attributed to overly sensitive immune systems. To continue with Jewell Franklin's narrative:

> *Here's an artist at Time magazine, the representation they've decided to use for the immune system. Does the way they depicted it make sense to you?*
> It makes sense to me. I think it's rather infantile, I think my explanation was better. (Laughs.) You know why? Because, at least to me, it leaves everybody hanging, you know. Well where did this white cell wonder come from? What's responsible for that? How do we promote more of it if it's so necessary, and do people even understand that if there's too much of it, that we have another disease. Too many white blood cells is not good. So people might think, Oh gee, if I go out and get some white blood cells, than I can fight viruses. Where can I buy them? I mean, we have a mentality like that out there.

To work effectively, a nonlinear system must be in constant change. Like Jewell Franklin, other people talk about how elements of the immune system increase or decrease (Joan Breslau), about how the defences of the body must be variable to deal with the many types of viruses, which leads to the 'tremendous effort required to keep me in equilibrium' (Brian Torok). Gillian Lewis explains how she sees the various components of the immune system changing over time.

> I'll just say, when the white blood count is up, then there's a virus. That's about all I know. . . . And there's a T helper and a T suppresser. And they've got to be healthy and suppressing something. I guess it must be the white blood cells, and like maybe there's too many T suppresser cells, so that makes the white blood count go down, and that's why there's not enough white blood cells to fight off disease. You have a lower blood count, white blood count, when you have HIV. You're not capable of fighting off viruses, you know, like most people can.

One of the most striking images of the immune system in change is that of a perpetual motion machine:

> When I think about it in my head, I think of, you know, amoeba-like shapes moving through the body, being helpful when there's an issue or a crisis, or a contact point that's weakened, or something like that. And I think that's constant. For me I guess the best thing would be the perpetual motion machines. They always say that you can't invent a perpetual motion machine, but really, until we die, the bodies kind of are. That's what I think of it; I think of movement.
>
> (Wendy Marshall)

In what kind of change are these fluctuating mechanisms engaged? They are producing the different, specific things that the system needs at different times to handle whatever challenges it meets. In one account:

> White blood cells are just a sort of generic fighters of whatever foreign matter enters the body, and antibodies are specific for certain types of viruses that come in. It's like a lock and key type thing, where the antibody is only a certain size and shape and it has to find the right size and shape. It has to fit a certain type of virus, or it won't work.
>
> (Marsha Wilmslow)

In one imaginative description, that the body specifically designs different products, is attributed to a team of engineers:

> Now this is just my understanding, the way that it can identify foreign substance. Duplicate it, and then send it somewhere for processing, to say, OK, now how do we get rid of this? And then this team of engineers breaks in and says 'Oh, we can do this, we can do this, we can do this, we can do this. Oh great. OK, well let's build it and send it out there'. And then the new whatever it is that your body has created sends it, and it kills it.
>
> (Phillip Monroe)

In these and many other ways, people stressed the ability of the immune system constantly to change what it is producing to respond in a precise way to the constantly changing challenges presented. People told us that T cells can handle the unknown, even chemicals produced in a laboratory (Franklin Lamont); that, to handle viruses that are changing all the time, the immune system draws on an 'inventory of resistance' (Gary Sullivan); that the immune system is differentiated, specialised, and always changing (Sally Felton); that the immune system is 'continuously active' (Stephen Mattson); that the immune system shapes its response to fit, building things up so that they fit perfectly (Daniel Crofton).

Although people may or may not give the proper scientific names to the various components of the immune system (as scientists understand it), they readily and vividly convey their sense that the immune system is a complex system in interaction with other complex systems inside the body, a system that changes constantly in order to produce the specific things necessary to meet every challenge.

It is plain how detailed and ingenious people's accounts of the immune system can be. But what the words alone cannot convey is the tone in which they are said. Are people bored and indifferent, describing something they see as mundane? Are they filled with distaste or wariness, describing something they see as sinister? Or are they excited and awed, describing something they see as marvellous? In most cases, people spoke about the immune system with at least energetic interest. Quite often people would remark that they 'valued' or 'respected' their immune system. A few times people came forth with extended expressions of the awe in which they held it: 'Just that, this is the immune system, and it helps you fight disease. . . . That to me is one of the miracles of life itself . . . I become speechless when I think of things like that' (Phillip Monroe).

> To me, the body is so mysterious. I think that there's elegance to it, its solutions to problems, the fact that it compensates so well. But I don't pretend to understand the mechanics of how it works – how antibodies recognise foreign objects, how they detect them, how they shape themselves. I don't know how the antibodies shape themselves. You see these drawings in scientific shows where the virus is like this, and [the antibodies] build up just so they fit just perfectly in there.
>
> (Daniel Crofton)

This is going to sound hokey and all, but it really does make me marvel at what God has done for humans in things like the immune system and antibodies and things like that. That we are able to fight off infections, and kick them out, and prevent them from ever being hazardous again to us, things like that. And then you think about how frail people are, I mean, in reality how frail they really are. How one little germ or one little microscopic organism can put an end to life. So, like I said, it sounds hokey, but . . .

Yeah, it is pretty amazing. Just the whole orchestration of things going on, you know . . .

How everything works – to perfection. At least, for the most part.

(George Millar)

Notes

1   A previous version of this chapter appeared in Martin (1994) *Flexible bodies: tracking immunity in American Culture – from the days of polio to the age of AIDS*, Boston, MA: Beacon Press. Every effort has been made to clear copyright.
2   For a more thorough analysis of what a complex system is and what it entails see Martin (1994).

References

Haraway, D. (1991) *Simians, Cyborgs and Women: the reinvention of nature*, New York: Routledge.
Martin, E. (1994) *Flexible Bodies: tracking immunity in American Culture – from the days of polio to the age of AIDS*, Boston, MA: Beacon Press.

Chapter 4

'Feeling letdown'

An exploration of an embodied sensation associated with breastfeeding

Cathryn Britton

The breast in everyday life has received attention from various disciplines such as medicine, sociology, anthropology, psychology and politics. The focus has been on the unwell breast, for example, breast cancer (Becvar 1996; Straughan and Seow 1995; Wilkinson and Kitzinger 1994; Fallowfield 1991; Dawson 1990); the well breast featured in health promotion (Stoppard 1996; McConville 1994; Cirket 1992); breasts and sex (McConville 1994; Richardson 1990); the breast and cosmetic surgery (Allen and Oberle 1996; Davis 1995); and breastfeeding (Carter 1995; Stuart-Macadam and Dettwyler 1995; Renfrew *et al.* 1990; Palmer 1988). The focus of this chapter will be to explore in detail a common phenomenon for breastfeeding women, the letdown reflex. The letdown reflex is, in physiological terms, a neuro-hormonal response produced by stimulation of the nipple during breastfeeding, resulting in the flow of milk from milk-secreting cells in the breast tissue to the baby's mouth.[1] It is considered to be a universal response, even if a woman is unaware of its occurrence. However, letdown is not governed by the hormonal response alone but is also affected by psychological experience.

A woman's transition to motherhood is not confined to the process of birth itself but includes other components associated with mothering. The ability to breastfeed is often seen as part of the successful transition to being a 'good' mother (Carter 1995). Breastfeeding is an experience which will not be encountered in the life cycle of a woman before she gives birth therefore, prior to the event, some women try to gain information to prepare themselves for the experience. This information is gained from a variety of sources, for example friends, family and health professionals (Britton 1998, 1997). The discourse of medicine tends to reproduce a hierarchy of knowledge, presenting scientific evidence and professional knowledge as superior to learning by experience. It neglects the variability and personal significance of experience which in many cases leads to a contradiction between expectations and the reality of breastfeeding.

Women who choose to breastfeed may find themselves confronting a barrage of new sensations and emotions for which they are unprepared; one such sensation is the letdown reflex. An examination of this process, in its wider cultural contexts, provides an excellent illustration of the need to transcend narrowly reductionist accounts of embodied human experience (Csordas 1994; Lyon and Barbalet 1994; Shilling 1993). Illustrative talk from a qualitative study of women's experiences of letdown will show how social, biological and emotional factors became integrated into their experience of breastfeeding to give meaning to, and make sense of, this embodied sensation in the context of everyday lives.

Three themes have been incorporated into this chapter. The first theme explores the expectations, realities and meaning of the sensation of letdown in relation to the influence of a biological approach on the information which the women had received about breastfeeding in general and about letdown in particular. The second theme examines how women described and coped with milk leaking from the breast, and the third explores the significance attributed by the mothers to breastfeeding as a means of nourishing their babies.

The sample and method

After the birth of my child I became involved with a group of local mothers for mutual support. Through informal discussions I had with these women it became apparent that breastfeeding could be an incredibly satisfying activity but also one of concern. This led to the development of this qualitative research study in which I asked women in focus groups to talk about their breastfeeding experiences. Thirty postnatal women living in England who had breastfed agreed to participate in this initial study. The mothers were aged between 20 and 39 years and from a variety of backgrounds in terms of class, region and ethnicity. Twenty-four were first-time mothers and six were second-time mothers. The age of the babies at interview ranged from 15 days to 20 weeks. The duration of breastfeeding varied from five days to ongoing.

The women were recruited into the study by approaching existing postnatal groups. Five groups from four different areas in the south-east of England agreed to participate. Focus group interviews were considered an appropriate means by which to obtain data about the women's opinions and experiences (Kitzinger 1995; Taylor *et al.* 1995). The interviews were tape recorded and subsequently transcribed. I became familiar with the content of the interviews by listening to the tapes several times and with the transcripts by extensive close reading. The text was then sorted into thematic categories (Bernard 1995).

Sources of information about letdown

In modern industrialised societies the transmission of traditional women's lore has declined, through the fragmentation of kin networks by social and geographical mobility. Many women have neither had the opportunity to observe other women breastfeeding, nor spoken to other women about it before their own experience. Women may refer to textual accounts of breastfeeding information to help them make sense of the sensations they are experiencing and understand the bodily changes they are witnessing. In both medical and lay literature letdown is described mainly in biological terms.[2] The texts concentrate on the physiology of the letdown reflex, its function and the sensations the woman may feel. Physiologically, letdown is described as a neuro-hormonal reflex which can be inhibited by psychological influences (Palmer 1988; Llewellyn-Jones 1983; Jolly 1977). The function of the letdown reflex is explained as being necessary for the flow of milk from milk-secreting cells to the baby's mouth (Health Education Authority 1992; Ebrahim 1991; Royal College of Midwives (RCM) 1991; Renfrew *et al.* 1990). Writers often place alongside the scientific explanations of letdown details of the sensations a women may feel, as guidance as to how she can monitor her body. The sensations of letdown are not, however, described consistently across different medical texts. They have variously been described as: 'a tingling sensation or heaviness' (Ebrahim 1991: 12); 'sharp pain' (Ebrahim 1991: 15); 'needle-like pain', 'tingling sensation' or 'no sensation at all' (RCM 1991: 2). In the lay literature letdown was often described as a pleasant sensation: 'Some women feel . . . a tingle in their breasts . . . others will not feel it at all' (Renfrew *et al.* 1990: 73); '[a] sensation of milk rushing in' (Jolly 1977: 77);

'[a] tingling sensation of the milk pouring from within the breast' (Palmer 1988: 28). Even Maher (1992), in an anthropological text, suggests it is pleasurable and fails to mention differences between women, either individually or across cultures. Hence women are exposed to a proliferation of discourses which are often in contradiction with each other.

Making sense of letdown

When examining how the women made sense of the sensation of letdown the interrelationship of biological, social and emotional factors are well demonstrated. First, this section provides the woman's descriptions of letdown where they linked their expectations about the sensation with reality, the here and now. The second part demonstrates the fragile relationship of the emotions with the physical response and how the women may attempt to control the erratic leakage of breast milk to prevent their embarrassment. Third, the women's concerns with adequately nourishing their baby highlights the significance of the sensation to mothering a new baby.

Describing the sensation

When describing the immediately embodied experiences of the letdown sensation, many women struggled to find words to describe the sensations they felt, often using metaphors to illustrate their meaning. Metaphors are a way that individuals make sense of their world (Fernandez 1986), conveying the actual experience in a culturally meaningful way (Low 1994). Several authors have given examples of how individuals use metaphors to describe chronic illness and distress (Jenkins and Valiente 1994; Radley 1993; Sontag 1979) as well as 'normal' bodily processes (Martin 1987). The women assimilated these new experiences into their familiar experiential world, the metaphors provided maps for the outer edges of subjective experience. Their use of metaphor relates to two categories of experience: the descriptions of the initial sensation of letdown and the flow of milk from their body.

The descriptive terms, 'tightening' and 'tingling', occurred in the books the women had read to describe the initial sensation of letdown. Some women reproduced these terms in their narratives, as it was the dominant discourse available to them (Martin 1987), but it was evident to them and to me that they did not necessarily convey the feeling adequately as the women would add further layers to the description to communicate the individuality of the sensation.

> It is difficult to describe it. It was almost like a tightening and a, a sort of tingling, tightening, as it occurred. Quite intense, but very gentle.
>
> (Gillian)

> It was if small shards of glass were being drawn through the breast, you know, an intense sort of feeling, yeah, as though a pane of glass had been cracked inside you and was being forced out.
>
> (Andrea)

> It is a tingly sensation with an edge to it . . . something like sparks going off inside you. As though little electric currents are going off inside you that can set your teeth on edge.
>
> (Rebecca)

> There is this feeling you get inside when you know it's coming. Then it wells up causing your breasts to go hard as rocks, and you can see the breast under the skin, all bumpy and lumpy. It is this intense tightening that is like a cramp but different, something you've never experienced before. And you think 'this is coming from inside me!', it's wonderful, but boy! it can be uncomfortable sometimes.
>
> (Helen)

Uncomfortable sensations described as 'bursting', 'pain', 'hurt' were not expected by the women. They had not been prepared for this and considered whether the sensation was normal.

> I don't know how to describe it. It feels like a, I don't know, like a very strong tingling sensation. Yeh, sort of like pins and needles or like a, don't know, like a sort of, I don't know, it's really hard to explain actually. Sort of a tingling, and sometimes it hurts if your breasts are very full. And then you wonder if everything is all right.
>
> (Sarah)

> That's one of the things in the early stages that I wished they'd mentioned at the antenatal classes, and in some of the literature I read. I found the letdown reflex incredibly painful and it came

as a complete surprise because I thought it would be, yes I thought there'd be some sensation but nothing as strong, or in my case painful, and when I repeated this to a friend she said 'Oh yes, red hot wires brushing your nipples' and I said 'Yes! that's it!' I thought yes, that's put it into words now. That might've put me off if I hadn't been so determined to do it. I can understand why mothers who are undecided would find that physical discomfort sufficient to deter them. So I think a little bit more warning about that. And yet some mothers feel nothing at all. . . . [pause] Yes, that was a complete surprise.

(Abigail)

Several women described situations which reminded them of the discomfort they experienced with letdown. All the accounts were occasions when the women were away from their baby. There seemed to be an emotional association with letdown expressed as a feeling within the woman's body which she interpreted as a significant reminder of the dependency the child had on its mother.

I went shopping on my own and left him [the baby] at home with Terry. While I was at the bakery I could hear this similar cry to his and I felt this pins and needles sensation, it just felt like everything was going to burst. I felt I had to rush back home to see him for some reason, I just felt as though, you know, it's somebody trying to tell you something, your baby needs you.

(Maggie)

And then, I had to go out so I fed her before I left and I rushed out the door and ran to the lift. I got apprehensive when I was out 'cos they [breasts] started to tingle, so I rushed back and said 'is she alright', like that. She hadn't moved, she was still asleep, you know. But I shouldn't've done it, I couldn't leave her again. It wasn't right. I don't know what I'd've done if she'd been screaming when I got back. It would break my heart.

(Tracey)

During the interviews women remarked, with surprise, on the wide variations in women's experiences, believing that other women would be perceiving, or describing, a similar sensation.

Metaphors used by the women to describe the flow of milk in the breast were linked to a mechanistic paradigm of the body, using the familiar to make sense of unfamiliar sensations. Some women appeared to apply the 'plumbing' model of the body (Helman 1994) which could be attributed to other experiences in their domestic space.

> Well, I always imagined it would be like, I mean it sounds silly, but it would be like petrol when you had to, you put the pump in, then you press the thing, then it goes, it clicks-in sort of thing. I always imagine I feel a pumping sensation.
>
> (Charlotte)

> I'd say it was tingling. I mean, you'd have the feeling of moving obviously, the milk moving through when she was feeding.
>
> (Sharon)

> It was a flooding sort of, especially when you were full, you could feel it sort of draining.
>
> (Tracey)

> I expected to feel some movement inside, like a drainage or something maybe. When he went to drink it would just sort of squirt out, you know, in a sort of stream sort of thing. It was like the breast was pumping it out and I had to get him plugged in quick so that he could get the milk. Sometimes it [the milk] came out so fast it was like an overflow, and he'd be covered with milk – so messy!
>
> (Penny)

The embodied experience of letdown is highly variable, reproduced in language by grappling with terms that give meaning to the user and convey the individual experience to others. The use of metaphors helped the women to make sense of the sensations and provided illustrative accounts of these embodied experiences.

Letdown: 'a mind of its own'

In this second part the emotional self becomes more visible within the discussions of the unpredictable nature of letdown and associated embarrassment particularly in the context of bodily control, presentation of self and the leakage of body fluids. The expectation that letdown would occur during the process of feeding the baby was usually welcomed by the women. However, the delayed response or ill-timed occurrence of letdown led some women to talk of it as having a separate identity which needed to be controlled. Several women felt unprepared for the unpredictable nature of letdown which might not occur during the breastfeed as expected, or could occur unforeseeably in response to another baby's cry or for no apparent reason in a public setting: 'it was on its own kind of schedule, a mind of its own' (Rebecca).

One consequence of this unpredictability was that the mother might have had to 'work' at achieving the necessary response. A paradox of control in the context of breastfeeding is that to breastfeed effectively involves relaxation and *allowing, letting,* letdown occur, rather than trying to force it in an instrumental goal-centred way. [3] Some women recognised factors that inhibited letdown such as anxiety, anger or tiredness, and identified strategies to enable them to relax to encourage letdown to occur.

> Stephanie: I found it very difficult in other people's company and I could feel I didn't get it that often and I think that's when my problems with breastfeeding really began. At Christmas we went down to my parents-in-law, who I don't know that well, and I found it really difficult breastfeeding in front of them. I could actually feel that I was never getting the letdown.
> CB: *What were you expecting to feel?*
> Stephanie: I thought it was just continuous. I just thought that when the baby was on the nipple it was just continuous milk. I didn't realise that it was anything to do with your emotional being. But I could tell as soon as someone came into the room, I could feel it stop. Because I'd be tense and I was embarrassed. All I could say was, when I was relaxed again it would happen. I had to really think hard, and encourage it to come and quite often I used to close my eyes and I'd think [pause] and then suddenly I'd feel a tingle and then a sort of filling up.

Another repercussion of its unpredictability was that their breasts sometimes leaked breastmilk. The external presence of their breastmilk affected women in different ways. A few women experienced very little leaking of breastmilk while breastfeeding. While they were pleased they were spared the embarrassment of dealing with a 'messy' fluid, it caused some to wonder if they had sufficient milk to nourish their baby.

I had minimal amounts of leaking, I mean at times when he would cry, yes, that would sort of stimulate it. But I don't think I ever had the quantity of milk that was sort of free to leak away, there wasn't that amount there. But in the shower and things it would leak from time to time but not, I don't think to the degree of being soaked or anything.

(Rosie)

For some women it was a reassuring sign of breastfeeding success, a reminder of their body's ability to nourish their baby.

I only really leaked at night, it would be in the morning, that's when I'd notice it. During the day not too much really, I found the breast pads soaked up as much as came out. I mean, it sounds silly, but I used to be quite glad when I leaked because I used to think, oh yes, I've got milk. I was so paranoid that I didn't have enough milk to feed her, because, you know, people in the medical profession were making me feel that she wasn't putting on the weight that she should be and therefore it was all my fault. But I used to be really glad, I used to think, oh well I have got milk, and it's there and it was evidence, so.

(Stephanie)

I didn't leak much anyhow apart from during the night if she hadn't woken up. It didn't bother me as I kind of felt I must be doing it properly. I felt sort of pleased that I had something to show. I was desperate to get those breast pads in (laughter). I had a friend that said, 'You know I'd wake up in the morning and there was milk spurting everywhere', and I thought this was going to happen to me. It never did.

(Daphne)

For a couple of women, the idea that breastfeeding was 'natural' and leaking a part of the course of breastfeeding enabled them to transcend their worries about discrediting themselves in public.

I don't think leaking ever bothered me though, I think if I've had a patch I've just thought 'Oh sod it' sort of thing, I think I've got to the stage where I just think well, this is natural and if other people don't like it they can lump it.

(Ailsa)

My sweater would be wet down one side, but I never used to let it get me down or anything because I used to think 'Oh, it's just part of it'. The thing is, it wouldn't have bothered me, if I was at someone's house, I think people who know me would have totally understood.

(Charlotte)

Women found the prospect of leaking not only would confirm the presence of breastmilk and provide reassurance, but also meant that the visibility of their breastmilk became an embarrassment. Breastmilk that leaks from the breast and is visible on clothes may be considered 'out of place' (Douglas 1984) as it has crossed a body boundary. All the women used breast pads inside their bras to absorb any leakages from the breast. They found it irritating that their clothes were sometimes stained by milk and embarrassed if this was seen by others, especially strangers.

I was embarrassed by it because the whole front of my shirt was covered, I had no idea! It was just so obvious, and I was unaware it was there and I just wondered how long I had paraded around looking like that, because I went through my breast pads like you would not believe it.

(Rebecca)

And that's another problem I thought, is the leaking, you know, if you forgot to put breast pads in it's quite embarrassing, you may need to keep changing your clothes.

(Amy)

I had a very embarrassing situation. Suddenly, that was it, I felt it [letdown] and I thought, 'Oh my God' and there it was, leaked all over the place. My breast pads had failed me. I had two great big wet patches. . . . I didn't want it to happen and it did, typical.

(Theresa)

I don't think I would have liked to have walked down the street with everyone else looking at me. I had very little leakage anyway but I mean I would have felt very embarrassed by it.

(Penny)

There were many accounts about how this aspect of breastfeeding necessitated being in control of an uncontrollable, unpredictable fluid by using devices (such as breast pads) to conceal the uncontrolled from others. This became an issue especially when in the public eye where the woman wanted to be successful at managing her body in public.

> Leaking has never really bothered me. I mean I still wear breastpads when I'm out. A couple of times it was quite embarrassing like, I'd open the door to the postman or something and I'd shut it and I'd realise like there's this big stain or something. He must have thought, but you know, it doesn't matter. It didn't bother me, no. I wouldn't say that I leaked that much that when I went out, I never leaked through the pad. It didn't bother me at all.
>
> (Tracey)

> I am surprised I didn't drown in the night! I was so cold because I would wake up and be so wet. You know I never knew I was spurting . . . you know I just had to keep changing those breast pads. I think the worst thing about breast feeding was sleeping with a bra on and having these things [breast pads] packed in you.
>
> (Rebecca)

> Jean: I don't actually think they [breast pads] work very well either.
> Sally: Yeh, I've had a few accidents, they won't stay in. I kept thinking I had odd shaped boobs or something because they didn't fit.
> Jean: And I couldn't understand why I had all these wet patches, you know, and some days I'd have, like, so many [breast pads] in there I'd be like Dolly Parton because I've big boobs, plus about five breast pads in there, and still they'd let me down.

The discussions about the use of breast pads created an impression that the women invested trust in these products to protect them from embarrassing emissions, keeping breastmilk invisible from others. This enabled them to maintain the appearance of a well-controlled civilised body, albeit one which has the capacity to disgust (Lupton 1995). Breast pads are marketed as 'specially developed to control the *problem* of excess and leaking milk'; to 'protect your clothes from wetness and staining'; coloured white 'for greater discretion'; to 'ensure comfort and *security*' (my emphasis). Similar wording is used for the advertising of panty liners or sanitary wear – products concerned with vaginal discharge, incontinence or menstruation and associated with the fear some women have of leaking urine or blood in public (Britton 1996). Hence, these marketing strategies emphasise the avoidance of being discredited in public and the soaking up of unpredictable leaking female fluids.

> [Leaking] is not very nice, it's sort of like wetting yourself really. You don't want stains round your clothes, especially if you've got a blouse or something on when it can really show up. Yeh, like I say, it's like wetting yourself, isn't it? It's an involuntary thing. You wouldn't want people to see wet knickers in public, so you don't want people to see this either.
>
> (Sally)

Although few women spoke of a correlation between breastmilk and excretion further exploration of this concept may provide a valuable contribution to the issue of embarrassment.

First, these accounts illustrate how the body may be constructed as being out of control, discrediting and embarrassing the woman in public, an example of how normal physiological processes can be construed as violating norms of 'civilised' bodily comportment (cf. Elias 1978; Goffman 1968). Second, these differences of bodily control illustrate how breastfeeding operates on the edge of human agency, in a context where medical discourses provide mothers with mixed messages about the individuality of control. On the one hand medical descriptions of letdown constitute it as a *reflex* determined by stimulus/response linkages and operating within the autonomic nervous system. This is reinforced by the mechanistic flavour of the hydraulic metaphors embodied in the terms draught, milk ejection and letdown reflex. On the other hand, health education discourse provides information to women in order to foster enhanced rational, individual and instrumental control over bodily processes (Lupton 1995).

The significance of letdown

This part focuses attention on the significance of letdown to the women and identifies clues the women may use to gauge whether their bodies are functioning normally. Texts describe letdown as necessary for the physiology of lactation but rarely indicate when it may be first experienced. The women in the study were confused about when they should first expect to feel the letdown sensation. They commented that this information was lacking in the texts. Some women expected to feel the sensation of letdown soon after birth but did not experience it until several weeks postnatally, a few did not feel it at all.

> Angela: I can honestly say I didn't feel anything.
> *CB: Were you expecting to feel something?*
> Angela: Yes, a great rush like a waterfall. But nothing.

The absence of the sensation created some anxiety and bewilderment about how the baby could be nourished, especially as it is promoted as being necessary for the physiology of lactation.

> They [books] describe it that you'll definitely know when it is happening and I sat there and thought, 'oh I wonder when this will happen'. ... I was conscious that something was going to happen but it took several weeks ... I was thinking 'oh I wonder if I have got a letdown' and then it did happen.
>
> (Daphne)

> I felt as though it was about five weeks until I really got my milk through. Until then she hadn't been taking it very well, she probably wasn't getting much, then I started to feel full ... getting that ache and a sort of pins and needles pain ... but it took me five weeks, I was very worried that she was getting nothing.
>
> (Dympna)

> It was about six weeks before I was ever, *ever* aware of a letdown. I mean I used to think quite often she wasn't getting any milk because I, I wasn't feeling something all the time. I thought that I'd feel the whole time when the milk was coming

out and I was . . . amazed that she'd put on any weight, because I used to think, 'Oh she's just sucking and sucking air'.

(Stephanie)

When, after a few weeks, letdown was eventually felt by the majority, the women often expressed relief that they had a sign, even though the sensation may have been uncomfortable, as they viewed this as an indicator that the infant was receiving milk and would become satisfied. A couple of mothers in the study blamed the lack of success with breastfeeding on the fact that they had not felt letdown and assumed, therefore, that the baby had obtained insufficient milk. The women sometimes doubted their ability to feed their baby, even though the baby appeared content and thriving, because they placed greater emphasis on the sensations occurring (or not) in their body. One woman, though, was unconcerned: 'I certainly don't feel this reflex thing at all. But, I mean, he certainly seems to be getting the milk, he seems satisfied' (Jean).

Other women looked for clues from their baby to monitor the occurrence of letdown, for example: a satisfied baby during feed and after, noises baby makes, movements and actions of babies.

She's not frantic any more, it's obviously there, she's more controlled.

(Daphne)

She makes moaning noises when it hasn't come and that stops as soon as letdown comes in.

(Ailsa)

You can see that they are actually getting more, can't you? The gulping noise. I find that, you know, when he starts to gulp you feel he's getting a good feed. It means something, to actually feel it.

(Helen)

He bashes the breast, until it occurs, it's almost like he's demanding it to come in, he's sort of saying 'come on, give me my milk now'.

(Vanessa)

Therefore, some women look for clues that their body is functioning properly by means of observations of the body of another.

Discussion

In this chapter, the letdown reflex has been used to illustrate some aspects of the social, emotional and physical everyday lives of breastfeeding women. The accounts of the sensations associated with letdown are wide ranging and convey a multiplicity of meanings about the significance of this event. The experiential approach of this study facilitated the exploration of these embodied experiences and how they are constructed by the women.

In the analysis of the information available to the women about letdown, it became clear that there was a strong reliance on science to explain and give meaning to this sensation. Medicine has contributed to breastfeeding knowledge and advice in a significant way. For example, there are scientific explanations for the physiology of lactation (Sauer 1987; Woolridge 1986), and the properties and components of breastmilk (Silverton 1993; Wood and Walker-Smith 1981). This knowledge is then transmitted to women by health professionals as reliable, scientific information. The power of the medical discourse is that it is clothed in an aura of science and thought to represent objective truth. It gains a privileged position in relation to other discourses about the body. The dominance of 'information giving' based on scientific knowledge treats the individual as existing in a social vacuum and fails to confront the complex social world in which subjectivity is constructed (Lupton 1995). Whilst there have been moves in medical practice towards greater recognition of the experience of the lay individual (Clark and Mishler 1992; Kleinman 1988; Armstrong 1984), these moves have been very partial and uneven, especially in relation to the recognition of female experience. The medical/biological approach underpinning health education models treats women as a homogeneous group and breastfeeding as a biological process. This creates a gap in knowledge because it stops short of an understanding of collective, shared beliefs and values about the body, and of variations in individual experience.

The medical conceptualisation of the female body has been born out of the dominance of authoritative, scientific models. The language used to describe female bodily functions simulates industrial metaphors concerned with production and control (Martin 1987; Corea 1985). Since the 1950s an increase in medical intervention in childbirth has occurred (Reissman 1992) demonstrating how the unpredictable character of the female body seemingly needs to be disciplined by medicine. Alongside this medicalisation of childbirth an interest in holistic medicine and lifestyles has also developed initially amongst women (Coward 1989). In contrast to the medicalisation of childbirth, holistic discourses may influence the woman to listen to her body, to be guided by her own intuition and to have faith in her abilities as a woman.

This research reveals that women struggle to make sense of the experiences of breastfeeding, including the attempt to avoid embarrassment, and are involved in a creative cognitive process which includes the use of *figurative* language. This indicates a need, for the analyst as well as the lay person, to transcend the *conceptual* systems of biological medicine which tend to iron out the diversity of experience. A key role for research on this and other forms of embodied experience should be to recognise this creativity in the ways that women make sense of their experiences. It should also distil and reflect back to women the results of these cognitive explorations enabling them to benefit from a pooling of embodied knowledge.

Notes

1 The letdown reflex may also be called the draught reflex or milk ejection reflex. The women in this study commonly used the term 'letdown' rather than the medical term 'letdown reflex'. The former will now be used throughout the text.
2 Medical texts are those primarily written for and used by health workers but may be consulted by mothers. Lay texts are those written expressly for mothers, but the authors are commonly health professionals or psychologists.
3 Similarities can be seen with the male erection. It is well documented that erection failure can be associated with performance anxiety, stress and poor self-image. The more a man wants the erection, the more elusive it may become.

References

Allen, M. and Oberle, K. (1996) 'Augmentation mammoplasty: a complex choice', *Health Care for Women International* **17**, 1, 81–90.
Armstrong, D. (1984) 'The patient's view', *Social Science and Medicine* **18**, 9, 737–44.
Becvar, D. (1996) 'I am a woman first: a message about breast cancer', *Families, Systems and Health* **14**, 1, 83–8.
Bernard, H.R. (1995) *Research Methods in Anthropology*, London: Altamira.
Britton, C. (1996) 'Learning about "the curse": an anthropological perspective on experiences of menstruation', *Women's Studies International Forum* **19**, 6, 645–53.

Britton, C. (1997) 'Letting it go, letting it flow: women's experiential accounts of the letdown reflex', *Social Sciences in Health* **3**, 3, 176–87.

Britton, C. (1998) 'The influence of antenatal information on breast-feeding experiences', *British Journal of Midwifery* (in press).

Carter, P. (1995) *Feminism, Breasts and Breast-feeding*, London: Macmillan.

Cirket, C. (1992) *A Woman's Guide to Breast Health*, London: Thorsons.

Clark, J. and Mishler, E. (1992) 'Attending to patients' stories: reframing the clinical task', *Sociology of Health and Illness* **14**, 3, 344–72.

Corea, G. (1985) *The Mother Machine: reproductive technologies from artificial insemination to artificial wombs*, New York: Harper and Row.

Coward, R. (1989) *The Whole Truth: the myth of alternative health*, London: Faber and Faber.

Csordas, T. (1994) 'Introduction: the body as representation and being-in-the-world', in Csordas, T. (ed.) *Embodiment and Experience: the existential ground of self and culture*, Cambridge: Cambridge University Press.

Davis, K. (1995) *Reshaping the Female Body*, London: Routledge.

Dawson, D. (1990) *Women's Cancers*, London: Piatkus.

Douglas, M. (1984) *Purity and Danger*, London: Ark Paperbacks.

Ebrahim, G. (1991) *Breastfeeding: the biological option*, London: Macmillan.

Elias, N. (1978) *The Civilising Process: the history of manners*, Oxford: Blackwell.

Fallowfield, L., with Clark, A. (1991) *Breast Cancer*, London: Routledge.

Fernandez, J. (1986) *Persuasions and Performances*, Bloomington, IN: Indiana University Press.

Goffman, E. (1968) *Stigma: notes on the management of spoiled identity*, Harmondsworth: Penguin.

Health Education Authority (1992) *Birth to Five*, London: HEA.

Helman, C. (1994) *Culture, Health and Illness*, Oxford: Butterworth Heinemann.

Jenkins, J. and Valiente, M. (1994) 'Bodily transactions of the passions: el calor among Salvadoran women refugees', in Csordas, T. (ed.) *Embodiment and Experience: the existential ground of self and culture*, Cambridge: Cambridge University Press.

Jolly, H. (1977) *Book of Child Care*, London: Sphere Books.

Kitzinger, J. (1995) 'Introducing focus groups', *British Medical Journal* **311**, 299–302.

Kleinman, A. (1988) *The Illness Narratives*, New York: Basic Books.

Llewellyn-Jones, D. (1983) *Breastfeeding – How to Succeed: questions and answers for mothers*, London: Faber and Faber.

Low, S. (1994) 'Embodied metaphors: nerves as lived experience', in Csordas, T. (ed.) *Embodiment and Experience: the existential ground of self and culture*, Cambridge: Cambridge University Press.

Lupton, D. (1995) *The Imperative of Health: public health and the regulated body*, London: Sage.

Lyon, M. and Barbalet, J. (1994) 'Society's body: emotion and the "soma-tization" of social theory', in Csordas, T. (ed.) *Embodiment and Experience: the existential ground of self and culture*, Cambridge: Cambridge University Press.

McConville, B. (1994) *Mixed Messages: our breasts in our lives*, Harmondsworth: Penguin.

Maher, V. (1992) 'Breast-feeding in cross-cultural perspective: paradoxes and proposals', in Maher, V. (ed.) *The Anthropology of Breast-feeding: natural law or social construct*, Oxford: Berg.

Martin, E. (1987) *The Woman in the Body*, Milton Keynes: Open University Press.

Palmer, G. (1988) *The Politics of Breastfeeding*, London: Pandora.

Radley, A. (1993) 'The role of metaphor in adjustment to chronic illness', in Radley, A. (ed.) *Worlds of Illness: biographical and cultural perspectives on health and disease*, London: Routledge.

Reissman, C.K. (1992) 'Women and medicalisation: a new perspective', in Kirkup, G. and Kellor, L.S. (eds) *Inventing Women: science, technology and gender*, Cambridge: Polity Press.

Renfrew, M., Fisher, C., Arms, C. (1990) *Bestfeeding: getting breastfeeding right for you*, Berkeley, CA: Celestial Arts.

Richardson, D. (1990) *Safer Sex*, London: Pandora.

Royal College of Midwives (1991) *Successful Breastfeeding*, 2nd edn, Edinburgh: Churchill Livingstone.

Sauer, H.J. (1987) 'Physiology of lactation and factors affecting lactation', *Obstetrics and Gynecology Clinics of North America*, **14**, 3, 615–22.

Shilling, C. (1993) *The Body and Social Theory*, London: Sage.

Silverton, L (1993) *The Art and Science of Midwifery*, Hemel Hempstead: Prentice Hall.

Sontag, S. (1979) *Illness as Metaphor*, London: Allen Lane.

Stoppard, M. (1996) *Breast Book*, London: Dorling Kindersley.

Straughan, P. and Seow, A. (1995) 'Barriers to mammography among Chinese women in Singapore: a focus group approach', *Health Education Research* **10**, 4, 431–41.

Stuart-Macadam, P. and Dettwyler, K. (1995) *Breastfeeding: biocultural perspectives*, New York: Aldine de Gruyter.

Taylor, M., Farmer, A., Craig, C. (1995) 'The focus group: is this an acceptable method of exploring women's knowledge of the oral contraceptive?' *British Journal of Family Planning* **21**, 25–6.

Wilkinson, S. and Kitzinger, J. (1994) 'Towards a feminist approach to breast cancer', in Wilkinson, S. and Kitzinger, J. (eds) *Women and Health: feminist perspectives*, London: Taylor and Francis.

Wood, C.B.S. and Walker-Smith, J.A. (1981) *Mackeith's Infant Feeding and Feeding Difficulties*, Edinburgh: Churchill Livingstone.

Woolridge, M.W. (1986) 'The "anatomy" of infant sucking', *Midwifery* **2**, 164–71.

Chapter 5

Going with the flow

Some central discourses in conceptualising and articulating the embodiment of emotional states

Deborah Lupton

Individuals' understandings of their sense of self, or their subjectivity, are strongly shaped via emotional experiences. At a time in which people in western societies are both encouraged to 'display' and 'confess' their emotions but also to 'manage' their emotions carefully by conforming to expectations about the expression of emotional states in specific social settings, the emotions are integral to the conduct of social life and relationships with others. So too, the emotions are integral to notions of embodiment, or the ways in which people live and experience their bodies. Rosaldo, for example, describes emotions as 'embodied thoughts'; 'thoughts somehow "felt" in flushes, pulses, "movements" of our lives, minds, hearts, stomachs, skin' (1984: 142). The emotions, therefore, present an area of inquiry which emphasises embodied responses as well as their construction through culture. Byron Good has noted that

> Disease occurs not only in the body – in the sense of an ontological order in the great chain of being – but in time, in place, in history, and in the context of lived experience and the social world. Its effect is on the body in the world.
>
> (Good 1994: 131)

The same might also be said of the emotions. As writers on the sociology of the body have contended (see Featherstone and Turner (1995) for a review of the literature), bodily states themselves are complex intertwinings of anatomy and society/culture. Like the body itself, emotional states serve to bring together nature and culture in a seamless intermingling in which it is difficult to argue where one ends and the other begins.

One way to understand the socio-cultural nature of emotions is to look at the discourses surrounding them, or the patterned ways of rendering embodied sensations or internal states of feeling into words or images so as to convey their properties to others. Via discourse, physical sensations produced by our bodies (rushes of blood, sweating, visceral clutches, bristling hairs, increased heart beat) are interpreted as emotions. These physical sensations are themselves produced through discourse in specific cultural and historical contexts. The blushing associated with the emotion of embarrassment, for example, is created through an individual's awareness that she or he has behaved inappropriately according to the norms of a particular social context. This is not to assert that discourse is the *only* means of constructing and expressing emotion (non-verbal bodily phenomena themselves, such as blushing and weeping, are clearly important indicators of emotional states), but rather to argue for its central role. Indeed, language can frequently sadly fail our needs when we try to articulate our feelings to another person, and facial expressions or bodily movements can often be far better indicators of a person's emotional state than words.

Method

In this chapter I discuss some of the ways in which people under-stand the relationship between subjectivity, the body and the emotions, drawing upon data collected in an empirical study to do so. The study involved semi-structured individual interviews conducted in 1995 with forty-one women and men living in Sydney. Twenty-three women and eighteen men participated, ranging in age from 19 to 72 years. They were asked to discuss features of the emotions, including what they thought an emotion was, how emotions were generally felt bodily, where they thought emotions came from, the importance of controlling emotions, whether different types of people were different in the ways they felt and expressed emotions, what they thought happened if people do not express their emotions and the purposes that emotions served. The interviewees were also asked questions relating to the experience of emotion in their own lives, including whether they saw themselves as an emotional person, whether there had ever been times when they had lost control of their emotions and whether there were any conventions about emotional expression in their family of origin. As well, they were asked to describe the earliest and a more recent memory of a strong emotion they had felt.

The interviews were audio taped and later transcribed. The transcripts were analysed using a discourse analysis approach influenced by post-structuralist theoretical perspectives on subjectivity. The idea was to combine the focus on exploring individuals' lived experiences of everyday life that has been a central emphasis in traditional phenomenological research, with the interest in the constitutive role played by discourse that has emerged from post-structuralist perspectives. The focus of analysis is therefore not so much onto what extent respondents are conveying an 'objective' reality, but how they express their understandings and experiences of reality incorporating both contradictory and overlapping discourses. Such discourses may be identified and theorised with the understanding that they are ways of allowing people to 'make sense' of phenomena and to convey narratives of their experiences to others.

From this perspective, it is considered important not to view the interviews as simply transparent reproductions of 'what the interviewees think' or 'what the interviewees have done'. Rather, it was assumed that in any empirical inquiry into people's beliefs, attitudes and behaviours (whether quantitative, 'tick-the-box' types of methods or qualitative methods are adopted), the means of collecting the data will inevitably shape the findings. What sorts of questions are asked, how much time or space is given to the participants to answer these questions, to what extent they are asked to elaborate upon their answers or to go off onto tangents, the social context in which the research takes place, all shape the findings in various ways. In the case of such a potentially sensitive topic as one's emotional feelings and experiences, the demeanour of the interviewer is vital to how the interviewees express themselves and what they choose to divulge.[1] The data derived from empirical research such as one-to-one interviews are treated as simultaneously a means by which the participants articulate and convey some of their understandings and experiences in relation to the issues in question, but also as themselves a social product, produced together by the interviewer and the interviewee in a particular social context (see Denzin (1994) for a useful overview of this approach). The ways that the data are then analysed by the researcher, how they are selected, interpreted and presented, is also part of their construction.

As is generally the case with in-depth research, the interviews produced a mass of rich and fascinating data that are far too extensive to cover in detail in a single chapter-length piece.[2] I focus here on some central discourses employed by the participants when discussing how they experience and understand feelings and emotional states in terms of embodiment. In doing so, I make some comments about the antecedents of contemporary discourses on emotions, seeking to engage in a diagnosis of the contemporary condition of the self, to reflect upon the interrelationship between 'personhood', subjectivity, embodiment and discourse. Such an analysis seeks to disrupt taken-for-granted assumptions about how we tend to understand subjectivity and embodiment and to identify the conditions in which these assumptions are developed and reproduced (Rose 1996: 41).

Embodiment and the emotions

The ways in which individuals understand, experience and talk about emotions is highly related to their sense of body-image. As Grosz explains it, the body-image

> is a map or representation of the degree of narcissistic investment of the subject in its own body and body parts. It is a differentiated, gridded, and ever-changing registration of the degrees of intensity the subject experiences, measuring not only the psychical but also the physiological changes the body undergoes in its day-to-day actions and performances.
>
> (Grosz 1994: 83)

The body-image shapes the ways in which individuals understand and experience physical sensations and locate themselves in social space, how they conceptualise themselves as separated from other physical phenomena, how they carry themselves, how they distinguish outside from inside and invest themselves as subject or object. Body-images are first developed from the earliest stages of infancy, but are subject to continual changes as the individual moves through life (Grosz 1994: 83–5).

The interviewees clearly drew upon dominant shared understandings of the emotion–body relationship when describing how they personally experienced emotions. For example, one 30-year-old man described happiness as having the following bodily effects:

'physically I feel energetic and positive and optimistic. I have higher energy levels, I'm more likely to be jumping around doing things.' When feeling sad, he said, 'I tend to be much more lethargic', while when he is feeling anger, 'your heart beats faster, your breathing obviously changes and that affects your voice and you tend to clench your muscles'. Similarly, a 31-year-old woman described happiness in terms of the body floating, feeling lighter, almost transcending the bonds of gravity:

> Extreme happiness makes me feel very elated, and almost lifted above the ground, above reality, as if you're bouncing along instead of walking under gravity. It's a light sort of feeling, a floating sort of feeling, and just a very uplifting sort of feeling.

Her explanation of anger, in contrast, drew upon metaphors of tightness and tenseness:

> When I'm feeling very angry, there's a sort of tightness of the body. My body feels really tight, I feel muscular tightness almost as if I need to move, or to hit out or hit somebody or throw something. I feel like shouting – I often do when I'm very angry – or slamming doors, or something physical like that.

Another woman, aged 41, described the physical restlessness she experienced when she learnt that her marriage had irretrievably broken down: 'I had to keep walking, my body wouldn't let me stay still, I just walked'.

Other emotions appeared to be more elusive in terms of individuals being able to describe how they are experienced bodily. A 44-year-old man found it difficult to describe the emotion of jealousy in specific terms of how it affected his body, but was clear about the incapacity of the mind to control such an emotion:

> To actually describe the feeling would be difficult. It would be something that would be felt through your veins and circulation system right through to your skin. It would impact on your brain, and perhaps raise your heart beat and blood pressure, maybe cause you to sweat. And so there's this overwhelming inner welling up that is associated with all those physical sensations that would go beyond your ability to

control. So that even though your mind might say, 'This is silly', you can't deny that fact that this sensation is happening physically within you and so it is very strong and above you, above your rationality.

As this man's words suggest, the emotions are often described as overwhelming, taking over in ways that are experienced as a loss of control of the body/self. In another example, a 46-year-old woman described the process by which she had a nervous breakdown:

It's just when you're completely, your emotions just take over so much, there's no turning back, your body just says 'I've had it'. And it's just overwhelming . . . it so bowls you over that you're frightened and you think, 'Oh, there's nothing I can do about it'. And it fills you with overwhelming sadness and over-whelming anger, the whole feeling is just overwhelming.

A central discourse upon which the interviewees drew when attempting to describe the emotions is the 'outside' and 'inside' opposition. When responding to the question asking them to explain where emotions 'come from', there was no strong agree-ment among the interviewees as to what roles were played by the mind, the heart or the soul, and how they interrelated with each other. Nonetheless, the notion that emotions somehow 'come from within', and then are expressed to the outside world, was very dominant:

I think they're generated, like through your soul, 'cause I think everybody has a soul. And it comes from somewhere deep within you and I don't necessarily don't think it comes from the mind so much. I mean the mind is thinking, but I think it is the soul for me that generates those feelings.

(36-year-old woman)

Emotions have to come from the mind, because there's so much of emotion that you can't really touch . . . I don't mean that your mind rules your emotions, because if your mind ruled your emotions then you probably wouldn't have them. But it's probably between how you feel in your heart and how your mind processes that feeling.

(49-year-old woman)

The interviewees therefore generally held on to the mind–body dualism, contending that emotions were the product of both: at some times subject to greater mental control and at other times stemming more from the body:

> An emotion for me is a feeling. It's a sort of physical experi-ence that has physical sort of effects that you feel. It's also a state of mind and there's an interrelationship between the two, so that usually it's the state of mind that leads to physical effects, although sometimes physical effects can affect your state of mind. So if you're feeling tired, or run down or jet-lagged or something, then that can have a real effect on your state of mind and make you feel perhaps a bit depressed, or down. So it sort of goes the other way as well.
>
> (31-year-old woman)

Emotions were also commonly described as a response to some sort of stimulus, generally originating from events or encounters taking place outside the body and then creating changes or sensa-tions within the body:

> Emotions come from within, obviously, they're part of who we are, they're part of our nature. So they're there all the time but we don't experience them all the time. So I guess they're triggered by us in a sense finding ourselves in a context or a relationship with people where there are triggers that generate one or the other.
>
> (44-year-old man)

This discourse is related to the 'open/closed' opposition, which most people adopted to discuss the ways in which one's emotions are either revealed, and therefore 'opened' to others, or kept within oneself, and therefore 'closed' to others. According to the inter-viewees' accounts, some emotions appear to be more 'to the surface' and therefore easily felt and expressed, while others are more 'buried' or built up over a longer period of time:

> I think there has to be a build-up over a bit of time, espe-cially for sadness. I mean, happy's kind of more instant . . . but hurt's got to be built up. So I think it's over a process of time really, that they build up.
>
> (30-year-old woman)

This same person argued that anger, in particular, was a more 'surface' emotion that was therefore difficult to control: 'it's kind of like an instant thing that just goes "Aaaaah!" and comes straight out'.

The ways in which we speak about and experience emotional states also draw very strongly on a discourse of 'loss' in relation to the regulation of the body, which itself builds on the 'inside/outside' binary opposition. People are said to 'lose control' or to 'lose it' if they openly demonstrate their emotions, particularly the more socially proscribed emotions such as anger. To 'lose your temper' is to relinquish control, to unleash unacceptable feelings from within the body and to let them loose upon the external world. Similarly, maintaining control is understood to involve 'holding onto' or 'in' an emotion. This use of language suggests that emotions are commonly thought of as entities that have their own power and force and which require some sort of energy from the individual who possesses them to control. The interviewees commonly alluded to the ways that they or others 'held' emotions 'in' or let them 'out'. In some cases it is believed good to allow the emotions to 'come out' of the body and be revealed for what they are. Such a release of the emotions was commonly described as a more 'honest' process, allowing the air to be cleared and letting others know how one feels about things. Here again, emotions are conceptualised as entities, as things that one can allow to come out of the self and to show to others.

So too, interviewees used the trope of 'covering' up emotions to express the ways in which emotions that are felt 'inside' are hidden from others. People themselves were described as 'open' in feeling and expressing their emotions or as more 'closed' and contained. The common expression, articulated by several of the interviewees, of people 'wearing their hearts (or emotions) on their sleeve' is a particularly vivid use of this metaphor. To 'wear your heart on your sleeve' is to display your emotions in public, open to the view of everyone, to be particularly free in expressing one's emotion. Interviewees made particular reference to women when describing the type of person who is likely to be so open. As a 45-year-old man remarked, 'Women are much better at expressing their emotion, in a general sense, they are more prone to wear their heart on their sleeves'.

The interviewees also tended to use wet and dry oppositions when describing feelings and emotional states. Being able to let go of one's emotions was described as a fluid or even gushy experience, even if it is not directly related to crying. Emotions are believed to 'well up' just as tears well up in one's eyes. Emotions therefore flow in various levels throughout the body and into the outside world. As one 47-year-old woman put it, 'normally it's good to go with the flow, to go with the way you feel'. The interviewees often drew distinctions between people using this binary opposition, describing those who tended to release their emotions as 'wet' or 'gushy' and those who held them in as 'dry'. For example, one 24-year-old man described his mother as a 'gushy' person, which he regarded as a negative attribute because he viewed her emotions as excessive. In contrast, a 49-year-old woman described herself as emotional and perhaps too soft-hearted, but added, 'I wouldn't like to be the sort of person that was cut and dried all the time'.

There is a related temperature metaphor, in which an emotional person, or someone who expresses their emotions freely, are often described as a 'warm' person, or a 'hot-blooded' or 'hot-tempered' person, while the opposite extreme is described as 'cold'. So too, some individuals are described as 'bubbly', meaning happy and optimistic, which is again a liquid metaphor that recalls movement: boiling or effervescent fluids. The oft-used phrase, 'stiff upper lip' to describe the supposed (particularly male) Anglo-Saxon approach to controlling emotion is a particularly vivid example of metaphor in portraying an image of a tightly held body part, kept from quivering, kept stiff rather than fluid, in the process of maintaining emotional control.

Related to this central discourse of fluidity are the embodied feelings that people experience around emotions which, as noted above, are often articulated in terms of the 'tightness' or 'pressure' that they feel in their bodies. Just as fluids must be 'bottled' to keep them in place and orderly, so too are emotions described as 'bottled' up to keep them under control. We feel the emotion welling up within us, against which we may struggle to exert control, or else give in to it by letting it 'out' of the body. Anger or anxiety in particular are embodied in such a way (cf. the comments made by Lakoff (1987) on the metaphors of anger). It was remarked by most people that sometimes the 'pressure' of the emotions is such that even if the individual tries to hold them in, or 'keep a lid' on them, they escape anyway. This use of language recalls the dam metaphor, where the body is conceptualised as an inner, fluid or gaseous mass of emotions that are held back by the external skin and the will. The 'steam' metaphor is also frequently employed to conceptualise emotion. Steam is both wet and hot, the result of a boiling liquid. When one expresses particularly strong emotions, such as anger, one is said to 'let off steam', as if the body were a kettle or engine. As a 50-year-old woman described her response to tension and stress: 'There's been times when really, as I say to the doctor, I feel as if my head's going to blow off, you know, like a kettle or something'.

Emotions themselves are described in terms of temperature and how they affect embodiment. Anger may be described as either cold or hot, depending on the way it is expressed. If kept within and demonstrated through the withholding of emotional expression, anger is described as cold. If released in an outburst of rage, an 'explosion', anger is hot:

> anger is a very overwhelming feeling, that for me feels like just like a rush, a rush of emotions that's very heated. And when I get angry I almost feel like I'm about to explode . . . just sort of a boiling sort of feeling of just feeling overwhelmed by this tension, a lot of feelings that I then need to release.
>
> (31-year-old woman)

Love is typically described in terms of warmth – to speak of a 'cold love' is an oxymoron. Joy and happiness are also commonly described as 'warm' emotions. A 30-year-old woman, for example, described love as 'just a nice warm feeling, nice sort of glow all over, positive thoughts about everything'. A 45-year-old man described how he was recently overwhelmed by his love and pride for his daughter performing in a school concert in a way that combined the liquid and warm discourses:

> My eyes bubbled up in tears, and it was beautiful, I was so proud, just so proud, it made me feel great. It's just that nurturing emotion you have when you have your own kids, it was just a wonderful warm feeling, a feeling of pride, a feeling of immense love, it's just very special.

The notion that holding in emotional states is bad for one's health has received a great deal of attention since the 1970s in popular culture, particularly in relation to 'stress'. As Sontag (1989) points out, both tuberculosis and cancer have been regarded as diseases of passion. In the nineteenth century the tubercular personality was portrayed as being consumed with an inward passion, a frustrated ardour leading to the dissolution of the body. Such emotions are understood to 'turn in' upon the body, to invade and destroy tissue because they are not released: 'Passion moves inward, striking and blighting the deepest cellular recesses' (Sontag 1989: 46). By contrast, cancer is conceptualised as a disease of insufficient passion, afflicting those who are unable to express sexuality or spontaneous violent emotions such as anger. The contemporary 'cancer personality' is portrayed as an isolated and lonely individual who denies her or his negative feelings and does not share them with others because she or he lacks meaningful relationships (Sontag 1989: 51).

In the interviews, this association between ill-health and emotional repression was a very dominant discourse. Nearly all the interviewees made the link between holding in one's emotions, not expressing them openly, and suffering psychological or physical problems or illnesses. They were not able to be very precise about the actual mechanisms involved, the chain of cause and effect, but were quite convinced that the repressing of the emotions often led to ill-health. As a 30-year-old woman said, failing to express strong emotions 'creates diseases inside. I just think that it creates diseases, it creates situations that are really negative'. In attempting to explain how this relationship is manifested, the dam metaphor was often used to describe the process by which emotions can be physically or mentally destructive, again representing emotions as liquid or steam. As a 34-year-old man put it: 'what can happen, if people bottle it all up and don't release their emotions, well they can become physically and mentally ill.' The idea was that the pressure of pent-up emotions could become so great as to cause damage within the body. Alternatively, a discourse was articulated adopting the concept of pent-up emotions as parasitic, turning 'bad' inside the body if not released and 'eating' away at or attacking body tissue: '[emotions] eat you up, I think that if you're continually not expressing them, they will eat you up inside. They could become ulcers, arthritis' (49-year-old man). One man, a tree lopper by trade, used the metaphor of 'dry rot' to describe the process by which repressed emotions may turn physically destructive.

The link of emotional repression and cancer was directly made by some interviewees. A 47-year-old woman described a friend of hers who had gone through a painful divorce after she had discovered her husband was having an affair 'and she was really bitter and twisted about it'. The friend had recently died of cancer, which this interviewee traced back to her first troubles in her marriage. She argued that her friend had lost the will to fight the illness because of her despair over her marriage breakdown:

> I think that part of her just didn't want to get better anyway, because she just didn't really care how she felt anymore. She didn't care about her health, she didn't care about what she ate, she didn't care about how she looked after herself, she didn't care about her medical treatment and things, and really, she just let herself die.

A 49-year-old man similarly voiced his opinion that his brother, who died of cancer at the age of 42, was affected by his negative emotions: 'the angst that is created through anxiety can affect you greatly, particularly the stomach, the nerves. That's what happened to my brother − his cancer was basically created through his grief and his anxiety.'

On the other hand, if expressed, emotions themselves are conceptualised as a means of releasing pressure, creating a sense of well-being and encouraging good health:

> I feel that they are an outlet, to keep us from becoming insane. Tears are for joyousness and sadness − I've cried for happiness and sadness and usually about ten minutes after doing it, one feels so much better, so obviously it can only be good.
>
> (46-year-old woman)

A delicate balance must be maintained, however, as the wholesale release of the emotions can cause social disarray and reveal negative feelings inappropriately to others. A 50-year-old woman noted:

> I think it's important to control your emotions, but if you over control them you probably would suffer in other ways. Because I think your emotions are there as a safety valve to allow you to be able to get over that thing. . . . You can't let your emotions control you, but you've got to let your emotions be expressed.

Contextualising emotion discourses: some speculations

How have we come to rely so strongly on discourses of fluidity, temperature and pressure in articulating emotional states? Some clues may lie in previous notions about the constitution of the body. Contemporary understandings of the emotions appear to draw, if perhaps somewhat obliquely, upon the humoral model of the body. Notions of health states, the flow of bodily fluids and their relationship to the emotions have been evident in European literature for many centuries, and date back to ancient Greek notions of the body and health. From ancient times until well into the eighteenth century in European cultures, the four humours – blood, phlegm, black bile and yellow bile – were believed to circulate in the body, related to an individual's diet and the environment. It was thought that an excess of one humour over the others resulted in an imbalance that could cause illness, and also in the expression of certain personality traits (Nutton 1992). Notions about temperature were also incorporated into the humoral model. 'Heat' and 'cold' were core concepts in both classical Greek and Islamic notions of the body and medicine, and they remain important in contemporary understandings about health and the body in areas such as Latin America and Southeast Asia. The concept of 'heat' centres around the transformation of the 'natural' into the 'vital'. It is believed that food, after it is eaten, is 'heated' or 'cooked' in the stomach and then in the liver, where it is transformed into the four humours (Good 1994: 103).

As scientific medicine gained hold in Europe in post-Enlightenment times, physicians progressively abandoned humoralism as an explanation for illness. Nonetheless, the legacy of the humoral model was the notion that the flow of fluids, and their relationship to 'heat' and 'cold' states were vital to health and bodily functioning. In her book on concepts of the female body in eighteenth-century Germany, Barbara Duden observes that emotional states were considered potentially to cause blockages in the body:

> Anger as an inner poison drove the women, caused a quick, hot surge, an inner cramp, a choking, a congestion in the womb. If anger swelled too much, it could stagnate the inside, the womb. Anger was the heated, internal upwelling that caused a multitude of pains.
>
> (Duden 1991: 142–3)

To deal with these problems, women typically consulted physicians for prescriptions to release the anger by opening the body, allowing it to flow out through purging, sweating, bleeding or drawing plasters. There was, therefore, a perception of negative emotions dwelling inside the body where they must be worked upon to allow their release, or else they could get 'stuck' and poison the inside (Duden 1991: 144). At this time it was also commonly believed that a fright could cause a blockage or stagnation of bodily flows. It was thought that fright caused the blood to drive from the limbs to the heart, causing tightening of the heart, while anger caused the blood to surge to the periphery, where it caused cramps (Duden 1991: 149).

It is not only concerns about health that influence ideas about the importance of managing emotions, but also concerns about self-presentation and self-management. The body is often experienced as 'absent'; that is, we are not consciously aware of our bodies unless an experience of hunger, pain or other sensation occurs (Leder 1990). Emotional states bring the body into consciousness by virtue of their sensual dimensions. Indeed, in moments of extreme emotional experience bodily sensations are experienced as overwhelming cognitive or 'rational' processes. In anger, for example, the quickened heart rate, the tensed muscles, the rush of adrenaline combine to produce a heightened sense of embodiment. The blush of embarrassment, the churning stomach of nervousness, the elation of joy are all experienced as the body coming to the fore, making itself known, slipping beyond the bonds of the mind or will's control. There are similarities here with the way that the body that is in pain, ill or disabled is often conceptualised as both self and not-self, as threatening self-control and rationality. People experiencing such bodily extremes often speak about a symptom of physical distress or part of the body causing pain, sickness or dysfunction as something other than themselves; they externalise the sensation or bodily part while also acknowledging that it is part of oneself. Pain, for example, may be described as a demon, a monster lurking within, a force which streaks around the body and attacks it but also as a betrayal by one's own body. For those experiencing strong pain, there is often a sense of a split subjectivity, the self against the self (Good 1994: 124).

The bodily sensations and feelings associated with emotional states may be enjoyed for their sheer spontaneity, the freedom they seem to give from the bounds of the mind and self-control, but perhaps more often they are perceived and therefore experienced more negatively for their very evidence of a loss of self-regulation. The emotions are culturally associated with chaos, with excess, disorder, unpredictability and irrationality, and even with some degree of social or physical risk for both oneself and others: 'The chaotic energy of emotions makes them dangerous to anyone in their vicinity and weakens the person experiencing them' (Lutz 1986: 291). The emotions may be experienced as beyond the control of the self, as 'taking over' and therefore as both part of and separate to subjectivity.

In western societies we rarely feel sanguine about losing control of the body. As suggested in the discourses drawn upon by the interviewees in the study here reported, the essence of the self is conceptualised as harboured in individual bodies that are differentiated and separate from others' bodies and selves. Maintaining this sense of separateness is an integral aspect of everyday life and self-management. The contemporary logic of self-management is predicated upon the ascetic avoidance of excess, the quest for rationality, the transcendence of desire and the flesh. Emotional states, according to this logic, are impure, defiling, animalistic (Heywood 1996). The emotional body is often represented as a grotesque body, a body that is able to contain itself in socially acceptable ways, a body that threatens to burst apart its boundaries: 'open to the world in all its orifices, unbounded, abusive, devouring, and nurturing' (Greenblatt 1982: 5).

Here again, there are clear antecedents for these ideas in past notions of embodiment and selfhood. In Judaeo-Christian writings, the body has traditionally been portrayed as source of corruption via the temptations of the flesh, a means of drawing people's attention away from their spiritual devotions. Nonetheless, early modern understandings of the body tended to view it as far more open to the world. In her study of body-images in early modern German culture, the historian Lyndall Roper noted a 'literature of excess' in which the body is imagined as

> a container for a series of processes: defecation, sexual pollution, vomiting. Fluids course about within the body, erupting out of it, leaving their mark on the world outside. The body is not so much a collection of joints and limbs, or a skeletal structure, as a container of fluids, bursting out in every direction to impact on the environment.
>
> (Roper 1994: 23)

The 'civilizing process' (Elias 1978) taking place from the Renaissance onwards gradually served to contain excess and privilege decorum and self-containment. Where, in medieval times, the opportunity to revel in the delights of the grotesque body, to celebrate excess, the crossing of boundaries and engagement in socially proscribed activities was often taken and enjoyed, particularly in times of carnival (Bakhtin 1984; Greenblatt 1982), in contemporary western societies such grotesqueries are now rarely allowed.

The fluidity and volatility of emotions are problematic in that they tend to dissolve the boundaries between outside and inside. They may therefore be conceptualised as polluting in their challenging of bodily boundaries, inspiring horror and fear. Like body fluids, emotions 'flow, they seep, they infiltrate; their control is a matter of vigilance, never guaranteed' (Grosz 1994: 194). The body without boundaries, the permeable body, the liminal body, the leaking, fluid body has become a site of horror, dread and fear for its transgressive nature (see Tudor's (1995) discussion of horror movies and Lupton's (1996) commentary on the menopausal body). This loss is highly gendered because of the cultural associations that link women with uncontrolled embodiment, liquidity and softness and men with rational control, dryness and hardness. For men particularly, the dissolving into tears is evidence of a 'leaky' body, a body that is vulnerable and permeable, and which is feminised in the breaking down of boundaries between 'inside' and 'outside' (Jones 1993).

Contemporary discourses on emotions, embodiment and subjectivity, therefore, evince a continual oscillation between acknowledging the importance of carefully regulating and controlling the highly fluid and volatile emotions, and the need to express them, to allow them to 'escape' from the body. Emotions threaten order and propriety, they are undignified, they render one open and vulnerable. They potentially lead to a loss of containment of the self. Hence the discourse on emotions that refers to the fragmentation, the 'breakdown' of the self that can occur in heightened emotional states, the references to 'pulling oneself together' and 'picking up the pieces' that are the after-effects of losing self-control. However, too much regulation is viewed as potentially damaging, for the emotions may become 'blocked' or 'stuck' in the body through repression, causing tension and pressure which may lead to ill-health. Emotional release is important, but must be carried out in a way that as far as possible avoids the loss of self-containment. Both concepts of the emotions draw upon a culturally specific model of the self which sees it as residing within a 'body-container' filled with intensities and flows and surrounded with borders that requires constant vigilance to police, allowing certain phenomena 'in' and others the passage 'out'.

Notes

1 In the case of the research reported here, I was fortunate to have the assistance of a very capable and sensitive interviewer, Else Lackey. I thank her and the interviewees in the study for their participation.
2 The study is part of a book currently in progress, provisionally entitled *The Emotional Self: a sociocultural exploration*, due to be published by Sage, London, in early 1998.

References

Bakhtin, M. (1984 [1968]) *Rabelais and his World*, Cambridge, MA: MIT Press.
Denzin, N. (1994) 'The art and politics of interpretation', in Denzin, N. and Lincoln, Y. (eds) *Handbook of Qualitative Research*, Thousand Oaks, CA: Sage.
Duden, B. (1991) *The Woman Beneath the Skin: a doctor's patients in eighteenth-century Germany*, Cambridge, MA: Harvard University Press.
Elias, N. (1978) *The Civilizing Process*, New York: Urizen.
Featherstone, M. and Turner, B. (1995) 'Body and society: an introduction', *Body and Society* 1, 1, 1–12.
Good, B. (1994) *Medicine, Rationality, and Experience: an anthropological perspective*, Cambridge: Cambridge University Press.
Greenblatt, S. (1982) 'Filthy rites', *Daedalus* 3, 1–16.
Grosz, E. (1994) *Volatile Bodies: toward a corporeal feminism*, Sydney: Allen and Unwin.
Heywood, L. (1996) *Dedication to Hunger: the anorexic aesthetic in modern cultures*, Berkeley: University of California Press.
Jones, A. (1993) 'Defending the border: men's bodies and vulnerability', *Cultural Studies from Birmingham* 2, 77–123.
Lakoff, G. (1987) *Women, Fire and Dangerous Things: what categories reveal about the mind*, Chicago: University of Chicago Press.
Leder, D. (1990) *The Absent Body*, Chicago: University of Chicago Press.
Lupton, D. (1996) 'Constructing the menopausal body: the discourses on hormonal replacement therapy', *Body and Society* 2, 1, 91–7.
Lutz, C. (1986) 'Emotion, thought, and estrangement: emotion as a cultural category', *Cultural Anthropology* 1, 3, 287–309.
Nutton, V. (1992) 'Healers in the medical market place: towards a social history of Graeco-Roman medicine', in Wear, A. (ed.) *Medicine in Society: historical essays*, Cambridge: Cambridge University Press.

Roper, L. (1994) *Oedipus and the Devil: witchcraft, sexuality and religion in early modern Europe*, London: Routledge.

Rosaldo, M. (1984) 'Toward an anthropology of self and feeling', in Shweder, R. and Levine, R. (eds) *Culture Theory: essays on mind, self and emotion*, Cambridge: Cambridge University Press.

Rose, N. (1996) *Inventing Our Selves: psychology, power, and personhood*, Cambridge: Cambridge University Press.

Sontag, S. (1989) *Illness as Metaphor and AIDS and its Metaphors*, New York: Anchor.

Tudor, A. (1995) 'Unruly bodies, unquiet minds', *Body and Society* **1**, 1, 25–41.

Part II

Health and illness

Chapter 6

Malignant bodies

Children's beliefs about health, cancer and risk

Simon J. Williams and
Gillian A. Bendelow

Our starting point in this chapter concerns Douglas's (1970, 1966) contention that the social body constrains the way in which the physical body is perceived, and the physical experience of the body sustains a particular view of society. From this viewpoint, the body is a model which stands for any bounded system and its boundaries can represent any borders which become threatened or endangered. Whenever the boundaries of the social collectivity or people are threatened, these anxieties are mirrored in the degrees of care exercised over the physical body. Bodily orifices, for example, together with the 'marginal stuff' issuing from them, are potent symbols of power and danger, pollution and taboo. Ideas about demarcating, separating and punishing transgression have, therefore, as their main function, the imposition of a system of symbolic 'order' on what is, in effect, an essentially 'messy' or 'untidy' experience: ritually (re)ordering this 'matter out of place' as a means of protecting and guarding the threatened borders and vulnerable margins of the broader body politic.

Sontag (1977) echoes these themes in her discussion of the metaphorical status of illness, and the negative symbolism and ritualistic taboos surrounding the cancerous body. As Herzlich and Pierret state:

> The expressions used by many people to speak of it [cancer] have their roots in the distant past, the days of great epidemics, and revive archaic representations of illness, such as the suddenness and severity of disease, its unpredictable and incurable nature and sudden death. ... Like diseases of the past, cancer is also fraught with phantasms of rot invading the body, as well as animals that gnaw and destroy it. ... In this context,

> it is not surprising that the fear it arouses today, *a fear shared by everyone*, bears some resemblances to the great obsessive fears of the past.
>
> (Herzlich and Pierret 1987: 56, our emphasis)

Certainly the relationship between the body and society, 'healthy' or 'diseased', has received a good deal of attention since the late 1980s, leading to a re-reading of many traditional sociological themes in a new, more 'corporeal', light. This, in turn, has opened the way for a critical questioning of seemingly ossified conceptual forms and dominant binarised modes of western thought, including mind/body, nature/culture, biology/society, reason/emotion, public/private and so on (Benton 1991). Whilst much of this literature has tended, to date, to be *about* rather than *from* bodies, stressing *representational* (i.e. social constructionist) over *experiential* (i.e. existential/phenomenological) issues (Csordas 1994), it is nonetheless clear that the sociology of the body is now entering a new 'synthesising' phase in which formerly opposed positions are starting to be reconciled in the interest of more integrated analytical frameworks concerning human embodiment: one in which emotions are proving central (Williams and Bendelow, 1998; Bendelow and Williams 1997).

Whilst many of these debates have proved highly illuminating – countering centuries of disembodied, 'unreasonable' (male) theorising – there nonetheless remains a dearth of empirical evidence with which to test these corporeal claims and analytical insights. Discourses on risk, consumption and the 'reflexive' body, for example, continue to be pitched, for the most part, at the level of broad claims and sweeping generalisations with little concern for empirical detail or with how precisely these categories mesh with everyday experience. Kroker and Kroker (1988), for example, claim that in the era of AIDS, 'panic' bodies emerge through a form of 'Body McCarthyism' regarding the exchange of 'clean' and 'unclean' body fluids. Similarly, Turner (1992) claims that the body has become an 'apocalyptic site' of 'contamination', 'toxicity' and 'waste'; one which is needful of constant surveillance, regulation and control.[1]

This, in turn, relates to a broader set of issues concerning the nature of life in so-called 'risk society' (Beck 1992). To be sure, life has always been a 'risky business' – from the battles of medieval warrior nobility to the great plagues of past centuries – but the nature, scope and intensity of contemporary risks have all, it is argued, profoundly altered as a consequence of human interventions of many different sorts (i.e. 'manufactured' risks and uncertainties), including the globalising tendencies of late modernity (Giddens 1994, 1991).

In this chapter, we take a closer look at these issues through a focus on the neglected topic of children's bodies, health and risk. Taking cancer as a paradigmatic example, we seek to explore, through a critical analysis of children's writings and drawings, the following key questions: first, what does it mean to children to be 'healthy' or 'unhealthy' and what relationship does this have to prevailing discourses on health and risk, consumption and lifestyles? Second, moving from the general to the specific, in what ways do children depict the 'cancerous' body, and how do these images relate to age-old metaphors of 'chaos' and 'disorder', 'pollution' and 'taboo'? Finally, what does all this tell us about the relationship between biology and society, the (corporeal) 'interior' and the 'exterior', the 'active' and the 'passive', 'responsibility' and 'blame'?

As we shall see, children possess considerable knowledge about the factors contributing to 'good' and 'bad' health, including the causes and prevention of cancers, especially smoking and lung cancer. Within these 'malignant' discourses, notions of the 'monstrous', 'dys-figured', 'combustible', 'pathological' and 'mortal' body loom large, reflecting and reinforcing the centuries of fear and negative symbolism associated with this most 'dreaded' of diseases. Here, personal and environmental factors are frequently blurred, suggesting a lack of distinction in children's minds between those factors under individual control, and those stemming from broader living conditions and the material circumstances of their lives.

Before turning to these corporeal themes, however, a brief word about 'researching children' and the nature of the present study is required as a methodological backdrop to the discussion which follows.

Researching children

Not only have children's bodies been peculiarly 'absent' in much of the (adult-centred) sociological discussion of the body and society to date, but also much of the health education and promotion directed *at* them has not been based on what they themselves know, believe or want to know. There has, in short, been a tendency for children's embodied voices and concerns, feelings and emotions, to remain silent or under-researched. Whilst the role of children as *active* constructors of their own health-related behaviours and understandings is beginning to be addressed (Mayall 1996, 1993; Roberts *et al.* 1995; Brannen *et al.* 1994), much still remains to be done in order to redress this traditional imbalance. Though research data can undoubtedly be collected from children using well-established methodologies, there is also a need to develop new more 'child-centred' methods in order to encourage children to provide information on the ways in which they see health (Backett and Alexander 1991). Whilst a number of surveys, for instance, have been conducted in order to elicit children and young people's beliefs about cancer (Mabe *et al.* 1987; Treiber *et al.* 1986; Michielutte *et al.* 1979; Charlton 1977), only one study, to our knowledge – an Art Competition for 15 year olds, organised by Ann Charlton (1979) on behalf of the Wellcome Foundation, with the title 'What does cancer mean to me' – has attempted to explore these issues in a more detailed, embodied, rather authoritarian, 'top-down', manner. In doing so, Charlton identified four key themes in these children's paintings: cigarette smoking, bodies with cancer, parts of the body, and what she termed more 'abstract ideas'.

Building on these issues, the data upon which this chapter reports were drawn from children aged 9–10 in six mixed-sex primary schools in the south-east and north-west of England (Kent, Surrey, Inner London – from here on referred to collectively as children in the 'SE' – and Inner Manchester, Didsbury and Lancashire – from here on referred to collectively as children in the 'NW').[2] A mix of group interviews and discussions were carried out with a total of 179 children in the six schools. Access was negotiated through the headteachers, relevant class teachers and the children themselves, although half the schools approached did not, initially, want to participate in the research as they thought cancer too sensitive a topic for young children to discuss. In each school, the researcher (GB) was given free access to one class for 90 minutes, although teachers (and sometimes helpers) were often present. An interview schedule, derived from the 'draw and write technique', pioneered by Williams *et al.* (1988) and adapted to include simple questions about cancer and health, was given to each child. The children were guided through the schedule, and then the researcher held a group discussion, the purpose of which was both to gain more information about the context of children's health beliefs and knowledge, and to allay any anxieties that may have arisen from discussing this 'sensitive topic' with the children. Several children in one class, for example, were worried whether having a nosebleed meant they had leukaemia, as a character in their favourite soap opera, who was dying from the disease, complained of constant nosebleeds.

All the children (179) who were present on the days the research was carried out in the schools completed the interview schedules and took part in the group discussions. The written answers were entered onto a D-base package, and the children's drawings were scanned and entered onto a database using an Apple flatbed scanner and Ofoto software, which stores and reproduces the graphic images on screen.

In these and many other ways, as our data show, researching children can be a richly rewarding experience. Not only does this challenge prevailing notions of children as 'incompetent' actors and 'irrational' agents, but also it shows that children *can* provide detailed information about their perceptions and beliefs regarding health in general and cancer in particular. In doing so, this more grounded approach can build upon and consolidate more general methodological strategies which emerge *from* bodies, rather than simply being *about* them.

'Healthy' and 'unhealthy' bodies: consumption, risk and lifestyles

In order to 'gently' lead into the sensitive topic of cancer, children were asked if they could write or draw anything that happened in their lives on a day-to-day basis which they thought might be 'healthy' or 'unhealthy'. Whilst, in common with previous studies (Mayall 1993; Williams *et al.* 1988) the notion of 'good health' appeared to be more or less centred around exercise and healthy eating, so-called 'risky factors' in terms of ill-health were conceptualised in a much more wide-ranging and subtle and sophisticated manner. Although individual factors such as smoking and bad diet were cited most often as 'unhealthy' behaviours – the latter including 'being fat', fatty meats, sugar, salt, fizzy pop or drinks, burgers, fast foods, crisps, fatty foods, cakes, meat, chocolate, sugary food, red meat, 'too much food', school dinners, beans, 'Weetabix and lemon custard', 'fish salad', rape seed oil, dieting, no food and anorexia – there was much more emphasis on external and structural aspects of the children's world which were beyond their control.

In the category of 'environmental factors', for example, were 'smelly odours', smog, pollution, petrol, bad gasses, car fumes, acid, ozone layer, motorways, cars, running in the road, microwaves, cutting down rain forests, toxic waste, swimming in chlorine, bad water, dustbins, sun, heat, fire, lack of fresh air, computers, litter and poison. 'Violence' also included mention of cuts, mugging, stabbing, knives, fighting, 'dangerous drunks', guns, nuclear arms, bombs, wars and tanks. These factors, in turn, were seen to impinge on different groups of children in differing ways: environmental and pollution factors, for example, were more frequently mentioned by children in the inner-city schools, and boys were more likely than girls to mention both violence and hygiene. Bodily representations, mainly in the form of stick–figures, centred largely around exercise, accidents, eating and drinking, although, as Figure 6.1 shows, there were references to self-harm and mutilation.

The 'miscellaneous' category also contained an interesting mix of 'other' factors associated with ill-health. This included 'not sleeping', laziness, overwork, constipation, posture, fleas, doctors, teachers, school, police, John Major, being homeless, bedsits, winter, sex (without condoms), spitting, 'burping', 'farting', reading while eating, Sundays, 'my brother', 'my sister', sharks, 'dog pooh' and 'food shopping'.

It was in relation to cancer, however, that the metaphorical status of the body, and its relationship to the broader body/politic, became particularly striking.

'Malignant' bodies

When asked what types of cancer children had heard of, lung cancer was most frequently mentioned (56 per cent), although this varied regionally, with only a quarter of the children in the NW, compared to three-quarters in the SE mentioning it. Breast cancer was the second most common form (43 per cent), followed by leukaemia (37 per cent) – often called 'blood cancer', mentioned by almost half in the NW and a quarter in the SE – and skin cancer (23 per cent) – which, again, was more familiar to children in the NW. There was also some confusion about parts of the body affected by cancer, with cancer of the heart (23 per cent),

Figure 6.1 Beliefs about causes of ill health, girl aged 11, rural school in NW England

head (16 per cent), arms and legs (9 per cent) mentioned, as well as cancer of the hair, neck, back and 'breath' indicated by a few children (1–2 per cent). Cancer of the 'private bits' (5 per cent) and pets (2 per cent) also received some attention in the SE, whereas children in the NW were more likely to confuse other illnesses such as AIDS, eczema and asthma with cancer.

On a blank page of the interview schedule, children were asked to write or draw anything at all they might know about cancer. As in Charlton's (1979) study, mentioned earlier, abstract ideas were frequently expressed, and these were not, in principle, scientifically speaking, 'incorrect' or 'ill-informed' – apart, perhaps, from the intriguing suggestion that 'You get it having a baby' and the notion that 'People say you've got cancer if your hand is bigger than your face'. Generally, the responses given, whether textually or visually, portray quite vividly the complex, multifaceted relationship, between 'scientific' and cultural beliefs about the body and risk. As with their ideas about health and illness, it was possible to make analytical distinctions here between 'internal' and 'external' factors, although these were frequently blurred in children's own minds. From this, it was possible to identify five distinct, though frequently overlapping, themes in children's writing and drawings on 'malignant bodies'.

'Monstrous'/'demonic' bodies

Echoing Charlton's (1979) findings, a major theme in children's drawings was the abstract depiction of cancer as a frightening disease, portrayed through vivid images of the 'monstrous' or 'demonic' body. These images were often expressed in a 'free-floating' way through unpleasant faces showing a menacing quality; expressions which evoked feelings of helplessness and fear of being 'taken-over' by sinister forces.

Themes of chaos and disorder figured strongly here, the body 'horrible' displaying a chilling, Kafkaesque/nightmarish quality; one which resonates with archaic images of dark, mysterious forces and a maelstrom of 'pre-scientific' beliefs, taboos and superstitions (Figure 6.2).

So strong, powerful and threatening were these beliefs, that a handful of children felt cancer to be too frightening to write or draw anything about; one child actually wrote 'It's too horrible. I can't say anything'.

Figure 6.2 Ideas of cancer as 'monstrous', boy aged 11, inner city London school

'Dys-figured'/'absent' bodies

Closely allied to these issues was the theme of the 'dys-figured' or 'absent' bodies, the most prominent example being hair loss (Figure 6.3) which over a third of children depicted in drawings or commentary as a great source of anxiety for all concerned.

There may be many reasons for this finding: children in the SE rural school, for example, mentioned a pupil (not in their own class), with leukaemia, whose hair had taken six months to grow

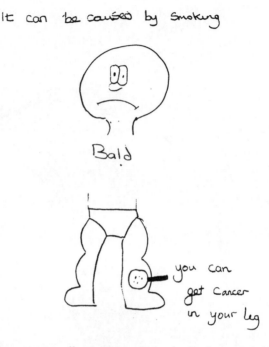

Figure 6.3 How cancer affects parts of the body, boy aged 10, sub-urban school in SE England

back following radiotherapy. TV drama, especially soap operas, have also repeatedly been shown to be important sources of health education (Oakley *et al.* 1995; Brannen *et al.* 1994), and the Australian tea-time 'soaps' were particularly popular with this age group. At the time of carrying out the study, for example, a story in *Home and Away* featured a young woman suffering from leukaemia. This character had long blonde hair, which gave rise to great concern in discussion about the adverse effects of treatment (though she did not actually lose her hair).

Certainly disfigurement to the external surfaces of the body and the disruptive effects of cancer in terms of bodily appearance, caused much anxiety and concern. Many drawings depicted tumours and bits of the body affected by cancer, often arms and legs (Figure 6.3), and amputation was frequently indicated, as in the child who wrote: 'You can have cancer in any part of the body and you have to get it chopped out or you can die'.

if your smoke youcan get cancer and some
times you can get bald and you can die sometime.

Figure 6.4 Smoking and cancer, boy aged 10, suburban school in SE
England

Other disfigurements detailed problems with the skin, in the
form of rashes, spots, bumps and bruises, and several children drew
or mentioned 'going white' (cf. the inner fire, burning passion and
romantic imagery surrounding the tubercular patients in the late
nineteenth and early twentieth centuries). Again themes of chaos
and disorder were prevalent here; themes played out through the
external manifestations of disease.

'Combustible' bodies

Smoking, perhaps unsurprisingly, featured strongly in a third of
children's written and pictorial responses to cancer. Similarly, more
than three-quarters of their ideas concerning prevention were
centred on the avoidance of smoking – a far higher proportion
than any other risk factor (Figure 6.4).

Figure 6.5 Cancer as 'fires in the body', girl aged 11, inner city London school

In contrast to 'monstrous' and 'dys-figured' bodies, however, responsibility and blame were common themes, and many children mentioned the need to avoid passive smoking. Again, the role of the media was important here: fourteen children, for example, mentioned the high media profile of Roy Castle, as a non-smoker, in this connection.[3]

Emphasis on the exterior surfaces and structures of the body also gave way, in these depictions, to a concentration on the corporeal interior; a concern most frequently depicted in terms of smoke and fires within the lungs and thoracic cavity (Figure 6.5).

Other influences, besides smoking, included the avoidance of sunburn, pollution, alcohol and drugs, eating 'healthy'/'good' food, condoms, and keeping 'healthy' generally; factors which, in turn, resonate with broader notions of the carcinogenic effects of external agents upon the physical body. More puzzling recommendations for cancer prevention included comments such as the following: 'Don't have a baby', by a girl in the rural SE school, and 'Don't let ladies touch your body', by a boy in the NW suburban school!

'Pathological' bodies

Although greatest concern appeared to be expressed over the external manifestations of disease, the internal workings of the body nonetheless gave rise to considerable concern, again echoing Sontag's (1977) earlier discussion of the metaphors of 'invasion' and 'mutation'. Cancer, for example, was often depicted in oncogenic terms as cells which take over and destroy the body wreaking havoc from within (Figure 6.6). As one child remarked: 'It's on the inside, it's not on the outside'. Other metaphors, mentioned earlier, were also invoked, such as cancer being caused by 'bad blood', or 'an "airy liquid" which gets in and out of your lungs

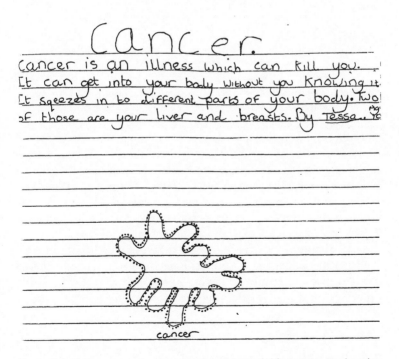

Figure 6.6 Cancer as a group of cells, girl aged 10, inner city London school

Some-times by smoking!
You lose your hair
your body gets bad blood inside you
It is rare People Survife from it
Most People die from it Cancer
Its an afull disese

Cancer
Ward

Figure 6.7 Treatment of cancer, boy aged 10, inner city Manchester school

and suffocates you'. Despite this focus on 'internal', intra-corporeal issues, heredity did not figure strongly in these children's writing or drawings on the 'malignant' body; rather a more heavy emphasis appeared to be placed on external 'triggers' to internal disorder.

In conjunction with cancer being a disease which 'attacks' the body, either from within or outside, treatments were often, as Figure 6.7 shows, portrayed in highly physical terms, in the form of chemotherapy, radiotherapy (often confused with physiotherapy), medicines and injections. Indeed, over a third of children thought that taking pills or having injections could stop or 'cure' cancer. In doing so, death could be 'postponed' if not avoided.

'Mortal' bodies

This issue of death brings us to the last, and indeed most prominent, theme to emerge in children's writing and drawings of cancer,

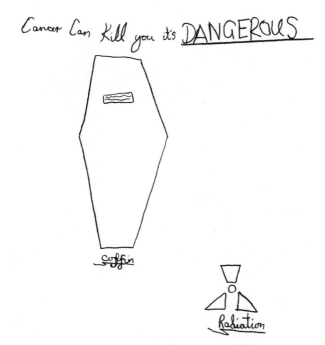

Figure 6.8 Death and cancer, boy aged 11, rural school in NW England

namely the 'mortal' body. Here a central paradox emerged: whilst over a third of children saw cancer as 'fatal', only one in ten thought that death was inevitable. Children, in other words, were more likely to say 'You *can* die', than 'You *will* die', although inner city children, and boys rather than girls, were notably more likely to see death as inevitable.

Prominent imagery here included coffins, tombstones and angels of death (Figures 6.8–6.10), with some very poignant writing around pictures of the coffins and gravestones, such as 'It is very rare that people survive cancer – people can die from cancer. It is a terrible situation for them and their mothers to suffer too'.

Children were often writing and drawing here from their own personal experience: over half the sample said they knew someone who has had cancer, and in some cases who had died as a result. Taboos surrounding death – what Aries (1976) has referred to as the 'veil of silence' in western societies – therefore appeared to be lifted, albeit temporarily, through children's candour and frankness

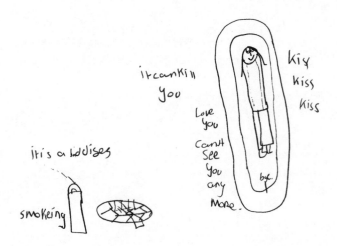

Figure 6.9 Death and cancer, girl aged 11, suburban school in NW England

on this most personal and emotive of topics.[4] Whilst notions of responsibility were sometimes invoked here – again mainly as a result of lifestyle factors such as smoking – people with cancer, by and large, were depicted in blameless, sympathetic terms. Death, in short, was as both 'untimely' and 'unjust'.

Figure 6.10 Death and cancer, boy aged 11, inner city Manchester school

Discussion and conclusion

Researching children is a richly rewarding experience. The use of drawings in collecting data from children shows that this is indeed a valuable research tool. From a methodological viewpoint, our study therefore makes a contribution to developing techniques for research *on* and *with* children within the evolving discipline of 'children's studies'. Seen in these terms, children are not 'incompetent actors' or 'irrational' social agents. Rather, like their adult counterparts, they are active, reflexive, constructors of their own health-related knowledge, beliefs and behaviours, albeit in an adult-centred world with limited degrees of freedom across the public/private divide.

As we have seen, children's notions of health, risk and the body are often complex, subtle and sophisticated. Whilst notions of 'good health' tended to centre around issues such as exercise and diet, factors associated with 'ill-health' were often conceived in broader, more wide-ranging terms, including external and structural aspects of children's lives – from school to unemployment, John Major to environmental pollution – which were beyond their control. In this respect, children tended to operate with insightful and well-informed multifactorial models of risk: models which extend far beyond the individual realm of victim blaming ideologies. Indeed, this integration of personal and environmental factors in children's perceptions of 'good' and 'bad' health, suggests a lack of distinction, in their own minds, between those factors under individual control and those stemming from broader living conditions.

But what of 'cancerous' or 'malignant' bodies? At the beginning of this chapter we introduced a number of theoretical perspectives which emphasised the metaphorical status of the (diseased) body, including the notion of 'apocalyptic' or 'panic' bodies at the turn of the century. Certainly there appears, on the one hand, to be plenty of evidence to support these contentions in this chapter. 'Monstrous', 'dys-figured', 'combustible' and 'mortal' bodies, especially when confused with other illnesses such as AIDS, suggest important elements of fear and anxiety, pollution and taboo. In this respect, children's perceptions of cancer may be interpreted as part and parcel of a broader, age-old picture in which so-called 'accurate' (i.e. 'scientific') understandings are 'obstructed' by cultural metaphors of fatality, contagion and blame. The pervasive role of metaphor and metonymy in social life (Lakoff and Johnson 1980), however, suggests that calls such as Sontag's (1977) to rid disease of this 'cultural baggage' are at best overly optimistic and at worst downright naive.

On the other hand, the very fact that children were asked to reflect on such a highly charged, emotive topic as cancer cannot be taken as a general indicator of somatic concern or 'panic bodies' at the turn of the century. Indeed, contra such interpretations, it is perhaps worth noting that, like social life itself, our relationship to our bodies is, for the most part, a largely taken-for-granted one. Bodies, in other words, in the normal course of events, tend to 'recede from view': only when we encounter 'resistances' of various kinds, including episodes of pain and sickness, do they 're-appear', or more accurately, '*dys-*' appear (Leder 1990). This, of course, may be more or less true of children's 'volatile' bodies – where processes of biological and social maturation proceed *a pace* – but it does nonetheless point to a certain (phenomenological) universality of embodied experience. This, coupled with a largely 'balanced' view of health – one in which, at least in older age groups, health competes with a number of other priorities in young people's lives, including the avoidance of unemployment and the forging of satisfactory relationships (Oakley *et al.* 1995; Brannen *et al.* 1994) – and the complex intermixing of lay beliefs and scientific knowledge (i.e. the dialectic of social and scientific rationality: Beck 1992), suggests that the wilder claims of postmodern theorists such as Kroker and Kroker (1988) need to be tempered by a more realistic assessment of so-called 'panic' bodies at the turn of the century. Indeed, despite their fears, the scope for (cancer) prevention was, at least in these children's minds, considerable, suggesting a degree of rational control rather than panic-stricken anxiety. This, in turn, suggests a further paradox. The more the body is subject to rational mechanisms of control, the more 'uncertain' it becomes and the more anxious and insecure we feel about those 'vulnerable margins', including cancer and AIDS, that elude control. Seen in these terms rational control creates its own doubts and uncertainties.

Children also displayed quite detailed 'scientific' knowledge about differing types of cancer, including cancer of the lung, leukaemia, breast and skin cancer. Perhaps the most interesting thing here, however, was a concern with not only the outward manifestations of disease, but also the internal workings of the body – although not heredity or genetics – including images of 'mutating cells' and pathogenic agents silently 'taking over' and 'destroying' the body from within. Here we glimpse again the complex, (inter)relationship between the corporeal 'inside' and 'outside', this time in terms of oncogenic and exogenic factors.

This also serves as a paradigmatic example of how popular cultural as well as scientific categories, including metaphors of mutation and invasion, 'map' not simply the corporeal exterior but also the physical interior of the human body. Bodies, in short, are inscribed both outside in and inside out. This, in turn, links up with a broader set of issues concerning not simply the role of the biological in social explanation – i.e. the 'return of the repressed' (Benton 1991) and the need for a non-reductionist 'socially pliable' biology rather than a reductionist socio-biology – but also the current cultural imaging of the immune system (Haraway 1991) and the need for 'flexible' bodies at the turn of the century: discourses in which, in neo-Darwinian terms, only the 'strongest', 'fittest' and most readily 'adaptable' will survive (Martin 1994).

Although children's knowledge was considerable, there is little in these data to suggest that this was a direct result of health education. Rather, television and other mass media were the most frequently cited sources of information regarding cancer, especially TV soaps. Educating children and young people directly about cancer is, however, feasible and important. Teachers and schools clearly have an important role to play as providers of such information – even if they are sometimes themselves considered to be 'bad for health' (Mayall 1993; Mayall et al. 1996)! Ultimately, however, as we have argued throughout this chapter, health education and health promotion should be based on what children and young people say they know and want to know, and on how their knowledge and understanding of health and illness differ according to factors such as class, gender and ethnicity. There is also, of course, a need to temper such information with the avoidance of undue anxiety creation.

To conclude, bodies, at the turn of the century, are becoming increasingly 'uncertain': both stability and flux, pleasure and pain, order and transgression, certainty and doubt. 'Malignant' bodies, like their 'immuno-deficient' counterparts, lie at the heart of these tensions and dilemmas, mapping a broader body/politic upon the external surfaces/internal workings of the fleshy body incarnate. In this respect, a central paradox emerges, whilst children, just like adults, are *active* constructors of their own health, their beliefs about 'cancerous' bodies reflect and reinforce age-old metaphors and dominant beliefs in western society: discourses which seek, in the face of *dys*-ease and *dys*-order, to discipline 'uncivilised' bodies, educate 'unruly' minds, and symbolically re-order any 'matter out of place'.

Acknowledgements

Thanks to Ann Oakley, Mary Buchannan, Dame Josephine Barnes, the Women's Nationwide Cancer Control Campaign (WNCCC), Mary Madden and, of course, the children themselves.

Notes

1   For empirical studies of these issues see Lupton *et al.* (1995) on 'panic' bodies and the HIV test, and Douglas and Calvez (1990) on the 'self as risk-taker: a cultural theory of contagion in relation to AIDS'.
2   The study was commissioned by the Women's Nationwide Cancer Control Campaign and was carried out between July 1992 and June 1994. Whilst quantitative data were also collected, the data presented here are mainly qualitative, focusing on children's writing and drawings, in order to explore themes pertaining to health, cancer and the body.
3   Roy Castle was a popular TV celebrity who was very publicly fighting lung cancer at the time of the research, blaming passive smoking as the cause. He died aged 62 in 1994.
4   See also Walter (1995) on the '*Revival of Death*' in late/postmodernity.

References

Aries, P. (1976) *Western Attitudes toward Death: from the Middle Ages to the present*, London: Marion Boyers.
Backett, K. and Alexander, H. (1991) 'Talking to young children about health: methods and findings', *Health Education Journal* **50**, 34–8.
Beck, U. (1992) *Risk Society: towards a new modernity*, London: Sage.
Bendelow, G. and Williams, S.J. (eds) (1997) *Emotions in Social Life: critical themes and contemporary issues*, London: Routledge.
Benton, T. (1991) 'Biology and social science: why the return of the repressed should be given a (cautious) welcome', *Sociology* **25**, 1: 1–29.
Brannen, J., Dodd, K., Oakley, A., Storey, P. (1994) *Young People, Health and Family Life*, Milton Keynes: Open University Press.
Charlton, A. (1977) 'Cancer: opinions of some secondary school pupils in Northern England', *International Journal of Health Education* **22**, 42–8.
Charlton, A. (1979) 'A penny for your thoughts: pupils' concepts of cancer expressed in pictures', *Journal of the Institute of Health Education* **17**, 2, 51–6.
Csordas, T.J. (ed.) (1994) *Embodiment and Experience: the existential basis of culture and self*, Cambridge: Cambridge University Press.
Douglas, M. (1966) *Purity and Danger: an analysis of the concepts of pollution and taboo*, London: Routledge and Kegan Paul.

Douglas, M. (1970) *Natural Symbols: explorations in cosmology*, London: Cresset Press.

Douglas, M. and Calvez, M. (1990) 'The self as risk-taker: a cultural theory of contagion in relation to AIDS', *Sociological Review* **38**, 3, 445–64.

Giddens, A. (1991) *Modernity and Self-Identity: self and society in the late modern age*, Cambridge: Polity Press.

Giddens, A. (1994) *Beyond Left and Right*, Cambridge: Polity Press.

Haraway, D. (1991) *Simians, Cyborgs and Women*. London: Free Association Books.

Herzlich, C. and Pierret, J. (1987) *Illness and Self in Society*, Baltimore, MD and London: Academic Press.

Kroker, A. and Kroker, M. (1988) *Body Invaders: sexuality and the post-modern condition*, London: Macmillan.

Lakoff, G. and Johnson, M. (1980) *Metaphors We Live By*, Chicago: University of Chicago Press.

Leder, D. (1990) *The Absent Body*, Chicago: Chicago University Press.

Lupton, D., McCarthy, S., Chapman, S. (1995) '"Panic bodies": discourses on risk and HIV antibody testing', *Sociology of Health and Illness* **17**, 1, 89–108.

Mabe, P., Riley, W., Treiber, F. (1987) 'Cancer knowledge and acceptance of children with cancer', *Journal of School Health* **57**, 59–63.

Martin, E. (1994) *Flexible Bodies*, Boston, MA: Beacon Press.

Mayall, B. (1993) 'Keeping healthy at home and at school', *Sociology of Health and Illness* **15**, 4, 464–88.

Mayall, B. (1996) *Children, Health and the Social Order*, Buckingham: Open University Press.

Mayall, B., Bendelow, G., Barker, S., Storey, P., Veltman, M. (1996) *Health in Primary Schools*, London: Falmer Press.

Michielutte, R., Diseker, R., Hayes, D. (1979) 'Knowledge of cancer: a cross-cultural comparison among students in the US and the UK', *International Journal of Health Education* **22**, 242–8.

Oakley, A., Bendelow, G., Barnes, J., Buchanan, M., Hussain, O. (1995) 'Health and cancer prevention: knowledge and beliefs of children and young people', *British Medical Journal* **310**, 1029–33.

Roberts, H., Smith, S.J., Bryce, C. (1995) *Children at Risk? Safety as a social value*, Buckingham: Open University Press.

Sontag, S. (1977) *Illness as Metaphor*, Harmondsworth: Penguin.

Treiber, F., Schramm, L., Mabe, P. (1986) 'Children's knowledge and concerns towards a peer with cancer: a workshop intervention', *Child Psychiatry and Human Development* **16**, 273–85.

Turner, B.S. (1992) *Regulating Bodies: essays in medical sociology*, London: Routledge.

Walter, T. (1995) *The Revival of Death*, London: Routledge.

Williams, S.J. and Bendelow, G. (1998) *'Embodying Sociology': critical perspectives on the dualist legacies*, London: Routledge.

Williams, T., Wetton, N., Moon, A. (1988) *A Picture of Health*, London: Health Education Authority.

Chapter 7

Falling out with my shadow

Lay perceptions of the body in the context of arthritis

Bethan Williams and Julie H. Barlow

This chapter presents an exploration of lay perceptions of the body in the context of a common chronic disease, arthritis. The chapter opens with an introduction to arthritis and the impact the disease has on the body. Experience of the body among people with arthritis is examined in a descriptive study based on in-depth interviews. Findings are presented and discussed with respect to the impact of the disease and its treatment on the body and movement; social and emotional well-being; and the maintenance of positive body perceptions.

Background

Arthritis is a chronic, debilitating disease that is the principal cause of physical disability in the UK (Badley and Tenant 1993). The term 'arthritis' is used as a generic diagnostic label encompassing over 200 different types of musculoskeletal, connective tissue and non-articular conditions with the most prevalent forms in adults being rheumatoid arthritis (RA), osteoarthritis (OA) and ankylosing spondylitis (AS) (Taal *et al.* 1993).

Contrary to popular belief, arthritis is not solely a disease of old age; it can develop in children and young adults. Although arthritis is primarily a disease of the joints, there are a number of types of arthritis that affect bones, tendons, muscles, the skin and internal organs. Onset may be sudden or gradual, with symptoms often not given a specific diagnostic label for many years. Arthritis is characterised by pain, fatigue, stiffness, inflammation, and limited physical functioning. For some, chronic symptomatology can lead to joint degeneration. Posture, gait and general mobility (e.g. ascending and descending stairs, rising in and out of chairs) are often affected, thus posture can become stooped and compensatory walking patterns (e.g. limping and knee flexion) are often adopted unconsciously in order to protect painful joints. The disease course is cyclic in nature, following an unpredictable pattern with periods of exacerbation (i.e. flare-ups) and remission. Arthritis can be invisible; however for many, the pain, inflammation, joint deformity, alterations in gait, and restricted general mobility can be all too evident. Although these visible consequences of the disease can be temporary, persistent inflammation can give rise to permanent changes of the body.

Body experience within the context of arthritis

The impact of arthritis on the body has been an area of much neglect despite considerable research focusing on the psychosocial aspects of the disease such as pain, psychological well-being, social support, and coping strategies (e.g. Young 1992; Liang et al. 1984). Several studies have shown that people with arthritis are concerned with the alterations that they experience to their physical appearance (Bauman et al. 1989; Liang et al. 1984; Rogers et al. 1982). Of the few studies that have explored this issue in greater depth, the focus of attention has been to explain the impact of disease severity on bodily satisfaction and feelings of attractiveness.

Carr and Thompson (1995) found that the body parts most affected by RA strongly influenced perceived levels of satisfaction. High levels of dissatisfaction with the hands and legs were expressed by those with visible hand deformities and abnormal gaits, respectively. In addition, they found a significant relationship between high levels of dissatisfaction and low levels of emotional quality of life.

The relationship between disease severity and body-image among people with AS was explored by Barlow (1993) and showed that concern with appearance was predominantly centred on the spine and the degree of curvature exhibited. Greater disease severity (e.g. pain, stiffness, fatigue) was associated with greater psychological distress and negative evaluations of the body, whereas less disease severity was associated with more positive psychological well-being and evaluations of the body. Furthermore, perceptions of personal control were central to the prediction of psychological adjustment: high perceived control of AS was associated with a more positive body-image.

Cornwell and Schmitt (1990) conducted a comparative study between two different types of arthritis, RA and systemic lupus erythematosus (SLE), and healthy subjects. SLE is an inflammatory form of arthritis that affects the skin, internal organ systems as well as the joints. The greatest dissatisfaction was attributed to the parts of the body most affected by their condition. People with RA expressed more negative feelings towards their eyes, hands, feet and muscle strength, whereas those with SLE expressed a more global dissatisfaction with their bodies encompassing their complexion, glands, heart, kidney, chest, energy and health (list not inclusive). This more global dissatisfaction resulted in the SLE sample having a more negative body-image than that exhibited by the RA and healthy samples whose overall body-image was similar to that of each other. Their findings revealed that differences emerged between RA and SLE. The authors concluded that certain conditions that fall under the umbrella of arthritis may promote more negative feelings towards the body than others.

The need to feel attractive has been shown to be an important concern for women with RA (Stenström *et al.* 1993). The restriction that RA imposed on their choice of clothing and footwear were viewed as 'obstacles' to the presentation of an attractive physical self. Concealment of swollen joints was frequently employed to mask both the pain and the disease. The importance of an attractive physical appearance was also found in a study exploring the perceptions of hand appearance in women with RA (Vamos 1990). Two factors emerged as powerful predictors of the desire for corrective surgical interventions: body-image concerns pertaining to unattractive hand appearance; and negative emotions provoked by hand appearance.

Although the cited studies have been instrumental in placing the body on the research agenda, they have provided only a superficial 'snapshot' of the impact that arthritis has on the body. Most studies identify it as a concern but fail to provide insight into the nature and experience of the body in the context of arthritis. In-depth explorations, centred upon lay perceptions pertaining to the meaning and relevance of the physical changes to the body, have largely been ignored.

Method

The sample was recruited through the Arthritis Care Branch network (Central Region), a local National Ankylosing Spondylitis

Society (NASS) group and a number of willing volunteers known to the Psychosocial Rheumatology Research Centre, Coventry University. A diagnosis of arthritis was the only selection criteria employed, thus the study was open to women and men across a wide age spectrum with varying disease duration and chronicity.

Fourteen interviews were conducted. The median age of the nine women and five men was 49.5 years (range, 28 to 86 years) and the median disease duration was 24.5 years (range, 9 to 60 years). Eight interviewees had RA, five had AS and one had OA. All participants were white/European, eight were married, seven did not have formal educational qualifications, eight were registered disabled, six were retired and two felt that they were unable to work because of their arthritis. Four participants reported psoriasis, scleroderma, juvenile chronic arthritis (JCA) and osteoporosis as secondary types of arthritis. Eight reported comorbidity, with stomach ulcers being the most common. Other additional health problems included asthma, emphysema, diabetes, and angina. Eleven were currently taking medication for their arthritis.

Data were collected by semi-structured interviews. An interview schedule, comprising open-ended questions, was developed from existing literature and exploratory conversations with the target population. The interviews focused on the impact of arthritis and its treatment on the body; body concerns; relationships with others; and ways to maintain positive feelings towards the body. The interviews lasted between 45 minutes and 120 minutes. All interviews were audio taped (with the participant's consent) and were transcribed verbatim.

The data were not entirely lacking in structure as preliminary categories were formed based on the themes addressed in the semi-structured interview schedule. Therefore, a 'middle-order' approach was employed to develop categories within the data (Becker and Geer 1982). This flexible approach for data-categorisation was favoured because it enables the analysis to move between a 'holistic' approach (Jones 1985), where broad categories are first identified, and a more detailed, grounded, 'line-by-line' approach as advocated by Strauss (1987).

To facilitate analysis, the data were initially filed as complete interviews for each participant. All data were repeatedly read and simultaneously annotated and coded to explore potential content-related and conceptual themes. Comments in response to the data and annotated notes were recorded as memos. The identification of prevalent themes through the process of data reduction resulted in key textual data from each participant being filed under each question asked on the semi-structured interview schedule. In addition, the meanings participants ascribed to each particular theme identified were depicted graphically. Filing the data in several formats enabled it to be read either as a whole data set for each participant, or, as responses to key questions asked during the interview across all participants. Once all data sets had been coded, broad categories were identified from distinctions within the data and from data confirmation of the preliminary set of categories derived from the interview schedule. Subcategories nested within the broad categories were then developed from more detailed investigations of the data.

Impact of arthritis and its treatment on the body and movement

Body parts

Not surprisingly, the principal concerns expressed focused on the body parts most affected by arthritis. For example, the women with RA were concerned with their hands, knees and feet. The visible swollen and disfigured appearance of these painful body parts were believed to be the underlying root of their dissatisfaction. In the words of one participant:

> My concern is with my swollen fingers, my swollen feet, which ever bit that decides to swell. My fingers are all twisted and you get this sort of gargoyle appearance. . . . I don't like my body, not the way it is, I mean who would? It is disfigured.

For the woman with OA, concern was with joint instability of the lower body and the pain experienced in the legs on initial movement. For the men with AS, concern centred on the degree of spinal curvature and the pain and stiffness in their neck, shoulders, back and legs. In contrast to the women with RA, their concern was not constant but surfaced only during active phases of their disease. An absence of pain signalled disease remission, and thus concerns receded. In the words of one participant: 'I am more concerned when my disease is active. When my shoulders, back and legs don't hurt, it doesn't enter my head . . . I am not conscious of it at all'.

In addition, the women reported that their feelings about individual parts of the body affected by arthritis generalised to perceptions about their body as a whole. As one participant eloquently expressed: 'With arthritis you are unhappy with a body part but you are also unhappy with the whole of your body'.

Posture

Arthritis can alter the natural alignment of the body. The head tends to lean forwards, curvature of the spine becomes more prominent, the shoulders tend to become more rounded and the lower body can become permanently flexed. Consequently, postural concerns in the context of both sitting and standing were prevalent amongst all of the participants. It was felt that a 'tense', 'rigid' and 'stooped' posture presented an 'abnormal' and 'unattractive' stature. As one participant expressed it:

> We may look at ourselves and feel unhappy about the way we look but for me, I'm not happy about the way I sit, the way my posture is, the way I stand. . . . My spine is more rounded, my shoulders are more hunched, my knees are bent . . . I am physically not as upright as I should be. I don't like the way I hold myself at all.

Movement

Difficulties experienced with gait and general mobility were expressed as a concern and were felt to be inextricably linked to posture. The participants felt that their gait, general mobility and movement of body parts were severely restricted by their arthritis. Body movements and mobility were believed to be 'slow', 'contrived' and 'awkward' in appearance and were felt to be more marked during episodes of active disease. The following illustrates the impact of arthritis on posture, movement and mobility:

> When my AS is very active I tend to adopt an ape-like walk because you are really bent, stooped, your arms are lower and you bend your knees to compensate for your spine. Physical movements become difficult and you are aware that you are

not standing as straight as you should be or walking as quickly or smoothly as you want to.

Many people with arthritis experience joint instability, difficulties in bearing weight on painful joints and have an inherent fear of falling. Thus, mobility can be severely restricted. The use of assistive devices such as canes, wheelchairs and/or scooters can protect joints, enhance feelings of safety and can improve mobility. As one participant conveyed:

> I use a walking stick outside and depending on how my arthritis is I do in the house . . . you know how arthritis fluctuates. It makes me feel a lot safer, a lot more secure. I can walk without it but I think what is the point because I am in more pain and it takes me twice as long to get there.

However, this view was not universal. Although the participants knew that their mobility may be enhanced through using assistive devices (e.g. walking sticks), several interviewees felt hesitant in their use. Self-consciousness, lost pride, and fears of losing their independence were identified as barriers.

Side-effects of treatment

Most of the women felt that in addition to the effect of arthritis *per se*, the treatment received to alleviate their condition had a negative impact on their appearance. For example, side-effects such as weight gain, dry, thin skin and facial rashes associated with the medication prescribed provoked negative perceptions of the body:

> The cortisone has caused me to put on excessive weight . . . my stomach and my bottom are the parts that upset me the most when I look at myself sideways in the mirror and then I look at photos of how I used to be and that really does upset me at times.

The restriction that arthritis imposes on the ability to lead a physically active life was felt to be a contributory factor resulting in weight gain. In contrast, one woman was more worried about weight loss due to muscle wastage rather than weight gain. Furthermore, for two participants, medication was viewed positively as it was felt to reduce inflammation and pain thus improving their movement, mobility and self-perceptions.

Social and emotional impact of arthritis

Body taboo and visibility

All participants felt that their feelings associated with the experience of bodily changes as a result of arthritis was a taboo area avoided both by close partners and friends as well as by health professionals. A lack of understanding and awareness, as well as uncertainty about how to approach such a sensitive topic and time constraints were identified as reinforcing the taboo. As one participant stated: 'Doctors care for your body but they don't care about how you feel about your body'.

The need for more communication about this underserved psychosocial impact of arthritis was clearly expressed and several of the younger participants felt that a support network for partners concerning body awareness would facilitate the expression of feelings about bodily change. As one participant said: 'In terms of my body, I don't know what my husband is thinking. Maybe that is because he doesn't tell me or that I dare not ask, I don't know.'

For the women with RA in this study, the visibility of disease provoked great anxiety, feelings of self-consciousness and negative emotion. They believed that the presence of a 'visible disease' was invasive, threatening their private and public self. These feelings were based on an underlying belief that people in their social worlds would see only the disease rather than the person within. Concealment assumed paramount importance, whereby items of clothing were selected and worn with the sole purpose of hiding the changes to the body. The art of concealment becomes a self-defence strategy, protecting people with arthritis from the outside world. As one participant eloquently expressed:

> You feel very very threatened. It is on display to everybody. It is not so much bodily threatening, it is your inner self . . . when there is swelling, you see people looking at it so you try and hide it. You wrap it up, you hide it away so that people can't see it. The swellings are like a visible effect of pain. You don't want people to see the pain that you are suffering.

Although concealment was effective in hiding visible changes to the body, most participants felt unable to disguise their mobility difficulties (i.e. how their body moved): 'With my hands, you can disguise that ... but with my walking, I know that people are looking and you cannot disguise it ... it makes you feel a bit of a freak at times'.

One participant felt more comfortable 'hiding' in her wheelchair in order to reduce the feelings of self-consciousness provoked by the 'staring eyes' of society as a result of her mobility difficulties.

Four participants believed that the visibility of bodily pain, the adoption of a stooped posture and their impaired mobility served to 'age' their bodily appearance beyond that expected for their chronological years. For one woman in her early forties, her impaired mobility made her feel one step behind her peer group when in social situations. Her need to sit down and rest further fuelled her feelings of being older than her years. As she explains:

> Movement wise, I can't stand up for long, I have to sit down. So if I am out shopping in town, I often have to look for somewhere to sit down. Usually this is with all the old dears resting their feet. This really makes me feel and probably look, a lot older than I actually am.

Another young woman in her twenties felt that she looked as if she was in her mid-forties or early fifties. She believed that the arthritis had 'robbed' her of twenty years of life.

For the women, the changes to their bodies had consequences for appearance-related issues that were of paramount importance to positive self-presentation. They felt that their physical symptoms such as swollen joints, limited hand dexterity and limited upper body movement imposed on their choice of clothes and their ability to wear both cosmetics and jewellery. They felt that their femininity was threatened. Consequently, clothes and jewellery were selected for ease of fit and ease of fastening (e.g. without buttons, hooks or catches). The following illustrate this view:

> I don't wear pretty blouses because of the cuffs, collars and buttons up the front. I wear looser clothes so that should I get the swellings, the clothes don't restrict it. You have to choose your clothes carefully, you choose clothes that you can cope with.

I can't wear jewellery, especially necklaces with catches because my arm movement is limited and there is no use in my fingers.

Among male participants this concern with self-presentation was manifest in relation to the loss of body fitness. Weight gain, muscle atrophy, loss of stamina and flexibility were all attributed to the restriction that arthritis placed on participation in active leisure pursuits, such as golf and football. A physically unfit body provoked feelings of self-consciousness and motivated the men to perform regular daily exercise routines designed to fight disease progression. Therefore, despite the physical limitations imposed by their condition, men placed body care and maintenance high on their agenda of disease management. As one participant put it:

> You have got to look after your body . . . I've got to be aware that I am upright whether I am sitting, driving or standing. I have got to do everything to the best that I can for my body as it is the only one I am going to get.

Social relationships

Within social contexts, participants, particularly the women, felt 'uncomfortable', 'embarrassed' and 'self-conscious' about the changes that have occurred to their bodies and their general mobility. These feelings derived from internal (i.e. self-perceptions and feelings) and external (i.e. others' perceptions and reactions). sources. As one participant expressed:

> I feel self-conscious movement wise. You feel as if you do things different to the way that other people do things, which draws attention to you. For instance, when we were on holiday we went to a cabaret show in the evening. When I got up to move, I couldn't move properly to start with. I had to stand there for a bit until I could get going and I know other people were looking at me and thinking that I was drunk. That's how you feel with strangers . . . that they will automatically think the worst of you.

This instilled an 'obsessional preoccupation' with the appearance of the body and engendered feelings of being different: 'being a fish out of water'. Participants employed avoidance strategies to protect themselves from having to deal with the reactions of others to their bodies. The following quotes illustrate this view:

> You feel very self-conscious, you try to hide your body and the swellings. You avoid things that take you into contact with people, you avoid places where you think you are going to meet friends . . . you avoid contact of any kind like the plague.

Within intimate and sexual contexts, several of the women felt that the visible changes that had occurred to their bodies had made them less attractive to their partners and potential partners. As one participant expressed:

> You don't feel so attractive at all. . . . You want to still feel attractive and still feel that he fancies you. . . . You hope that they think of you the same as you were, before all of this happened, but you don't feel as if they can. . . . You feel self-conscious of your body, you want to disguise it as much as you can.

Falling out with your shadow

Alterations to the body provoked negative emotions. Many of the participants felt angered by the changes to their bodies. Bodily pain, disfigurement and disability engendered depressed mood, self-hatred, sadness and feelings of being different to others. In the words of two participants:

> I get depression a lot. . . . I often feel annoyed and angry with myself. It is a self-destructive anger. . . . You have to try and get over that hating of yourself because it is inevitably going to happen, you are going to hate yourself but you have got to get through it and get on with your life. You can't just sit there all day with tears streaming down your face and thinking I wish I wasn't alive, I wish I was dead. Yes it does happen and if you have got arthritis it happens a lot because when you are in pain, terrific pain, it is not just a headache or whatever, it is severe body pain, you doubt yourself constantly.

> I sometimes get depressed about it. If the way that I look is bad, if somebody says something about it or if something goes

wrong you can fall out with yourself, them, your shadow, anything. Yes, when it is bad you can even fall out with your shadow.

Three of the women felt that they had lost control of their bodies with respect to both physical functioning and appearance. Decisions regarding self-presentation such as choice of clothing were felt to be governed by their arthritis rather than by personal choice. Consequently, loss of control, limited choice and memories of the body as it used to be prior to the onset of arthritis elicited depressed mood.

A further concern identified was that of the future appearance of their bodies. Arthritis was described as a disease of 'uncertainty'. The 'fear of the unknown' was unsettling and provoked great anxiety about posture, mobility, increasing periods of active disease and permanent disfigurement and disability. For all participants, the visible impact of arthritis on their bodies was central to their current and future concerns.

For one woman, the pain, restricted arm movement and concern with 'looking awkward' were barriers that prevented her from engaging in physical contact with men. She felt that this put a tremendous strain on her relationship with her partner and thus she tried to 'avoid intimacy at all costs'. In contrast, three of the participants who had developed arthritis prior to meeting their current partners, viewed their condition and the changes to their bodies as a 'new way of life' which had cemented and strengthened their relationship with their partner.

Positive perceptions of the body

Participants expressed that being with similar others, especially within a social, educational or group exercise environment promoted positive perceptions of the body. It was felt that experiences of this nature reduced feelings of isolation and fear of the future promoted proactive thinking and confidence. Being in a peer group was identified as a 'safe' place to freely express their feelings about the changes to their bodies with others who really understand. As one participant succinctly stated:

I think that the whole idea of body-image is something that people find difficult to talk about. That is why people benefit from talking with other people with arthritis. Sometimes it can be hurtful when you talk about your body to the people who are close to you.

Furthermore, sharing within a non-threatening environment was felt to be instrumental to accepting bodily change. In the words of several participants who attend self-help groups for exercise:

> Seeing other people with the same appearance as yourself helps you to come to terms with yourself and to realise that you are not alone in the world with the disease . . . the self-help group helps you to get over the idea that you may look a bit different but not that different. The group has helped me to accept the changes to my body. I saw myself in others and have seen how others perhaps look at me and it either doesn't look that bad or if it doesn't look that good you tell yourself that you can do better.

Social comparison with similar others was particularly evident for the men. Being in contact with similar others also promoted the adoption of self-help strategies to curtail disease progression. Several men with AS were keen to avoid the bodily changes they observed in others with the same condition: 'You see people who look as if they have bent over 90 degrees. They don't try to help themselves at all. That is something I want to avoid and that is why I do the exercises'.

The men viewed exercise as a means to achieve a positive perception of the body. It was felt that exercise reduced pain and stiffness and improved muscle tone and flexibility. Furthermore, they felt that by adopting a pattern of regular daily exercise, they were able to play an active role in controlling their disease, thus counter-balancing feelings of helplessness provoked by bodily changes.

In contrast, for the women, clothes, cosmetics, other grooming behaviours (e.g. nicely styled hair) and disguise of bodily change were assigned greater importance in achieving a positive perception of the body. As one participant expressed: 'I binge on clothes, compulsive shopping for clothes, make-up, and having my hair done. All to present an image that looks reasonably good'.

Discussion

Despite much emphasis being placed on the body within society today, within the context of arthritis, the body emerged as a 'taboo' area. Prior to the study, few participants had been able to voice their feelings and concerns about the impact of arthritis on their body and their bodily perceptions. A body branded with a chronic painful disease for which there is no known cure was felt by the participants to be a topic that others within clinical, home and social environments found 'too sensitive' to approach. In clinical settings, participants reported that the focus of attention tends to be on management of bodily manifestations of disease (e.g. pain) rather than on body perceptions and feelings. This finding suggests that the biomedical model still remains dominant within present-day clinical practice. Sensitivity concerning the impact of arthritis on the body coupled with fear of rejection was felt to impede communication within the home and social environments.

The findings from this study clearly demonstrate that regardless of gender, age, type of arthritis and disease duration, arthritis can have a profound impact on perceptions of the body. Chronic pain, inflammation, stiffness, restriction and deformity are all common consequences of the physical manifestations of arthritis on the body. In accordance with previous studies, concerns primarily centred on the body parts most affected by arthritis. Earlier studies addressed the impact of disease severity on levels of bodily satisfaction (Carr and Thompson 1995; Barlow 1993; Cornwell and Schmitt 1990), but ignored the totality of the body experience, focusing only on the body parts most affected. The present study has extended these findings by showing that the metamorphic experience of the body within the context of arthritis threatens not only individual body parts targeted by the disease, but also the totality of the body experience which consequently engenders dissatisfaction with the body as a whole.

The emotional impact of the body experience within the context of arthritis is far reaching. The wide spectrum of emotions included anger, anxiety, fear, depression, sadness, 'why me?', feelings of being different from others, and isolation. Perceptions of the body were further challenged by disease uncertainty. The disease course is unpredictable: disease symptomatology and bodily changes may be episodic and reversible, episodic and permanent, or chronic and permanent. Bodily changes may be visible or invisible to the self and others. Trapped within a body that may be fine one day but unbearable and unrecognisable in appearance and function the next day provoked much anxiety.

Several authors have noted that the 'body is an obvious, though sometimes ambiguous, point of reference for external labels' (Kelly and Field 1996: 251; Hutchinson 1982). Within the present study, people felt that the impact of disease on their body became the focus of attention in the social world, hiding the 'true' person inside. Bodily changes fuelled feelings of self-consciousness partic- ularly when in contact with strangers and current or prospective partners, provoked feelings of being different and highlighted fear of stigmatisation. Understandably, avoidance strategies were used as a means of self-protection in order to minimise self-consciousness and the pain of rejection. Paradoxically, when arthritis was not visible, emotional distress was also experienced. Explaining the underlying reason for physical difficulties and limitations was believed to be just as invasive as having a condition that is visible in nature. Furthermore, having a disease that oscillates between visibility and invisibility caused immense anxiety. Similar findings have emerged from studies of young people and children with arthritis (Barlow et al. 1997a; Barlow and Harrison 1996), suggesting that similar issues reverberate across the body experi- ence in arthritis, regardless of age.

Inextricably linked to visibility was the self-defence strategy of concealment. Concealment of visible disease is commensurate with the term 'covering' (Goffman 1990) as an 'adaptive technique' to minimise the 'obtrusiveness' of a visible stigma. Clothing was chosen and worn to mask bodily change to reduce feelings of self- consciousness and to maintain an appearance similar to that of same-aged peers. Thus concealment was employed to minimise the interference of visible symptomatology on social interaction in order to maintain one's social identity. Concealment was also related to the impact of arthritis on emotional well-being. Participants felt reluctant to disclose their feelings about the changes to their physical body because they wanted to maintain some degree of privacy as well as to shield family and friends from their inner pain and suffering.

Society places much emphasis on appearance with respect to youth, the 'body beautiful' and the attainment of the perfect body (Stone 1995; Featherstone 1982; Hutchinson 1982) and reinforces culturally determined stereotypes of male and female bodies. To some extent, culturally determined gender stereotypes were borne out in the findings. Although all of the participants were equally concerned with presenting a positive appearance that is deemed socially acceptable, the emphasis differed. For men, the main concern centred on loss of physical functioning and fitness together with a strong emphasis on body care and maintenance. In contrast, women were concerned about appearance-related issues, e.g. the visibility of arthritis, difficulties encountered with positive self-presentation involving cosmetics, jewellery and clothes (see also Saltonstall 1993). Barron states that 'having a physical impairment may mean having to come to terms with a body that departs from cultural norms of acceptability and attractiveness' (1997: 229). Thus the presence of a disease such as arthritis can challenge culturally determined gender stereotypes pertaining to appearance, physical attractiveness, femininity and masculinity, as well as an individual's quest for the 'perfect' body.

Although gender socialisation practices and culturally determined stereotypes influenced positive perceptions of the body, being with similar others within a social, educational or group exercise setting was universally regarded as promoting positive perceptions of the body. The benefits of sharing with similar others within a group format were widespread. Realising that you are not the only one instilled a sense of peer-belonging and being able to freely exchange coping strategies and feelings pertaining to bodily changes with others who 'really' understand enhanced body well-being. This finding provides further evidence of the beneficial power of sharing amongst people with arthritis (Barlow et al. 1997b).

For the men with AS, being with similar others also triggered social comparison with respect to physical health status, physical functioning and psychosocial adjustment, with others less fortunate than themselves (i.e. downward comparison). They felt that downward comparisons instilled the strength and motivation to cope, 'fight' and overcome disease progression, thus fostering body well-being.[1]

In conclusion, the body experience in arthritis confirms the fundamental inseparability of body and mind. As argued by Grosz (1994), the biological body is not simply mapped onto the psychosocial body to form a body-image. Neither is the psychosocial mapped onto the biological. Rather there is an interweaving of biological, psychological and social realms which has been well illustrated in the accounts described here. Our understanding of the fundamental nature of the totality of the body experience has been enhanced by powerful insights.

Acknowledgement

I would like to express my thanks to all of the participants for giving their views and their time so freely. Without your help this would not have been possible. Thank you.

Note

1   This finding is in accordance with Affleck *et al.* (1988) and DeVellis *et al.* (1990) who found downward comparison to be associated with self-enhancement and positive psychosocial well-being amongst people with RA.

References

Affleck, G., Tennen, H., Pfeiffer, C., Fifield, J. (1988) 'Social comparisons in rheumatoid arthritis: accuracy and adaptational significance', *Journal of Social and Clinical Psychology* **6**, 2, 219–34.

Badley, E.M. and Tenant A. (1993) 'Disablement associated with rheumatic disorders in a British population: problems with activities of daily living and level of support', *British Journal of Rheumatology* **32**, 601–8.

Barlow, J. (1993) 'Perceived control, self-efficacy and outcome expectations in the context of a chronic disease', unpublished PhD thesis, Coventry University.

Barlow, J.H. and Harrison, K. (1996) 'Focusing on empowerment: facilitating self-help in young people with arthritis through a disability organisation', *Disability and Society* **11**, 4, 540–551.

Barlow, J.H., Shaw, K., Harrison. K. (1997a) 'The psychosocial impact of juvenile chronic arthritis', *British Journal of Rheumatology* **36**, 4, 266.

Barlow, J.H., Cullen, L.A., Davies, S., Williams, B. (1997b) 'The hidden benefit of group education for people with arthritis', *British Journal of Therapy and Rehabilitation* **4**, 1, 38–41.

Barron, K. (1997) 'The bumpy road to womanhood', *Disability and Society* **12**, 2, 223–39.

Bauman, A., Barnes, C., Schrieber, L., Dunsmore, J., Brooks, P. (1989) 'The unmet needs of patients with systemic lupus erythematosus: planning for patient education', *Patient Education and Counselling* **14**, 235–42.

Becker, H. and Geer, B. (1982) 'Participant observation: the analysis of qualitative field data', in Burgess, R. (ed.) *Field Research: a sourcebook and field manual*, London: Allen and Unwin.

Carr, A.J. and Thompson, P.W. (1995) 'The impact of rheumatoid arthritis on body-image', *Arthritis and Rheumatism* **38**, 9, 387.

Cornwell, C.J. and Schmitt, M.H. (1990) 'Perceived health status, self-esteem and body-image in women with rheumatoid arthritis or systemic lupus erythematosus', *Research in Nursing and Health* **13**, 99–107.

DeVellis, R.F., Holt, K., Renner, B.R., Blalock, S.J., Blanchard, L.W., Cook, H.L., Klotz, M.L., Mikow, V., Harring, K. (1990) 'The relationship of social comparison to rheumatoid arthritis symptoms and affect', *Basic and Applied Social Psychology* **11**, 1, 1–18.

Featherstone, M. (1982) 'The body in consumer culture', *Theory, Culture and Society* **1**, 3, 18–33.

Goffman, E. (1990) *Stigma: notes on the management of spoiled identity*, Harmondsworth: Penguin Books.

Grosz, E. (1994) *Volatile Bodies*, Bloominton, IN: Indiana University Press.

Hutchinson, M.G. (1982) 'Transforming body image: your body, friend or foe?' *Women and Therapy*, **1**, 3, 59–67.

Jones, S. (1985) 'The analysis of depth interviews', in Walker, R. (ed.) *Applied Qualitative Research*, London: Gower.

Kelly, M.P. and Field, D. (1996) 'Medical sociology, chronic illness and the body', *Sociology of Health and Illness* **18**, 2, 241–57.

Liang, M.H., Rogers, M., Larson, M., Eaton, H.M., Murawski, B.J., Taylor, J.E., Swafford, J., Schur P.H. (1984) 'The psychosocial impact of systemic lupus erythematosus and rheumatoid arthritis', *Arthritis and Rheumatism* **27**, 1, 13–19.

Rogers, M.P., Liang, M.H., Partridge, A.J. (1982) 'Psychological care of adults with rheumatoid arthritis', *Annals of Internal Medicine* **96**, 344–8.

Saltonstall, R. (1993) 'Healthy bodies, social bodies: men's and women's concepts and practices of health in everyday life', *Social Science and Medicine* **36**, 1, 7–14.

Stenström, C.H., Bergman, B., Dahlgren, L.O. (1993) 'Everyday life with rheumatoid arthritis: a phenomenographic study', *Physiotherapy, Theory and Practice* **9**, 235–45.

Stone, S.D. (1995) 'The myth of bodily perfection', *Disability and Society* **10**, 4, 413–24.

Strauss, A.L. (1987) *Qualitative Analysis for Social Scientists*, Cambridge: Cambridge University Press.

Taal, E., Seydel, E.R., Rasker, J.J., Weigman, O. (1993) 'Psychosocial aspects of rheumatic diseases: introduction', *Patient Education and Counselling* **20**, 55–61.

Vamos, M. (1990) 'Body image in rheumatoid arthritis: the relevance of hand appearance to desire for surgery', *British Journal of Medical Psychology* **63**, 267–77.

Young, L.D. (1992) 'Psychological factors in rheumatoid arthritis', *Journal of Consulting and Clinical Psychology* **60**, 4, 619–27.

Chapter 8

The body, health and self in the middle years

Sarah Cunningham-Burley and Kathryn Backett-Milburn

In this chapter we report on a research project which investigated perceptions of health in the middle years. The middle years are likely to be a period of social, personal and biological change, as well as continuity, although as Hepworth (1987) has noted, there is little empirical research into the 'reality' of the midlife phase. The specific role transitions associated with middle age, conceptualised by the life cycle perspectives, have been challenged by life course theorists who take a more complex view of the middle years. The middle years will be variously experienced by individuals in different social locations and with different biographical experiences, and the cultural stereotypes of those who are 'middle aged' are now challenged and potentially being eroded.

The middle years are often pathologised, with much focus on ill-heath, change and loss. Certainly, in industrialised societies, mortality and morbidity rates rise at population level in the middle years, and individuals are more likely to encounter illness, sometimes serious, in themselves and others, and possibly face premature death amongst friends and relatives, or themselves. Yet most remain healthy, and this period is also portrayed as positive (Hunter and Sundel 1989). This juxtaposition of health and illness, continuity and change makes this period of the life course a particularly interesting one for an empirical study of the body, self and health.

The body is central to understanding the middle years, not as some pathological entity, but as the site of biographical experience, culturally mediated and socially located. The body both constitutes and is constituted by the social relations and circumstances in which people are embedded: its empirical study should shed light on the way in which individuals both make sense of and live with their changing bodies, in different spaces and at different times. As sociological theorising begins to take up the task of becoming truly embodied, it must begin with an examination of lived experience (Watson *et al.* 1996; Connell 1995; Csordas 1990; Freund 1990) or to theorise 'from the body up' (Frank 1991).

The middle years, then, are likely to be a period when the body is very much in biological evidence – corporeal and mortal. It may be getting sick, too fat or too thin, tired and even dying. In this period, people may also be concerned about management and maintaining their bodies, and perhaps those of others, for example older relatives. This may impact on their personal and social relationships as well as on their relations to those who mediate socially defined health concerns – doctors and health promoters. Moreover, individuals have to acknowledge and challenge the very conditions of their existence routinely in their everyday lives. The middle years may bring these processes into sharp focus, as one's body asserts itself in unforeseen or undesired ways. As Hepworth has noted:

> In the late twentieth century version of middle age, the 'bodily betrayals' which are its primary identifiers derive their significance from the fact that for the majority of men and women, there *is* a lot of life left to live.
>
> (Hepworth 1987: 137)

The research reported in this chapter was informed by a prior recognition of a need to investigate lay theorising about the body and health, in the same way that lay theorising has long been recognised as important for understanding health and illness. It is maintained that we have no direct or 'innocent' knowledge of our bodies but rather are always 'reading' our bodies through lenses of various interpretive schemes. The social construction of the physical body as a site for control and change mediated through biomedically driven 'lifestyle' directives has been considered a major way in which bodies are experienced (Scheper-Hughes and Lock 1987; Crawford 1984). We felt that more empirically based work on the body and physical change, over time, was necessary in order to address the following questions: what kind of interpretative schemes and models were people drawing on in relation to the no longer youthful but not yet old body during the middle years? How do people feel about their bodies in a culture which stresses youth, health and personal control over health and illness?

However, in attempting to answer these sorts of questions, we have to make 'the body' empirically accessible in order to generate theory of the body or bodies and health grounded in lay experience.

The study

Our research was carried out in central Scotland between 1992 and 1994. It aimed to investigate lay perceptions of health and health promotion in the middle years.[1] Aware that this period of life may be associated with negative cultural stereotypes, we avoided using any term to represent these years other than as the chosen age range, 45–60 years. We tried not to invoke the value judgements inherent in life cycle or life course approaches, and we hoped that any reference to negative or positive images would emerge in respondent accounts, rather than being explicitly reinforced by our framing. We did not wish to be seen to be contributing to the pathologising of experience and stressed our interest was in everyday experience and how it may be related to health. Although the study was a multi-method investigation, this chapter draws on data obtained from in-depth interviews with twenty-four men and twenty-seven women. After sensitising pilot work, involving three group interviews and four individual interviews, and also drawing on theoretical and conceptual groundwork, we developed an effective and grounded topic guide for the interviews. This covered respondents' views on health, their bodies, the life course, and change. The interviews lasted between one and two hours and were transcribed fully for subsequent analysis. Our analysis involved 'cut and paste' using a word-processing package, where segments of transcripts were collated into emergent themes. However, the researchers also used readings of whole transcripts to maintain an accurate sense of context throughout the analysis.

Accessing the body empirically

Critical of work which sees the body as text, we searched for a way to access lived experience, or to develop a phenomenology of the body (Csordas 1990). Although research on lay perceptions of health and illness is commonplace, with an associated awareness of the constraints and possibilities associated with the research process, empirical work which directly addressed people's perceptions of the body was, at the time we conducted the study, still quite limited. In sociological research, which relies heavily but not exclusively on verbal communication to generate data, knowledge and understanding, we are constrained by, yet can also creatively use language. Martin (1987) argues that language and conceptual metaphor are used to structure how we think and act. Accessing the body empirically, through interviews, demands the labelling of something truly intimate – 'bringing the body in', in the interview situation is almost like asking someone to get undressed in front of you. People deal with their bodies (and health) in a variety of ways, and ignoring them and keeping them covered up, actually and metaphorically, are two obvious practices. As Mead has noted 'We are trained by our society to keep our bodies out of our minds' (1949: 79, quoted in Synnott 1993: 246) – we were asking our study participants to give them attention.

We argue that this intimate terrain of the everyday lived experience of 'the body' is at least partially made accessible through accounts generated in one-to-one interviews. Language becomes both a topic and resource in the research process; the body both object and subject, as respondents use language to articulate embodied experience. In our sensitising pilot work we found that we could not ask people directly how they felt about their bodies: this was too sensitive and personal. Quite simply, the words we had, at that time, produced either non-response, bewilderment or embarrassment on the part of the respondents. We had to develop culturally acceptable but nonetheless challenging ways to ask about bodies. We found that focusing on the body and health was one way of making this task more permissible and acceptable, and our pilot work provided us with the language and everyday concepts with which to proceed.

Our fundamental concern with change/age and health, led to the formulation of the following routes of questioning of people about their bodies. First, we asked the respondent if he or she saw his or her body as having any strong or weak points. This was one way of attempting to bring the respondent's 'body' into the discussion, framed in language used in our pilot work. We then asked something along the lines of 'Do other people's bodies tell you anything about their health?'; in order to draw out culturally relevant constructions, and the signs and symbols of health and fitness which may be used to interpret 'others' bodies'. We then worked with the idea that people may 'read off' from their bodies in particular ways which are relevant to understanding health. Questions took the form of 'Would you say that your own body ever gives you signs or ever tells you anything about your health? Does it give you any messages about your health?' We also tried to probe around the relationship between emotions and physical symptoms, by asking about the impact of changes either physical or emotional. Finally, we asked respondents to reflect on their bodies and what they communicate now as compared to when they were in their twenties or thirties, in order to consider time and not to make assumptions about change. This could allow for the expression of continuity across the life course, as well as the articulation of change.

Although most people we spoke to were able to speak at some length about their bodies and health, a few still responded to our questions in a rather bemused way – and told us if they had not thought of their bodies in the way we were asking. As an intimate site, this was a sensitive area to probe and as a taken-for-granted part of lived experience, it is perhaps difficult to talk about. However, we also found that respondents felt able to ask for clarification about what was being asked or discussed. For these reasons we feel confident that respondents took the topic seriously, and provided accounts which were directly related to their personal experience, and how they lived with their bodies. We were attempting to reveal the taken-for-granted nature of one's body, and the routine ways it communicates about health. As one respondent herself noted:[2]

> *RK: What . . . does your own body ever tell you anything about your own health?*
> R9 (F45): Uhuh, yeah.
> *RK: How, how does it do that?*
> R9 (F45): Uh, intuition. I can always sort of tell it's funny how can I describe it? Um, like if I get constipated or anything like that I get a headache, like so I dinnae take tablets or anything for a headache, 'cause I know it's the constipation.
> *RK: Uhuh.*
> R9 (F45): Does that sound silly?
> *RK: No.*
> R9 (F45): Um, food er, I can look at food and I think well that'll make me ill, or that won't, even though I've never had it before, I can tell.

The uniqueness of lived experience, its very embeddedness and embodiment, means it is hard to call to mind and express in words. Yet, it is the task of a sociology of everyday life to take embodiment seriously. Investigating lay perceptions, the 'actor's' point of view, provides a starting point for developing grounded conceptualisations of the meanings of bodies and embodied experience. Our following analysis of lay accounts of the body and health and how these relate to the self in the middle years focuses on the following areas: first, we consider respondents' accounts of weak and strong points, which was one 'safe' way we developed of focusing talk on the body. Second, we examine how the respondents said that their body communicates to self. Third, we examine the respondents discussions of ageing and the body. Finally, we consider issues of choice and control in relation to bodily experience, and the importance of understanding human agency as the point at which the cultural, structural and personal meet.

The body and health

Knowing your body: weak and strong points

As we have already noted, we self-consciously brought bodies into the discussions in the interviews by asking people if they viewed their bodies having weak or strong points or spots. We were not requiring that people compartmentalised their bodies in that way, although the question derived from our pilot work which identified these practices: we offered the questions tentatively. In fact, a few people said that they did not view their bodies in that way at all, as this example from a 50-year-old woman illustrates:

> RK: Em, you know people sometimes talk about em, their bodies as having particular strong points or weak points, do you ever think of yourself in that way?
> R19 (F50): Not really, em, no, no, I haven't really ever considered it, not really.

However, later this respondent did identify a 'weak spot':

> R19 (F50): I think I'm fairly tough. I did have a bad accident and fell from a horse and injured my neck and that is, if you know, if anything is going to sort of feel achy you know that's

it, as a result of an injury a number of years but em, it doesn't, I mean I don't think about it in between times much at all.

On the whole, however, respondents could quite easily identify the weak points in their bodies; and the question itself seemed to make sense. For example, one 52-year-old female respondent answered firmly to the interviewer's question:

> *RK: You know how people sometimes talk about their bodies as having weak points or strong points; do you ever feel that way?*
> R17 (F52): Oh yes, I know that my chest, if I'm badly stressed or if I'm overworked and I'm going to get something, it will be bronchitis, and there have been times when I've had perhaps six bouts of bronchitis a year, every two months. It's not quite as bad now, maybe twice a year and my knees are my weak point now, partly to do with the overweight problem.

Others identified different parts of their bodies, or different types of proneness to illness. The former included knees, wrists, back or bladder:

> R33 (M45): I've got a weak back I think because even when I worked in the boatyard I had an accident to my back and still have trouble with my back in my work in the Power Station wi' daeing a lot of shovelling.

The latter might be cold sores, headaches, migraines or, as the following example illustrates, a proneness to sore throats:

> R29 (M48): The only weakness I have em is an odd thing that if I'm going to catch a cold it always starts in my throat so if I have a sore throat I'm destined to have a pretty nasty cold.

Still others described the specific impact of chronic illness, such as arthritis or multiple sclerosis (MS); although they could also identify other weak or strong points in the 'previous' body, or their body now with the illness bracketed.

> R2 (F48): I would have said before that [MS] my legs were my strongest point definitely.

The explanations for weak points, when provided, were rooted in experience. Sometimes, a specific incident, like the accident at work recounted in the example above, or an operation, was considered to have led to a specific weakness. Other explanations encompassed notions of heredity or genetic causes, for example weak knees like one's mother; or one's own build – a bad back could be due to height; or to the constant toil of work. As with the private accounts of illness derived through Cornwell's ethnographic work (1984), these accounts of one's body's weak points were richly contextualised.

The respondents less frequently mentioned strong points. Those that did tended to refer to overall health and fitness; to specific points of strength due to one's build; or to the effect of work or of exercise. The 52-year-old woman, who above has described her chest as a weak point, describes her back and gut as strong:

> R17 (F52): My back is very strong. It can take many burdens. Em, I've always felt that em, I can beat most things and travelling and em, like I can read in the car which apparently other people can't do and I'm not sick and I can – travelling doesn't bother me so I think my gut must be fairly robust.

A 48-year-old man said in response to the question:

> RK: Do you ever think of yourself in that way, particular strong points or . . . ?
> R29 (M48): Em, to an extent I suppose but almost in a negative way not having weak points so many people I know of my age have back trouble. I have never, touch wood, ever had back trouble. I've come to the conclusion that I must have a strong back.

While weak points are directly and obviously experienced, strong points do not routinely require reflection or attention. One may develop a sense of strong points through comparison with others, or because those parts of the body have withstood the 'burdens' of everyday life, as the example from R17 above poetically illustrates. Connell states 'Bodily experience is often central in memories of our own lives, and thus in our understanding of who and what we are' (1995: 53). It seems that most of our respondents carry with them an awareness of weak points to their bodies, which can be accounted for, and which help shape interpretations of symptoms, the effects of work; one's embodied relationship with the social world.

The communicating body: messages from within

Weak points more easily assert themselves, and communicate their presence through pain or other unpleasant sensation. Frank states that the talking body is the capacity of 'the body to express reflectively its conceptualization of its reality' (1990: 134). Hearing and responding to bodily communication is obviously an important component of bodily maintenance, but also a taken-for-granted way of living with and in your body. As noted above, our respondents did not so readily identify strong points, and, if they did, it was because of special circumstances or through explicit comparisons with others. On the whole, our respondents' accounts suggest that a body does not send messages to itself, or to the self, saying all is well: as with good health generally, it is literally 'unremarkable'. It is change or difference which demands attention. In response to being asked if your body ever told you anything about your own health, most respondents implicitly or explicitly drew on notions of change, sometimes associated with ageing. The following broad categories could be identified from their accounts: alterations in energy and strength; change in physical appearance and the occurrence of aches and pains.

Tiredness, lack of energy and loss of strength were commonly discussed. For example:

> RK: *Does your own body ever sort of tell you, give you messages about your health?*
> R39 (M52): As I say it's basically just the slowing down that's the problem, em possibly maybe even more often finding it difficult, no' difficult but harder to lift weights, my job . . .

Changes in physical appearance that were discussed often related to weight, especially weight gain, but also to changes in hair (hair loss), complexion and skin condition, most typically associated with ageing, but also possibly linked with illness:

> R4 (F45): I must say that I'm aware that my stomach's getting enormous and that's upset me but you know, but em, just generally what might be described as middle age spread I suppose.

Third, respondents described aches and pains, and these types of accounts are more obviously related to health or potential illness; reflecting the more urgent concerns of a threatened body:

> *RK: Well, what about then, to go, to . . . does you own body ever sort of tell you anything about your health?*
> R4 (F45): Well, you get aches and pains from time to time and you wonder, you know, like sometimes there's a strange pain in an arm or something . . . you wonder if it's a heart attack or something you know.

Many of the data suggest that the body, or your body, gives out messages which need to be interpreted and sometimes acted upon. It seemed from respondents' accounts that, in the middle years, one cannot easily ignore the messages and take for granted a restoration of equilibrium, but neither can one be overwhelmed by change. The female respondent quoted above went on to say:

> *RK: I mean would you say that you paid attention to these things?*
> R4 (F45): Again maybe a bit more now than I would have done in the past, yes. Now maybe this is partly, a bit of getting older and maybe taking a wee bit more responsibility and thinking that you ought to pay attention to these things.

To some extent, messages from one's body demand reaction – they are an 'action problem' to borrow Frank's terminology (1991). In her interviews with women, Martin identified one of the main metaphors as being that 'Your body sends you signals' (1987: 77). People are reflexively aware of their bodies and thus can articulate embodied experience through metaphorical language.

Change, age and the body

Bodily messages (the body communicating with self) are interpreted through a particular lens. Many of the accounts given about 'what your body is telling you' made reference to ageing, or getting older. People described their bodies as telling them to slow down, as sending out more serious messages, or telling them that they had overdone it. Asking people to compare these messages now to when they were in their twenties evoked immediate responses – respondents did not have to think about what was being asked here. The past body could easily be brought to mind, and the present interpreted in relation to it.

A few described little change in the nature of the 'communicating body':

> RK: *Would you say that those messages now are different from when you were in your twenties?*
> R6 (F46): No, I don't think so, I don't think, I think those same things would probably have occurred then as occasionally now . . . so I think those messages are probably the same messages but perhaps the degree is different, the frequency.

A few noted that the change was in the interpretation of the message, rather than in the message itself:

> R17 (F52): I think I'm prepared to listen to my body more.

Most, however, described differences and change:

> R51 (M55): Well frae well from I was 21, well I really cannae keep up the pace.

He goes on to say:

> R51 (M55): Och well you cannae dae what you used to dae years ago I mean I could gone out and dig all that back gairden and dae this, that and the next things, but . . . I still try and dae it but . . .

The ageing body provided a way of making sense of change, and reactions suggested a range of possible responses.

> R49 (M57): Yes, they certainly – I'm certainly more aware of that I'm older. . . . My body is telling me to slow down, take it easy em and of course, I suppose I don't take the message but I certainly get the message.

The following example shows that particular events may forcefully make someone aware that they are older:

> R43 (M58): I did do a bit of jogging for a few years but realised my hips were beginning to play me up so I thought

I'd better stop it, and I realised I wasn't as young as I used to be.

These accounts suggest that, as one's body changes through the life course, it makes claims on one's sense of self that at least have to be attended to, even if to be ignored. In some senses, the mind and body become more connected, but not in the taken-for-granted, seamless way of youth. However, they also seem more separated and the body seen as alienated from one's sense of self or self-image. This was expressed through reference to the body reflecting how you feel as a person, resonating with the 'mask of ageing' (Featherstone and Hepworth 1992). It is often referred to as an object, and as *not* reflecting how you feel as a person. The following examples succinctly illustrate this:

R41 (M59): I don't feel any older, it's no an issue but I am conscious, I'm aware of the fact that little things I put it down, it can only be due to the ageing process it's lots of little things, eh, a cup, you lift a cup and you put it down and you knock it against something. Now I've probably done that 20 years ago and it didn't register, it registers now and I'm saying to myself, your co-ordination's getting a bit sloppy so in that sense, yes, it certainly registers.

R9 (F45): People often say you know, um, how old do you feel? Well I still feel eighteen, but my body tells me I'm no eighteen.

As Giddens notes, 'The self, of course, is embodied' (1991: 56), and its 'reality is grasped through day-to-day praxis' (ibid.: 56). He goes on to write that control of the body underpins all social interaction, as the work of Goffman has so clearly shown. It is integral to daily life, and therefore to agency, rather than embodying the docility of Foucault's disciplinary power. Extending Giddens' analysis, it could be argued that the place of the self unproblematically 'in' the body is jeopardised in the middle years. Giddens asserts that 'Most people are absorbed in their bodies, and feel themselves to be a unified body and self' (ibid.: 59). He argues, following Laing, that when this unification breaks down, the self becomes a false self, and loses the individual's biographical narrative. However, our analysis suggests that some perceived separation of the body and self is part of the biographical narrative of those in their middle years. The body can no longer be completely trusted, its mirror image, or the image others see, is not what one might desire, nor what one really feels about oneself. Agency here involves challenging the intimate way in which the body and self is tied in self identity, although may also involve the kind of control and self-discipline familiar in Foucauldian analyses. As Martin notes, that 'Your self is separate from your body' is a central metaphor (1987: 77). It may be a way of maintaining a sense of control and agency and of challenging both the physical reality of the body and the socially mediated way in which it shapes both identity and experience.

Change, choice and control: responses to the communicating body

Our data show that people's responses, actions and interpretations are not infinitely variable; they operate within the contours of their life circumstances. How culture, structure, biology and biography intersect is individually experienced, and individuals, as active agents, respond. For some, the constraints of everyday life fore-closed choice, as this 49-year-old male suggests:

> R5 (M49): Some days, you're knackered, you cannae lift or . . .
> RK: Do you pay much attention to it?
> R5 (M49): Nuh.
> RK: Why not?
> R5 (M49): Because I've got to get the work done. I mean it is terrible, you've got to get the work done.

For others, constraints of work could be challenged and changed, if one had the resources, as this example suggests:

> R19 (F50): I definitely was beginning to go under then, and I just felt permanently tired em but I eventually went so as I say, they said well you know you haven't got an ulcer but if you don't do something about your lifestyle you probably will have an ulcer so I thought well . . .
> RK: So you did something about it . . .
> R19 (F50): Yes, I said, I thought well I think really it's time

to have a change and the symptoms all disappeared once I, you know, had been off work for a while and I was, I didn't work for about, it must have been nearly a year which was wonderful.

Others described a certain responsibility for one's body, and the personal ability to do something about how it changes, for example around 'middle-aged' spread:

R20 (F56): Some people when they reach 55, they're old. I'm no old, I don't look at myself as old but you meet someone you went to school with, same age as you, and they're old, and I mean it's the way they've let themsel' go.

Others seem to bracket off the effects of ageing, and either ignore them or focus on more positive aspects:

R29 (M48): I don't resent the fact that my body is getting older. I suppose if I'm honest, the negative bits about getting older are all to do with how one looks and I'd prefer not to have greying hair that's going white; I'd prefer not to have three chins and my skin losing its elasticity and putting on a bit of weight around the middle, but there's nothing you can do about it. The positive side is I do genuinely believe that you become older and wiser.

Although the ageing process was often described as defying personal control, many respondents indicated that the process could perhaps be moderated through attitude and behaviour. However, everyday morbidity was often talked about in terms of ageing, with aches and pains being seen as more common and the healing process slower than when they were younger:

R35 (M52): They say as you get older you cannae fight off infection the same as what you could when you're younger.

The experience of the ageing process in self, and in others, especially relatives, appeared to reinforce amongst respondents the need for good health at the very time it could suddenly or gradually deteriorate. The following female respondent provides a poignant reminder of this:

> R4 (F45): It's more a consciousness of the sort of things that might happen, and the fact that one is probably going to be going downhill.

There was an awareness amongst many that, during the middle years, perceptions of potentially new opportunities, unrestricted by childcare, could be marred by potential ill-health or impairment, altered social and personal circumstances, and lower energy levels.

Our research suggests that, in the middle years, there is a disjunction between the physical experience of ageing, and the actual or potential deterioration in health and function that this could bring, and one's sense of self. This has to be dealt with in some way:

> R29 (M48) I have this thought process that hits me every now and again that in my heart I'm 30 but of course in stark reality I'm not. And it's a niggling thought every now and again that should I start acting my age and should I start being less frivolous because of this age I am?

and

> R3 (F46): You look in the mirror and you see the lines . . . and yet inside yourself you're still the wee girl you were. I mean I don't think of myself as old, it's just my body and my face tell me I'm getting old but I don't feel old.

As we have noted earlier, in some sense the body and mind seem to become more connected during the middle years, because the body brings itself to the mind's attention through changes which are at least noticed. However, instead of supporting a cultural departure from mind–body dualism, one way of affirming one's identity is to separate one's body from how one describes how one feels as a person. In Frank's (1991) schema, the communicating body is dealing with self-relatedness on an axis of association and disassocation. Our analyses seem to suggest that this communication of the body with itself, or to one's consciousness, is an ambivalent process, and evokes different responses as individuals attempt to restore a comfortable relationship with their ageing body. While people have the capacity to monitor and interpret messages from their bodies, the degree of control over either the message or reaction to it is variable. Both internal and external factors may limit this. One response is to challenge one's body, another is to resign to its messages, and of course, for many the daily toils of existence (work and caring) put both body and self out of sight and mind.

Conclusion

People make sense of their bodies, health and change, and can both act upon and talk about this process. Scheper-Hughes and Lock pointed out in relation to sickness that it is:

> not just an isolated event, not an unfortunate brush with nature. It is a form of communication ... through which nature, society and culture speak simultaneously: The individual body should be seen as the most immediate, the proximate terrain where social truths and social contradictions are played out, as well as a basis of personal and social resistance, creativity and struggle.
>
> (Scheper-Hughes and Lock 1987: 31)

The same can be said for other bodily changes, such as those associated with ageing. We suggest our research identifies what Csordas calls somatic modes of attention – the processes in which we attend to and objectify our bodies. He says 'it is a truism that our bodies are always present, we do not always attend to and with them' (Csordas 1994: 139). Change and health in the middle years brings these moments, and their explication can promote an understanding of individuals' experience of this period of their lives.

In midlife, although the body may assert itself, and one may have to become more aware of it, this connection between the mind and body is not always comfortable. The body, one's own body, in some ways becomes separate and alienated: it has nothing to do with how one feels as a person: yet may still have a lot to do with how one *feels* in a physical and/or emotional sense. The processes relating to emotion, cognition and physicality run through the accounts in this study, but they do not merge – one may know something about one's body, but it may not affect how one feels; one may feel something, but disregard it.

We asked those who participated in our study to reflect on their bodies, change and health by focusing on the way in which the body communicates. The talking, communicating body, we suggest, is a starting point of any phenomenology of the body, and can serve to explore both the taken-for-grantedness of embodiment and when this is challenged. Our culture seems to be ill-equipped to deal with ageing, and the deteriorating body – and one way that people adjust or resist is to say they still feel young. The body is not fixed, as both it and the social processes which surround it change. In our research, we focused on bodies as they get older, and bodies in relation to health. We identified a range of ways in which one's body is brought to mind, asserting its physicality, presaging ill-health, decline or even mortality. Each person's biographical passage is to some extent unique, as external events and internal factors converge. Yet, some broad contours of cultural and social context can be highlighted: although aware of the body's needs, the body does not define or overwhelm the self. However, people also have to deal with their bodies' communications, either within themselves or by communicating with others. Such expertise in interpreting bodily change should be recognised not dismissed by all those involved with 'disciplining the body', otherwise fears and concerns will be trivialised and the 'mask of ageing' used as an excuse for victim blaming or insensitive healthcare provision.

Acknowledgements

The study was funded by the Scottish Office Department of Health, grant K/OPR/2/2D64, 1992–4. We would like to acknowledge this funding support, the work of the two researchers involved in the data collection and some of the analysis, and Morag Leitch for secretarial support.

Notes

1   The research involved two rounds of in-depth interviews, the first focusing on perceptions of health, the body and change, and the second on the experience of health services. We also conducted a postal questionnaire (n = 250) exploring factors which influenced health, caring and use of preventive services, and six discussion groups. This chapter draws only on the in-depth interviews. The interviews were carried out by Rose Kirk and the postal questionnaire designed and analysed by Steve Pavis.

2   Each quote is identified in the following way: RK is the interviewer. The respondent is identified by a number. The respondents' sex and age are then provided in parentheses.

References

Connell, R.W. (1995) *Masculinities*, Cambridge: Polity Press.

Cornwell, J. (1984) *Hard Earned Lives: accounts of health and illness from East London*, London: Tavistock.

Crawford, R. (1984) 'A cultural account of health, control, release and the social body', in McKinlay, J.B. (ed.) *Issues in the Political Economy of Health*, London: Tavistock.

Csordas, T.J. (1990) 'Embodiment as a paradigm for anthropology', *Ethos* **18**, 1, 5–47.

Csordas, T.J. (1994) *Embodiment and Experience: the existential ground of culture and self*, Cambridge: Cambridge University Press.

Featherstone, M. and Hepworth, M. (1992) 'The mask of ageing and the post modern life course', in Featherstone, M., Hepworth, M., Turner, B. (eds) *The Body, Social Processes and Cultural Theory*, London: Sage.

Frank, A.W. (1990) 'Bringing bodies back in: a decade review', *Theory, Culture and Society* **7**, 1, 131–62.

Frank, A.W. (1991) 'For a sociology of the body: an analytical review', in Featherstone, M. and Turner, B.S. (eds) *The Body: social process and cultural theory* London: Sage.

Freund, P.E.S. (1990) 'The expressive body: a common ground for the sociology of emotions and health and illness', *Sociology of Health and Illness* **12**, 4, 452–77.

Giddens, A. (1991) *Modernity and Self Identity*, Cambridge: Polity Press.

Hepworth, M. (1987) 'The mid-life phase', in Cohen, G. (ed.) *Social Change and the Life Course*, London: Tavistock.

Hunter, S. and Sundel, M. (1989) *Midlife Myths, Issues, Findings and Practice Implications*, London: Sage.

Martin, E. (1987) *The Woman in the Body*, Milton Keynes: Open University Press.

Mead, M. (1949) *Male and Female: a study of the sexes in a changing world*, New York: Morrow Quill.

Scheper-Hughes, N. and Lock, M.M. (1987) 'The mindful body: a prolegomenon to future work in medical anthropology', *Medical Anthropology Quarterly* **1**, 6–41.

Synnott, A. (1993) *The Body Social: symbolism, self and society*, London: Routledge.

Watson, J., Cunningham-Burley, S., Watson, N., Milburn, K. (1996) 'Lay theorizing about "the body" and implications for health promotion', *Health Education Research* **11**, 2, 161–72.

Part III

Gender

Chapter 9

Running around like a lunatic

Colin's body and the case of male embodiment

Jonathan Watson

Current knowledge of men's health is the product of anatomical, clinical, epidemiological, psychological and sociological research that has taken the male as object or subject. In the field of primary healthcare and health promotion such research has tended to generate and inform a mindset among healthcare professionals that poor health among men is a consequence of men having to live up to a macho image and that male lifestyles are dangerous to health. Assumptions about men's experience of health that flow from this perspective have rarely been critically challenged.

Against such a backdrop this chapter focuses on reporting empirical findings concerned with lay perceptions of the male body and health in order to demonstrate that male embodiment, in lay accounts, is experienced in ways that both resist and rework biological explanation, professional understanding and social theorising. There is also an attempt in this chapter to highlight some of the methodological implications of 'approaching' the body empirically. The study on which this chapter draws had thirty informants. The issues presented were generally common to all informant accounts though particular attention is given to one of the informants called 'Colin'. The accounts of these informants show how male embodiment is, even haphazardly, organised as a going concern in the everyday lives of the men who took part in the study.

Background

There has been a concern, particularly evident in the professional healthcare literature, to explain and account for poor health outcomes (mortality and morbidity) amongst men compared to women (Robertson 1995; Fareed 1994; Jackson 1991; Darbyshire

1987). The commonest explanation for differences in health outcomes between men and women is said to be that men adopt and maintain lifestyles that are more likely to be shaped by risk-taking and a lack of self-care.

This orthodox professional perspective has, to date, been influenced and supported by both medical and social research. For example, Verbrugge (1989, 1985) has examined a range of epidemiological evidence to highlight male disadvantage with regard to mortality data and, possibly, morbidity. Her central theoretical perspective is that sex differences in health derive from differential risks acquired from sex roles, stress, lifestyles and preventive health practices. Less important are psychosocial factors, for example, how men and women evaluate symptoms and the concomitant readiness to take therapeutic action. But both sets of risks are perceived to be grounded in a 'biological substrate' (Verbrugge 1989: 296). In the broader context of investigation of men's beliefs and behaviour, social scientists have suggested that men encounter an array of prescriptions and proscriptions through the impact of sex role norms (Kimmel 1987) and gender socialisation (Pleck 1981). Congruent with the resultant 'masculinity agenda' are tensions derived from age (Riley 1988) and status (Mortimer 1988); elements identified as being strong social determinants of unhealthy lifestyles (Abel 1991). By contrast, Annandale and Hunt (1990) have suggested, based on analysis of the 35-year-old cohort of the West of Scotland Twenty-07 Study (a longitudinal investigation of the processes generating social patterns in health), that masculine traits in both men and women could be implicated in more positive health outcomes. Yet, in terms of practice, if not of expectations, what it means to be male in our society is being challenged, for example, with regard to changing patterns of employment and the erosion of patriarchal dominance within families.

It will be argued in this chapter that the present medical and social debate around men's health is undermined and under-informed by a failure to explore men's perceptions of health as a personal, cultural and social phenomenon. The irony is that whilst we have moved towards a richer and subtler appreciation of women's health over the life course, a reassessment founded partly in the context of lay experience, one might argue that men have come to be defined, even constrained both by their physiology and related behavioural characteristics – as defined and measured by others. In this respect, Connell notes that 'true masculinity' is almost always thought to proceed from men's bodies, 'the body drives and directs action' (aggression and sex feed off testosterone) or 'sets limits to action' (men do not naturally take care of young children) (Connell 1995: 45).

Treated thus, the male body has a narrow and partial presence. Arguably the knowledge and understanding that flows from this contributes to normative constructions of the male body and behaviour which 'are disempowering at the level of individual experience of the body' (Watson *et al.* 1996: 170). Within the parameters of professional understanding male embodiment remains largely 'unproblematic'; fixed and immutable.

Notes on method

There are certain circumstances in which the researcher can approach the 'body' more directly than in others. For example, in accounts of chronic illness (Kleinman 1988; Murphy 1987) or women's experiences of pregnancy (Martin 1989). However, in the context of everyday life where bodies, and particularly male bodies, appear to be taken-for-granted a key methodological challenge is to develop conceptual tools that can facilitate the articulation of lay ideas about and experiences of the body that have previously been under-researched or treated as inexpressible.

In this study, the interview transcripts were analysed using a grounded theory approach (Glaser 1978; Glaser and Strauss 1967). The use of grounded theory is now well established in qualitative health research (Becker 1993; Charmaz 1990; Stern and Pyles 1986; Mullen and Reynolds 1978) and so will not be covered in detail here. In essence this method entails moving from data to theory through a general method of comparative analysis, rather than working from a predetermined hypothesis. That is, the data were not used to test a pre-existing hypothesis; rather, the starting point for analysis were the cultural categories that were located in informant accounts. In this sense, informant accounts are real in so far as informants believe them to be real. Thus, they have meaning even though informants may have been selective in what they disclosed to the researcher because the core elements remain consistent. That is, they appear repeatedly in informant accounts. Grounded theory is particularly appropriate in this respect because it works on the basis of identifying and verifying the consistency of categories and their properties through a process of constant comparison within and across data. The interview data were thus analysed in and for themselves; the data contained their own integrity. The researcher adopted a position of holding informant accounts to be data that 'display cultural realities which are neither biased nor accurate, but simply real' (Silverman 1985).

In this instance grounded theory provided a resolution to what were felt to be limitations with current theorising about the body and the neglect of men's personal experiences of health in qualitative social research. This is not to refute other methods of approaching and articulating embodied experience. Rather, in exploring issues of practice that are deeply embedded in the everyday world of informants, grounded theory provided a means of discovering and expressing something of the hidden side of men's experience of health. In addition, it can be seen to support Frank's assertion that empirical inquiry must 'grapple with theoretical issues' (Frank 1995: 187).

The empirical data reported in this chapter are drawn from a qualitative study of men's health beliefs carried out in the northeast of Scotland between April 1991 and October 1992, with a purposive sample of thirty predominantly middle-class men. All the informants were registered with a general medical practice in a community that lies to the south of Aberdeen and lived in the catchment area for the practice. Criteria for recruitment included being aged between 30 and 40, not having attended a well man clinic in the past three years, being in a stable relationship (though two of the men had separated from their wives by the end of the study), and having children either with a previous or current partner. Focusing on men meeting these criteria was done in order to explore the issue of how life course transitions such as marriage and parenthood might affect self and body-image. Once recruited, informants were interviewed at home on three separate occasions over an eighteen month period. Although many of the informants had a 'middle-class lifestyle' about half came from working-class backgrounds in Glasgow, north-east England, Aberdeen and its rural hinterland, and from crofting communities in the north of Scotland.

About 'Colin'

At the time when Colin was first interviewed he was 37 years old and had just previously been made redundant from his job working on oil-rigs in the North Sea. He had been born in London and brought up on a council estate. He left school at 16 with a few O levels and followed this with an apprenticeship. By the time we met, Colin had been married for twelve years (his wife worked part-time) and had a daughter aged 14. He had a mortgage, liked doing the *Telegraph* crossword and playing chess. A smoker and overweight, he said his only exercise was walking the dog and he thought that he usually ate 'all the wrong things'.

As an informant Colin was not untypical. Although all the informants were ultimately self-selecting this did not result in the recruitment of individuals who were necessarily health conscious. Of those recruited ten were cigarette smokers at the point of recruitment (though two gave up during the course of the study), four were ex-smokers and the rest had never smoked cigarettes or had experimented only when young. All the informants drank alcohol although there was no reported evidence that any currently drank above the then recommended sensible drinking levels of twenty-one units a week for men, although again, many had done so before marriage. Only seven of the informants took regular exercise. Six of the informants indicated that they had changed their diet during the course of the study. It is acknowledged that some of these changes may have occurred as a result of participation in the study but they were not sought or solicited by the researcher. Overall, participation in the study seemed to have sensitised some of the informants to reflect upon personal health beyond the attention it was perceived to merit in early informant accounts.

Empirical findings

As the process of analysing the first interviews began what was particularly evident was the presence, sometimes implied, at other times explicit, of the body. So, when respondents talked about health, particularly when conceptualised as a resource, as fitness, appearance or well-being, one of the places they located health was in the body – their own or the bodies of others. For example, take Colin on appearance:

> I have come out of the shower and there are six guys in your room and they say 'you better lose some weight you fat bastard or you'll be dead in a couple of years time'.

> I used to go [swimming] up until 3 years ago, take my daughter
> . . . teaching her to swim. It was a case of straight into the
> pool and hide the stomach under the water.

Colin is making an important point here about the facticity of
the body. His own is observed by others just as he is able to
observe the body of others. Thus, his mother is 'as thin as a rake'
or his grandfather 'as thin as a pole'. The realisation that informants were inserting the body into personal and general
experiences of health continued to emerge as analysis of first round
interviews progressed and so lay perceptions of the body became
a major focus for further exploration and clarification. In general,
the study found that informants' perceptions about the body and
health were grounded in three main areas: images of healthy and
unhealthy bodies; the embeddedness (one might say 'taken-for-
grantedness') of the body in daily life as located in marriage,
fatherhood and work; and in the material and physical nature of
the body.

Images of healthy and unhealthy bodies

The degree to which lay theorising about the body operates in
constructing self and others' health was explored by asking informants to describe people who they saw as being healthy and
unhealthy. When describing people who were healthy or unhealthy
– either a generic type or someone known to them personally –
informants generally gave descriptions that had three dimensions:
some reference to weight and/or height; reference to health-related
behaviours that are commonly associated with an overall orientation to personal healthcare; a degree of moral linkage between the
first two dimensions and a more or less explicitly imaged body
shape. For example, a healthy person (almost always masculine)
would be described as follows: 'He would be just the right weight
for his height. He wouldn't smoke or drink too much. He would
have regular exercise, regular amounts of sleep and health food'
(mechanical engineer: 40).

By contrast, an unhealthy person was described as:

> Someone who leads an unhealthy lifestyle never ever considers
> exercise. Wouldn't think about taking the car one hundred
> yards up the road. Someone who drinks, and eats to excess

all the wrong foods. Someone that is five feet four inches and fifteen stone. Totally gross!

(warehouse dispatcher: 31)

Taken together these dimensions combine to form symbolic shared images of male bodies. Sometimes, as in the last example, these were vivid images. The image of the grossly overweight type of person – whether male or female – tended to appear in most accounts of unhealthy people. Despite this image, some respondents did qualify the descriptions by suggesting that some people might not be able to help having the body they've got due to an underlying medical complaint unknown to the casual observer.

Similarly, analysis of informant accounts (as illustrated earlier) demonstrates that lifestyle has an acknowledged place in the shaping of bodies and thus the evaluation of other's health. The everyday context of that lifestyle was most evident when describing someone that they personally felt to be healthy or unhealthy, or when describing an unhealthy person. Descriptions of an ideal healthy person generally lacked an everyday context for their behaviour. A further embodied distinction apparent between healthy individuals known by the informant and (un)known unhealthy individuals was between active and passive embodiment. Thus, a father is described in the following manner: 'He had an outdoor job, which was fairly physical. He ate nearly every vegetable that he grew himself organically. He used to cycle to work, had plenty of exercise as well' (garage service manager: 32).

Although in this account one does not perceive body form, the body is clearly present. The father's embodiment is active in the sense that activity is projected from and centred on an embodied individual and that this activity takes place in an everyday context. However, some caution should be maintained regarding the salience of healthy as opposed to generalised lifestyles. For example, when related to personal experience and potential, a healthy lifestyle was felt to have only a marginal impact on the body.

Coincidentally, just before the final round of interviewing two Department of Health adverts appeared in newspapers and magazines across the UK to promote its *Health of the Nation* booklet for members of the public. The purpose of the adverts was to prompt people to write in or ring for a copy of the booklet as the first step in taking responsibility for their own health. The male advertisement, depicting a mesomorphic male body with cutaways of the limbs to show pistons, hydraulics and other machinery, used the metaphorical image of the body being like a machine and stated that the body, like a machine, needs looking after.

The advertisement was mentioned spontaneously by some informants and the others were shown a copy of it. A range of comments were forthcoming, ranging from the mildly indifferent to the openly critical. In particular, most informants questioned the effectiveness of the particular mesomorphic image of the 'health promoting body' shown in the advert and of the desirability and ability of developing and maintaining such a body in the context of everyday life. Informants were first asked to describe what they saw when shown the advert.

> Colin: The first thing I thought of when I saw it was what a poof, what a poser. It's the way he looks. He's a model for a start.
> JW: What do you mean?
> Colin: It's the way he looks, muscular. But that doesn't mean he's healthy. Any body could do that. You don't know what damage he's done to the other organs in his body, just with the physical exercise or the drugs. It's all for vanity . . . that's nothing to do with health.

The key point about the impact of this advert on the men in this study was that the image of the male body offered to them (not a normal everyday body) obscured the health education message (look after your body), which had been couched in terms of mechanical metaphors of the body i.e. of the body being like a machine and looking after it being related to notions of maintenance. A way of speaking about the body which the men in the study also used. The meanings embedded in such ideally rendered images of the male body evoked, for most of the informants, a fundamental tension between cultural notions of the perfectibility of the body and embodied personal and social obligations.

In particular, analysis pointed to the idea that marriage, fatherhood and work operating individually and together effectively marginalise the physical male body by placing greater value upon and reinforcing the social aspects of these male roles. That is, marriage and other adult male social roles affect a reworking of the salience of biological and social explanation in the status of

male embodiment. For example, when talking of their own experience or that of friends, informants would often remark on
marriage as a time of 'settling down' and 'letting go'. The consequences of this for health and the body are significant since marriage
is equated with loss of control or 'losing it'. There are obvious
echoes here of Mary Douglas's (1982) contention that the physical
body is a restricted medium of expression. A major factor in this
are the perceived constraints imposed by competing personal and
social obligations that such circumstances entail.

The body and daily living

Resistance can take many forms and it seems that lay theorising
about the body problematises the body for health professionals.
That is, although for the informants in this study, beliefs and actions
appear to be informed by cultural assumptions about the body and
health, they are also uniquely bound up in the everyday social
world of each informant. For example, on marriage: 'They seem
to settle down and just let themselves go ken. That's probably how
you get a lot of men that are overweight, misshapen and what
have you, ken? It's cause they let themselves go' (warehouse
dispatcher: 31).

A major factor in this loss of control are the perceived restrictions
on time that marriage and fatherhood entails. Another informant,
whose partner had recently left him, started off by reflecting the
argument given above when he said that 'you come home and get
into a routine. There's nothing happening to my body. A few years
ago I wasn't like this. Now I've got kids. I've got responsibilities
and no gallivanting'. At this point he recalls his new 'separate' status
and goes on: 'But now . . . I'm looking to get out and about. This
time next year I will be a lot fitter. There will be nobody telling
me I'm playing too much golf' (builder: 33).

So, this informant begins to see new opportunities emerging, or
perhaps old ones re-emerging. In reading these words, especially
where he observes that there is 'nothing happening' to his body,
one is reminded of Gagnon's comment that 'many men . . . sense
the absence of the testing of strength that direct physical competition
represents' (Gagnon 1974: 144). While such accounts may be
'public' justifications for not maintaining or adopting health behaviours, one should be careful about denying their legitimacy. In the
context of marriage it appears all too easy to lose the opportunities

to undertake exercise or sport, health practices which ground male experience of themselves, even fleetingly in the body.

Generally, informants found it relatively easy to explain how they were able to 'let go' of a conscious concern with the physical body, with keeping in shape. It could be argued that this 'settling down' phase is marked by a shift in the nature of the primary way in which individuals experience themselves as embodied. Earlier, in recounting reactions to a government advert promoting personal responsibility for health, what came through was that the image did not represent a 'normal everyday body'. What marriage, fatherhood, work and friendship appear to do is to place greater emphasis on a body that is functional (and indeterminately shaped) and able to address the particular demands of an everyday life in which these roles jostle and compete, rather than valuing the more 'unreal' cultural representations of ideal (and highly defined) male body types.

This functionality of male embodiment is strongly reflected in the way most informants talked about fitness. Although most informants acknowledged the importance of 'being fit' in order to cope with the demands of daily life, they did not tend to subscribe to standards of fitness commonly prescribed in health education literature, that is, at least three periods of exercise lasting a minimum of twenty minutes, every week. In contrast, the prevailing yardstick among informants was to have enough fitness to comfortably accomplish what was needed or expected of them as individuals. Thus, for Colin, as for other informants, there was a shared perspective that not only is form (the ideal healthy body) secondary to embodied function (essentially pragmatic; the normal everyday body) but also function and fitness are unique to the personal circumstances of each informant.

What Colin has to say about work is interesting in this context. I'd asked him what he liked about working offshore and he'd said 'having no responsibilities because there is nothing you can do about it. Your only obligation is to your work when your shift is on'. Colin goes on to say about life offshore that

> Quite a few people use them [gyms] but you tend to find that they are the guys who have not been using their bodies during the day. Roustabouts, roughnecks and derrickmen . . . they aren't going down to the gym in the evening. They are knackered from working during the day. Instrument engineers,

technicians, these sort of guys who have been sitting around on their bums all day, totally bored, they are the ones who use the gym. . . . I think they've probably got a different sense of lifestyle. Whereas, the guys – the roughnecks and derrickmen – still tend to be the type of guys who are going to the pub, read the *Sun* and bet. They still have the image they're working class guys.

This observation makes a distinction between use of the gym by manual and non-manual workers. Physical capital is acquired and expended by the former through the nature of their work. Function and fitness, located within work are experienced as coterminous. That same capital is acquired and expended primarily through exercise in the gym when off-shift primarily by some of the non-manual workers. For the latter form and function are also appropriately experienced within the work context but physical capital, if desired, is acquired in a para-work context (the offshore gym) or a recreational context (when onshore). The offshore life, with its two weeks on, two weeks off cycle, is an unusually restricted social environment. The husband/partner and father are effectively 'dis-located' from the family opening up space to indulge and/or improve the body. When onshore, the availability of spare time which is derived from re-incorporation into family arrangements that do not operate to the on/off work cycle, also appear to create an acceptable space and time for physical activity or other leisure pursuits.

Body maintenance

Douglas (1982), in talking of the two bodies (social and physical), has argued that in the ongoing exchange of meanings the physical body is a very restricted medium of expression. Similarly, among post-structuralists there exists an assumption that the physical body exists primarily, as a site for the investment of social order over individuals (see e.g. Turner 1984). Although, through work and family life, the physical body has come to be marginalised in most informants' lives, this is not to say that it also becomes an irrelevance. Corporeally, the body may be banished from what Geertz called 'the hard surfaces of life' yet these surfaces rest upon and bound up with 'biological and physical necessities' (Geertz 1973: 30).

Informant conceptualisations of the body – whilst supporting the idea of the existence of social and physical forms of embodiment and that the social body appears to operate as a wider medium of expression – also point to two differences with much social theorising about the body. First, informants are thoroughly conversant with a public health discourse that aims to 'construct healthy bodies' but appear to put more emphasis on responsibility in connection with the gendered nature of social roles and obligations. Second, their conceptualisations of the physical body (the memory of the body 'as it was', a body that 'fixes itself', and the fragmentary nature of their experience of the physical body through illness and disease) are far more prominent in accounts of personal experience and in the impact that they have on informants' responses to discourses on healthy bodies and healthy lifestyles than is suggested by the literature.

The key to seeing the relationship between physical and social bodies as problematic is found in the way informants conceptualise their own physical body. That is, the individual does not objectify his own body. For example, consider the way in which Colin comments on his fear of testicular cancer:

> Worrying about AIDS or any disease doesn't affect me. The only thing that affects me in that area is cancer. I've had a vasectomy and they say [the doctors] 'have a feel down there'. Saw the guy on TV examining himself and the guy said 'you can feel quite a few bumps'. It's like a can of worms down there chrissake. What the hell have I got in there like? I'm trying, in fact I have got little bumps on the back of my penis, see the blood vessels [*the offer was made and politely declined*] they keep coming up and I think 'bloody hell, what is this?' They go away after couple of weeks.

At a physical level, his body has an existence and subjectiveness of its own, the blisters on Colin's member come and go. His confusion, concern and sense of disempowerment is evident, and in this context, at least, differs from Saltonstall's findings from an American sample, which she felt demonstrated that men had a 'power-over' relationship to their bodies, that their bodies 'belonged' to them the same as an object belongs (Saltonstall 1993). This notion of a 'power-over' relationship between a man and his body comes across as more tenuous when informant accounts are considered. Although this should be qualified by saying that there were echoes of this position among the few informants who regularly exercised.

Saltonstall has also stated that the 'production of health for the self involves personal responsibility for body maintenance' (1993: 33). Yet, informants perceiving their own physical embodiment as having a largely independent existence from the social self also serves as a rationalisation against accepting personal responsibility for one's own body. Informants would shrug and say that 'you've got what you've got' or 'you're just the weight you are'. Thus, Colin says:

> Colin: I still eat all the wrong things and I don't think I would lose any weight. I get the feeling I'm fat anyway.
> *JW: Why do you think that?*
> Colin: . . . when I was about 15 or 19 I hardly ate a thing. I didn't drink much and I just kept putting on weight and I was exercising so much everyday. I was running about like a lunatic but the weight kept going on. I think I'm doomed to it, my metabolism, that's it.

This notion of having a 'natural' physical form and content appears to echo, in some respects, the idea that women have natural shapes that are distorted by patriarchal forces (Orbach 1988; Chernin 1983). Informant accounts would suggest that this constitutes almost a form of resistance to social pressure to adopt health-promoting behaviours, a notion previously found by Crawford (1984).

The emergent nature of the physical body and the emphasis on personal responsibility in relation to social practice as distinct from personal responsibility for health points, initially, towards a dialectical nature of embodiment such as that espoused by Shilling (1993), Giddens (1991) and Elias (1978). In informant accounts the nature of that intercourse appears to be pragmatic, ambiguous and highly contingent.

Discussion

In summing up informants' perceptions it is possible to identify some of the key features of male embodiment that are present in their accounts. To start with, informants talked about healthy and unhealthy bodies. They provided textual images of bodies that transmit prevailing values regarding masculinity and health. At the same time such accounts contained critiques of and resistance to ideal images of mesomorphic or androgenous men. In doing so they appear to make space for the body-I-am, the body-I-have ('a normal everyday body'). Their own embodiment was most obviously located in the social spaces of marriage, fatherhood and work. In these contexts the emphasis was on function (having normal, pragmatic everyday bodies) rather than appearance. That is, the body is located within gendered roles which create conditions in which it can live and recreate but which marginalise the physical body. Finally, as has been well documented elsewhere, the individual is embodied through disease, injury and illness. But the study opened up other layers of embodiment, especially those concerned with genes and maintenance. Ultimately, the living of daily lives is based on faith and resignation that deep down the body 'looks after itself' (body maintenance). This is related to basic physiological processes and informants' perceptions of the role of genes.

So we return to Connell, who says that a key task of 'social analysis is to arrive at an understanding of men's bodies and their relation to masculinity' (Connell 1995: 45). In doing so it is suggested that our understanding should take as its starting point the embodied experience of individuals. The author and others (Watson *et al.* 1995) have taken that position because of a belief that sociology of the body has been theoretically driven; that it bracketed out the individual; and that it was largely devoid of practical experiences of the body in everyday life.

This is not to say that there are not obvious reasons for such theorising. The emergence of the body as a major object of theoretical investigation, in part, reflected an agenda, sustained by feminist and Foucauldian analysis, to challenge the role of biological explanation, particularly in the area of social relations. Some reviews, such as those by Shilling (1993) and Nettleton (1995), have looked for ways to bridge or integrate the natural and social paradigms. Connell says that this is not possible because the two paradigms are not commensurate. Biology is always seen as more real, the more basic of the pair (Connell 1995: 52). By contrast, others (see particularly Gatens 1996; Lupton 1995) perceive a relationship between the body and society which resists the determinism of both biological and social explanation, which seeks to recast these differences in ways that are neither dichotomised or polarised. Both Connell, in his book *Masculinities* (1995), and Gatens in her book *Imaginary Bodies* (1996) assert the agency of bodies in social processes. Connell argues for a theoretical position in which bodies are seen as sharing in social agency, in generating and shaping courses of conduct. This is apparent from the findings presented above. The body is not a finished product, mechanical and unreasoning, as Descartes would have it. In a sense, as Gatens puts it, this is not the 'true nature' of the body, rather it is a process and its meanings and capacities will varying according to its context (1996: 57). Connell mirrors this position when he notes, quite vividly (in hyper-relativity mode), that in 1994 there were around 5.4 thousand million bodies, each with its own trajectory through time. Each one changing as it grows and ages, engulfed in and sustained by social processes that are also certain to change.

Ironically then, by starting from the embodied perspective of individuals one also questions the utility of a sociology of the body that seeks to construct ever increasing numbers of bodies (Watson and Shakespeare 1995). Rather, there may be more profit in addressing the changing experience of embodiment of individuals over culturally and temporally defined time periods. In particular, the challenge for those interested in men's health lies in both recognising and responding to the problems posed by individual embodiment where structural and everyday constraints interacting with social values shape and are shaped by the human experience of health, its maintenance and its loss.

References

Abel, T. (1991) 'Measuring health lifestyles in a comparative analysis: theoretical issues and empirical findings', *Social Science and Medicine* **32**, 8, 899–908.

Annandale, E. and Hunt, K. (1990) 'Masculinity, femininity and sex: an exploration of their relative contribution to explaining gender differences in health', *Sociology of Health and Illness* **12**, 24–45.

Becker, P.H. (1993) 'Common pitfalls in published grounded theory research', *Qualitative Health Research* **3**, 2, 254–60.

Charmaz, K. (1990) '"Discovering" chronic illness: using grounded theory', *Social Science and Medicine* **30**, 11, 1161–72.

Chernin, K. (1983) *Womansize: the tyranny of slenderness*, London: The Women's Press.

Connell, R.W. (1995) *Masculinities*, London: Polity Press.

Crawford, R. (1984) 'A cultural account of health, control, release and the social body', in McKinlay, J.B. (ed.) *Issues in the Political Economy of Health*, London: Tavistock.

Darbyshire, P. (1987) 'Danger man: the traditional male lifestyle and death rates', *Nursing Times* 30–2.

Douglas, M. (1982) *Natural Symbols: explorations in cosmology*, New York: Pantheon.

Elias, N. (1978 [1939]) *The Civilising Process, Volume 1, The History of Manners*, Oxford: Basil Blackwell.

Fareed, A. (1994) 'Equal rights for men', *Nursing Times* **90**, 5, 26–9.

Frank, A. (1995) 'Review symposium: as much as theory can say about bodies', *Body and Society* **1**, 1, 184–7.

Gagnon, J.H. (1974) 'Physical strength: once of significance', in Pleck, J.H. and Sawyer, J. (eds) *Men and Masculinity*, Englewood Cliffs, NJ: Prentice Hall.

Gatens, M. (1996) *Imaginary Bodies: ethics, power and corporeality*, London: Routledge.

Geertz, C. (1973) *The Interpretation of Cultures*, London: Fontana.

Giddens, A. (1991) *Modernity and Self-Identity: self and society in the late modern age*, London: Polity Press.

Glaser, B.G. (1978) *Theoretical Sensitivity*, Mill Valley, CA: Sociology Press.

Glaser, B.G. and Strauss, A.L. (1967) *The Discovery of Grounded Theory: strategies for qualitative research*, New York: Aldine de Gruyter.

Jackson, C. (1991) 'Men's health: opening the floodgates', *Health Visitor* **64**, 8, 265–6.

Kimmel, M.S. (1987) 'Rethinking masculinity: new directions in research', in Kimmel, M.S. (ed.) *Changing Men: new directions in research on men and masculinity*, London: Sage.

Kleinman, A. (1988) *The Illness Narratives: suffering, healing and the human condition*, New York: Basic Books.

Lupton, D. (1995) *The Imperative of Health: public health and the regulated body*, London: Sage.

Martin, E. (1989) *The Woman in the Body: a cultural analysis of reproduction*, Milton Keynes: Open University Press.

Mortimer, J.T. (1988) 'Work experience and psychological change throughout the lifecourse', in Riley,W. (ed.) *Social Structures and Human Lives*, London: Sage.

Mullen, P.J. and Reynolds, R. (1978) 'The potential of grounded theory for health education research', *Health Education Monographs* **6**, 208–303.

Murphy, R.F. (1987) *The Body Silent*, New York: Henry Holt.

Nettleton, S. (1995) *The Sociology of Health and Illness*, Cambridge: Polity Press.

Orbach, S. (1988) *Fat is a Feminist Issue*, London: Arrow.

Pleck, J. (1981) *The Myth of Masculinity*, London: MIT Press.

Riley, M.W. (1988) 'On the significance of age in sociology', in Riley (ed.) *Social Structures and Human Lives*, London: Sage.

Robertson, S. (1995) 'Men's health promotion in the UK: a hidden problem', *British Journal of Nursing* **4**, 7, 382, 399–401.

Saltonstall, R. (1993) 'Healthy bodies – social bodies: men's and women's concepts and practices of health in everyday life', *Social Science and Medicine* **36**, 1, 7–14.

Shilling, C. (1993) *The Body and Social Theory*, London: Sage.

Silverman, D. (1985) *Qualitative Methodology and Sociology*, Aldershot: Gower.

Stern, P.N. and Pyles, S.H. (1986) 'Using grounded theory methodology to study women's culturally-based decisions about health', in Stern, P.N. (ed.) *Women, Health and Culture*, London: Hemisphere.

Turner, B.S. (1984) *The Body and Society: explorations in social theory*, Oxford: Basil Blackwell.

Verbrugge, L.M. (1985) 'Gender and health: an update on hypotheses and evidence', *Journal of Health and Social Behaviour* **26**, 156–82.

Verbrugge, L.M. (1989) 'The twain meet: empirical explanations of sex differences in health and mortality', *Journal of Health and Social Behaviour* **30**, 282–304.

Watson, J., Cunningham-Burley, S., Watson, N. (1995) 'Lay theorising about the body and health', paper presented at the BSA Medical Sociology Group Conference, York, September.

Watson, J., Cunningham-Burley, S., Watson, N., Milburn, K. (1996) 'Lay theorizing about "the body" and implications for health promotion', *Health Education Research* **11**, 2, 161–72.

Watson, N. and Shakespeare, T. (1995) 'Habeamus corpus? Sociology of the body and the issue of impairment', paper presented to *Changing Organisms: organisms and change*, University of Aberdeen Quincentennial Conference on the History of Medicine, 29 June – 2 July.

Chapter 10

The body resists

Everyday clerking and unmilitary practice

Paul Higate

Biting cold, scorching heat, blistered feet, aching limbs; some or all will characterise the intensive period of military socialisation. The embodiment of these extremes is endured by all hopeful recruits, from cooks to combat soldiers. For them the body is at one and the same time a site of suffering and vital resource. The body, however, is a precarious resource and at any moment, debilitating injury might become conflated with corporal weakness. Here the 'bodies of men' (and less frequently, women) could be deemed unsuitable for the military life, their short-lived careers soon over. Alternatively, growing muscles, thickened skin and fitter hearts can spell success, the crystallisation of which is represented by synchronised bodies of (men) executing razor-sharp drill movement to the delight of gathered parents present at the 'passing out parade'.

In this chapter, I suggest that we might conceive of the military institution as colonised by a range of military *bodies*. In these terms, the trade of personnel administrator or 'clerk' in the Royal Air Force (RAF) may provide only limited outlet for the traditional embodied 'man-of-action' military image when contrasted with the combat soldier. A tension might exist between *preparation* for the military life, and how it is experienced at the everyday level. Thus, for many, basic and trade training are exciting, tough and challenging (and also particularly exhausting). Motivation and commitment are elicited through a perception that 'real' post-training military life will at times be similarly exhilarating – after all, why prepare in this way? With this in mind, it is entirely likely that physical inactivity apparent at the level of the daily administrative 'grind' could give way to frustration. Might this tension manifest itself at the somatic level for men deemed somewhat feminine on account of their official work? Can the body still provide a channel through which challenge and excitement is fostered within the constraints of the characteristically sedentary office-space?

A number of themes are developed in this chapter that turn directly on bodily symbolic display. In effect, they represented coping strategies within a (military) environment that demanded high levels of bodily control. That these were largely outwith discursive awareness underlines the difficulties facing sociology with regard to the embodiment of agency.

The bulk of the chapter draws on autobiographical material, and I suggest that it could provide a number of insights into the nature of the embodied experience within a relatively humdrum working environment. The backdrop is a particular military workplace coupled with the barely perceptible significance of status and meaning attached to the range of non-commissioned trades in the Royal Air Force (and no doubt other services). Here 'clerking', for reasons I expand on below, tended to occupy the lower reaches of the informal trade hierarchy. With this in mind, at the intersection of gender, hierarchy and everyday work experience, various strategies of resistance were noted. Significantly, workplace pressures were eased through 'bodily channels'. Indeed, some acts assumed a ritualised nature and in themselves signified status within the small oppositional subordinate group. First, however, we touch briefly on the problematic of body and method.

Problems: method and the body

Given the importance of 'the body' within the military environment (Scott and Morgan 1993; Mazur and Keating 1984; Foucault 1977) it makes a great deal of sense to analyse particular events from an embodied perspective. However, the somewhat 'peculiar' nature of the corporeal self – its simultaneous elusiveness and ubiquity, or its 'absent presence' (Shilling 1993) – render questions around its 'behaviour' as likely to significantly influence the specific bodily displays and their possible meaning(s) under scrutiny. Thus, the act of highlighting events usually carried out at the non-discursive level necessarily influences the nature of agent-engagement with the self-same phenomena subsequently. In the case of the body this remains especially pertinent as habitual bodily activity might move into the realm of consciousness or 'discursive awareness' (Giddens 1991).[1]

Autobiography

Are there theoretical resources within the sociological armoury that might help to illuminate everyday interaction from the very particular 'bodily' dimension? One approach might be that of auto-biography. Not only is it well established within the discipline (Stanley 1993, 1992; Benstock 1988; Morgan 1987) but it provides an opportunity to reflect on the everyday, perhaps mundane activity that constitutes any one element of the life course. Indeed, it may help us to reconsider events that appear(ed) entirely whimsical or seemingly meaningless, as well as more crucial life markers. In other words, it is to a large extent a useful tool offering great flexibility and potential. Moreover, it may facilitate greater insight into the subjective or experiential dimension as it is not preoccupied with a desire to be 'objective' (Morgan 1987; Plummer 1983). In these terms 'we may not wish to approach autobiography with ideas about its "objectivity" . . . but instead explore what it can tell us about our own "subjectivities"' (Ribbens 1993: 87). Similarly, for Friedman (1988) a 'critical and reflexive form of autobiography thus has the sociological potential for considering the extent to which our subjectivity is not something that gets in the way of our social analysis, but is itself social' (quoted in Ribbens 1993: 88).

Within the confines of this chapter then, subjectivity turns directly on the embodied behaviour of certain military personnel. The autobiographical events highlighted throughout represented crucial turning points in the shared lives of the subordinate group. Analysis of these important events oscillates between the gravity of the situation and the apparently trivial embodied coping strategies. Here, the pertinence of autobiography is in no doubt with regard to key life events. Bogdan (1974) states:

> The autobiography is unique in allowing us to view an individual in the context of his whole life . . . it can lead us to a fuller understanding of the stages and *critical periods in the processes of his development* . . . it permits us to view the intersection of the life history of [men] with their society, thereby enabling us to understand better the choices, contingencies and options open to the individual.
>
> (quoted in Plummer 1983: 69, my emphasis)

Not only does this approach offer a unique opportunity to treat elements of one's biography analytically (Morgan 1987), but it may

– through a range of recent theorising around the body – illuminate some of the ways in which individuals rely on the embodied characteristics of their 'selves'.

Within 'physical' environments (for example, sport, manual labour and the military) the bodily dimension remains hegemonic, size and shape of the embodied self can really matter.[2] Thus, we might bring the body 'in from the psychologistic cold' and begin to conceptualise it discursively against the backdrop of auto/biographical experience. Furthermore, there is a sense in which the 'bodies/auto/biography' linkage has long been recognised. Discussing Dilthey, Plummer states that 'lived life' is

> a dialectical compound of self and society and the organic matrix of body and mind ... we must acknowledge that experiencing individuals can never be isolated from their functioning bodies and their constraining social worlds – there is no room for a bodiless idealism or a mindless materialism. Body, mind, context, society – *all* are in constant engagement with each other, and *all* need to be taken into account.
>
> (Plummer 1983: 54, original emphasis)

However, there are limitations to using autobiography. Accounts given remain provisional, partial and one of many potential versions of parallel events (Morgan 1992, 1987). Coupled with this is the problem of memory, given that events detailed here unfolded in 1987.

For Morgan (1987), personal reflection represents the crucial interplay between past and present, so that 'autobiography is an occasioned activity ... that autobiographies are stories produced for particular occasions and that they are ... as much about these occasions as they are about the actual events recounted' (Morgan 1987: 5). Thus, autobiography is seen by Jay (1984) as a 'self-reflexive practice that does not constitute a summation of the past but an intervention in it' (quoted in Morgan 1987: 5). Though no doubt invoking extensive philosophical debate, this problematic can be treated straightforwardly enough and needs only minor explication. As one's sociological knowledge develops, might the social universe develop limitless explanatory horizons? In these terms, there has been an attempt to work within familiar frameworks, including discourses around masculinities, embodied experience and resistance to military rank hierarchy.

My social world, then, has been heavily influenced by the institution of the Royal Air Force. The following stories have been culled from personal experience and whilst unique, may throw light on similarly embodied resistance within 'body-conscious' institutions.[3] Finally, the following accounts are characterised by a mix of autobiography and biography. My absence from some of these incidents should not, however, detract from their overall importance. What remains at the centre of the analysis are the *meanings* attached by the group (absent or present) to these 'exemplar scenarios'. Gabriel states that stories (analogously gleaned from the workplace) 'present incidents as signs and symbols, rather than as information . . . information with its fixation on verifiability, objectivity and control . . . disregards context, it scorns meaning' (1995: 497). Throughout this chapter, subjective meaning remains of prime concern.

Context and structure

First, I detail the essentially routinised characteristics of administrative work within the 'Processing Office'. Military rank hierarchy is then discussed together with the ways in which lower ranks attempted to subvert and re-empower themselves through oppositional bodily practice. Next I sketch subordinate biographies and argue that apparently bizarre rituals had significant but rarely acknowledged meaning for members of the tight-knit group. 'Feminised' secretarial work (Pringle 1989) is shown to have energised a preoccupation with the condition of the body in an attempt to rekindle the 'man-of-action' military imagery. Bodily control is then discussed – both inadvertent and 'willed' within the context of autobiographical material; the legacy for authority is considered in the case of the former. Continuing the theme of authority, I then elucidate its fragility and somewhat negotiated nature (Hockey 1986) – even within the confines of a strict rank hierarchy. Bodily shape and size intervenes in everyday interaction, but assumes particular relevance in the military context where 'bodies' remain of crucial significance (Scott and Morgan 1993: 16). Before concluding, I provide instances in which the (apparent) evacuation of bodily waste provides an unexpected avenue for minor subversion of formal surveillance and work procedures. Within the military environment, personal expression in terms of widely varying hairstyles has formally enshrined limits. The motif of control over 'bodily functions' is continued together with the ways in which it might assume significance in the life of a serviceman keen to foster a civilian identity. In this way, bodily aesthetic becomes an important symbol of personal 'liberation' from oppressive bodily constraint.

The Processing Office

Operating at a Royal Air Force base in Britain during the late 1980s was what I will call the Processing Office. The mental exigencies of the office task were limited so that super- and subordinates alike quickly mastered the job. Indeed, the subordinate group referred increasingly to the 'sausage-machine', the invocation of a conveyor-belt repetitiveness resonant with the ultimate drudgery of the work. Not only did intense mundanity characterise the routinised task, but subordinates were vulnerable to near-constant surveillance from superiors on account of the 'classroom-like' layout of the office space. Ultimately this engendered frustrations on a range of fronts pivoting around both the superiors' and the broader institutions' perceived shortcomings (see Figure 10.1).

Royal Air Force rank hierarchy

It is worth drawing attention to a number of characteristics that made the Processing Office unique within the Royal Air Force. First, there was a distinct lack of commissioned officers. The thirteen person unit was autonomous, with the head office based some distance away. The Warrant Officer (WO) – the boss – had, therefore, greater discretionary powers than would normally be the case. His immediate deputy was the Flight Sergeant (FS) and continuing the rank descent was the female Corporal (Cpl(W)). The shopfloor workers (all but two civilians) were Senior Aircraftsmen/women (SAC/SACW: see Figure 10.2).

The rank of WO has a particular status within the RAF. It represents the hierarchical pinnacle amongst non-commissioned ranks and is usually bestowed on individuals only after a considerable number of exemplary years' service. For this reason, WOs are very rarely questioned with regard to their personal life or occupational competency. Indeed, in many ways, they are beyond question, aside, perhaps, from the occasional senior commissioned officer.

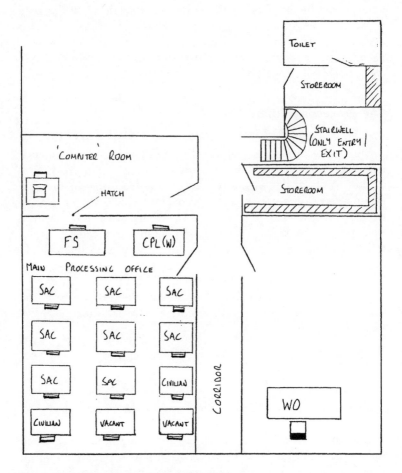

Figure 10.1 Plan of the Processing Office

The clearly defined rank hierarchy fosters a complexity of competitive dilemmas for those in the military. Thus, the FS operates on the periphery of the much aspired rank of WO, and could be preoccupied with the ultimate upward move, executed through a succession of highly favourable annual assessment gradings. The rank of Cpl is somewhat ambiguous. Friction from the shopfloor – the SACs – may be of particular note, whilst immediate superiors, in this case the FS, may apply pressure downwards through the rank structure. In many ways he or she may be caught in this status pincer

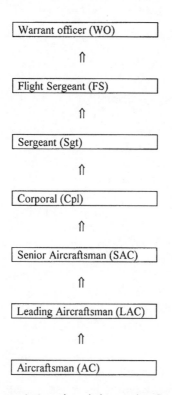

Figure 10.2 Non-commissioned rank hierarchy, Royal Air Force

Note: to denote female members of the RAF, affix 'W' to the rank title, e.g. Cpl(W).

movement, with shifting alliances continuously negotiated and renegotiated so as to facilitate effective junior command of the daily administrative task.

Next, I set the scene by recourse to a brief summary of biographies. This is important as it illustrates the solidarity of the subordinate group of four. Bodily ritual assumed particular meaning within this tightly bound context. It became a code of sorts and represented a mini-domain of exclusory understanding and therefore a diluted form of power within a formally disempowered status group.

The subordinate core – some biographies

It is my first day in the Processing Office. As I am introduced to my colleagues (the majority of which, like me, are SACs) I realise I have met Harry – one of the core – before enlisting into the RAF. After being court-martialled in Germany for what he describes as a 'questionable offence', he has become severely disillusioned with service life, as promotion to Cpl remains unlikely for many years. I then meet Steve, who has a reputation for 'poor attitude' to the service together with a penchant for collecting large debts incurred through credit cards. The service frowns on such behaviour and manages his income. Finally, I meet Sparky who has held the rank of SAC for seven years (promotion to Cpl in the trade of Personnel Administrator normally occurs between four and six years). He has been 'charged' on numerous occasions, and his attitude appears blasé, to say the least. My personal assessments (necessary for promotion to Cpl) were quite good on arrival in the Processing Office. This information has permeated through the entire office staff and been met with disdain and ambiguity by the subordinate group. Hitherto unquestioned promotional goals become increasingly problematised as I familiarise myself with an alternative orientation to the usually competitive service life. My alignment with group views hardens substantially when I discover that promotion to Cpl will not be forthcoming in the near future on account of an 'administrative error'. I experience a sense of great injustice.

Clerks and the 'bodies of men'

Aside from the clear disillusionment expressed by the subordinate core towards the Processing Office particularly, and the RAF generally, behaviour was characterised by a high degree of rumbustiousness. For example, risk taking behaviour was common (Canaan 1996), with cycling around the base in close formation at high speed representing one of the more dangerous activities. Further, there would be play-fighting in storerooms, and lunchtime runs or gym sessions. This is unsurprising given the importance of a fit and strong body in the military context 'Hence, appearance is unusually important in the military, especially when it is accompanied by strength and agility' (Mazur and Keating 1984, quoted in Willetts 1990: 15).

By its very nature, administrative duty within the RAF remained sedentary – the immobility of the body was crucial to desk-based activity. Though this seems like a rather obvious statement, it appears that for a number of military enlistees, consideration of bodily work-based constraints were overlooked (Hockey 1986). Basic military training represented the pinnacle of embodied experience for many, with clerking anathema to the military/physical/exhilaration nexus.

This was the experience of the subordinate core, but was rarely discussed. There was something 'not quite right' about men being clerks. The pervasive influence of military/masculinised self-identity and its grounding in the broader military context was captured in the nickname given to clerks – they were known as 'shinies'. Thus, the continuing friction of the seat would lead to a 'shining' of the RAF issued grey trousers. This term was considered derogatory by male clerks, and was only rarely applied to females within the trade. The name connoted unmanly 'inactivity', this in direct contrast to the 'man-of-action'. From clerk, it was only a short step to secretary and all that this represented in terms of femininity. As Pringle states, 'the ambiguity about what constitutes a secretary's work makes it easily 'available' for cultural redefinition . . . secretarial work is currently presented as quintessentially feminine' (1989: 3).

The contradictions around the man/clerk dichotomy rose to the surface from time to time. Here, Harry feels 'trapped' by his small desk; physical activity is necessarily curtailed. He recalls the FS's attempts to shorten the legs of some new desks. An over-shortening resulted from the failed bid to harmonise leg length, and led in Harry's words to 'big men being too big for little desks . . . !' He is often noted to lose his temper with these small desks, referring to 'big men' being 'trapped'. He bangs his fists and verbally denounces the FS's incompetence (only, however, when the latter is absent).

Contradictions and tensions around ambiguous identity were expressed through body. To be fit and strong countered the suggestion that clerks were somehow effeminate and weak. Size and shape of body is important in the military, and in the case of the subordinate core was used as resource to alleviate some of these contradictions. To be seen working out in the gymnasium, or running every day, helped to reaffirm the obscured man-of-action image. These tensions are echoed in the following account of Cockburn's Youth Training Scheme (YTS) male secretaries:

the real reason why men 'aren't secretaries' . . . was clearly not felt by the young women to be prejudice against them. It was, rather, the way men felt about themselves and about women. One young woman supposed that 'boys would like more active jobs', to be a man, 'do heavy work'. A second young woman said of secretarial work . . . 'I don't know, I suppose they think it's poofy' . . . 'Probably blokes [they] think it's a sissy job . . .' 'They'd be ashamed'.

(Cockburn 1987: 113)

Bodies, however, have been chosen as the locus of these organisational conflicts for a number of reasons. First, there was a specific connection to memory, so that in a sense the subordinate core had a particular bodily group identity – a repertoire of bodily actions that symbolised their difference from mainstream military value systems. Connerton states 'the body [should be seen] as socially constituted in the sense that it is culturally shaped in its actual practices and behaviour . . . and in particular habitual performances [as these are important] in sustaining memory' (1989: 104).

By virtue of their membership of the military, the subordinate core had experienced 'square-bashing', an endless round of synchronised marching, parading and so forth. Within the context of the Processing Office, oppositional bodily rituals developed that spoke of *disorder*. Though, undoubtedly bodily control was as involved if not more so than formally legitimised bodily display, its significance was in subversion of these regulated bodily movements.

Willed and unwilled bodily control

This next account deals with inadvertent lack of bodily control. The subject is the WO and for this reason the account may have been prone to exaggeration given his status. At stake here, however, is the WO's authority. Given that his deviant bodily display stemmed from over-consumption of alcohol, future sanctioning of subordinate alcohol excess became undermined. Harry relayed the following:

The WO was responsible for showing a relatively senior officer the office set-up. On this particular day, the office had been cleaned, and work had been duly apportioned so as to infuse the environment with an industrious atmosphere. The WO arrived mid-afternoon with the officer in attendance. He seemed rather unsteady on his feet and it appeared he was drunk. He was heard to slur his words, rendering them indecipherable. Shortly after the slurred speech was heard, he lost his footing and fell across a desk. There was suppressed giggling and surreptitious nods in recognition of his liquid lunch.

This next display also concerns disorder, but in this case willed disorder that sought to unwittingly undermine the appropriate levels of control and display over the military bodies' poise and predictability (the latter a crucial aim of military training). Within the military 'ordered' context, these rituals appeared to have little or no meaning. However, it is possible to see them as random 'pockets of bodily chaos' that served to comically subvert oppressive bodily control mechanisms. The first concerns Sparky: 'I am in the Processing Office, in the presence of Sparky. We are involved in a serious work-related conversation. Suddenly, he collapses, and falls to the floor. He apologises and states quite matter-of-factly that his " . . . legs stopped working . . ."'.

A derivative of this ritual was a simulated 'falling backwards', where the subordinate, with split second timing, falls backwards but prevents serious injury by landing carefully:

> I am in the storeroom one afternoon practising the move. I execute the most daring attempt yet, and in the process of adding danger, fail to look behind at my potential landing point. I narrowly miss a shocked looking FS who has just entered the storeroom.

It is worth reiterating that the physical exigencies of these rituals no doubt exceeded those required for many military drill movements. Similarly, they were innovative and deviant, and appeared spontaneous. Taken together, these three dimensions remain largely oppositional to the military environment and allowed the subordinate group a degree of bodily autonomy.

Hierarchy – status and size

These next accounts pivot around the linkage of size and status against the backdrop of the pervasive military rank hierarchy. The

first originates from direct experience, the second, perhaps embell-
ished somewhat, was relayed by Steve:

> I return to work the day after my gate guard duty. I am
> anxious as I believe the FS will 'want words'. He calls me
> into the storeroom and appears highly agitated. I note that he
> is sweating, and fleetingly become aware of his height (5' 4")
> and slim stature. My 6' 4" dwarfs him, and after uttering a
> few angry words he unexpectedly aims a blow at my head.
> Reflexively, I duck, and his hand strikes the wall. I scurry off
> towards the main office and my small desk.

> Harry has been called to see the FS for a minor misdemeanour.
> Like me, Harry is relatively tall in comparison to the FS. The
> combination of Harry's assertive striding and his height serve to
> erode the FS's authority. Though located temporarily in the
> WO's office, the FS's seniority is undermined for a crucial split-
> second. Whilst standing, the FS is forced to 'look up' to Harry.
>   Surprisingly, the FS appears rather conciliatory and moves
> behind the WO's desk presumably to both rekindle superiority
> and place a physical object between himself and his soon to
> be sanctioned subordinate.

Both these accounts illustrate how bodily difference blurred hierarchical difference. For example, drill instructors (those responsible for
teaching marching to recruits) are often selected with specific regard
to their bodily height and proportion; relative tallness remains an
implicit prerequisite for work of this nature. A further example is
characterised in the narrative section of the RAF annual formal
assessments, in which a description of bodily appearance is required.
Thus, in terms of hierarchy, Connerton states the following:

> almost every bodily movement we make changes our up–down
> orientation, maintains it, or in some way takes it into account.
> The direction upwards, against gravity, establishes the postural
> base in our experience of lived space for the dichotomous
> sense to which we attach values, such as those expressed in
> the oppositions between high and low, rise and fall, climbing
> and falling, superior and inferior, looking up to and looking
> down upon. It is through the essentially embodied nature of
> our social existence, and through the incorporated practices

based upon these embodyings, that these oppositional terms provide us with metaphors by which we think and live.

(Connerton 1989: 74)

The FS's slim build and relative shortness occasionally intervened in everyday interaction. The effect of 'looking down on someone' – both metaphorically and literally – permeated the more emotional situations in which rank-power was particularly manifest. It is at this point that we begin to grasp the elusiveness of the body's absent presence. In these micro-interactions, awareness of bodily difference and its legacy for control of subordinates was only rarely acknowledged at the discursive level. The bodily dimension represented the relatively fixed face of interaction. It served as a constant reminder that subordinates could experience superiority, most crucially during moments of confrontation.

In terms of status and size against the backdrop of bureaucratic organisations, the hitherto little considered bodily dimension remains significant. I have already provided substantive examples of the ways in which relatively (fixed) height and bodily ritual, together with bodily functioning provided meaning, challenge and identity to a formally disempowered subordinate group. The lead is taken from Scott and Morgan, who state:

> Bodies within organisation hierarchies are controlled and disciplined, their movements clearly defined in terms of time and space . . . little attention has been given to the bureaucratic body, its reproduction and the ways in which certain modes of bodily posture and deportment derive from and give solidity to organisational office. . . . [I]t is, perhaps, significant that lower participants in bureaucratically organised hierarchies such as the military are often referred to as bodies or just 'bods'.
>
> (Scott and Morgan 1993: 16)

More broadly, and it is stressed, in a barely perceptible 'everyday' sense, the body was utilised as resource. It provided loosely and spontaneously organised pathways to relative autonomy and control. Hockey's (1986) study of infantryman recruit training established strategies (similar in form – oppositional, but different in substance – for example 'skiving'). He states that, like the experiences of the subordinate core 'this alternative set of values justifies and propagates actions which constitute attempts by them [Army recruits] to achieve some form of *control* over an existence marked by a lack of autonomy and constraint' (1986: 158, my emphasis).

Though Hockey alludes to the ways in which infantry recruits empower themselves through bodily control (as, for example when marching proficiency is partly contingent on relationships with superiors), he does not overtly 'bring in the body' (Scott and Morgan 1993). This is not a criticism, but is, rather, suggestive of the potential for pursuing a sociology of the body across a wide range of contexts. There may be a degree of resistance from a number of established sociologists, however, who find an approach that places the body at the centre of analysis (as one of my former sociology lecturers put it), as rather 'modish'.

The fixed face of bodily functioning

This next account involves Harry. I visit him at home prior to his discharge from the RAF:

> Harry is looking particularly depressed as the FS has given him a full seven day spell of gate guard duties just prior to the onset of civilian life. A gleam comes into his eye, however, when he states that he is looking forward to growing his hair long and will no longer have to shave every day.

Given that this airman is about to be unemployed, and is potentially homeless, we might be surprised at his preoccupation with the loosening of constraints involving hairstyle. There is a real sense in which hair growth – something the body does outwith agent motivation (as far as we know)[4] – acts as metaphor for broader autonomous expression. It is at the intersection of biological functioning and the military rule-book that Harry experienced most pressure (during this particular moment, at least). Further examples of the biological/military requirements linkage might be considered in terms of the public nature of basic military training. Here pleasure through the body and space constraint are significantly heightened, 'Going to the toilet represents the one action where it is possible to be alone'. As one recruit, no doubt wistfully, explained, 'it's the only place you can have a wank in peace!' (Hockey 1986: 25).

Hockey's account might urge us to consider the importance of the toilet space. Within its confines the evacuation of bodily waste usually occurs.[5] Thus, there is just and general recognition that necessary and often unpredictable bodily functioning should remain outwith strict control in the workplace. Of note in the military context is the requirement for troops in hostile territory – often tasked to collect intelligence – to defecate into plastic bags. Here no evidence of their presence remains, as the waste is removed (see McNab 1994).

In this final account the requirements of the body form the backdrop against which Sparky manages to subvert superordinate surveillance. The sanctity of the toilet and its normal meaning acts as a ready excuse for his absence from the office. Who could argue with 'the urge to go'? Of interest here are the meanings the subordinate group attach to this activity which pivots directly on (apparent) compliance with bodily impulse:

> Considerable periods of time are spent in the toilet avoiding work. Members of the subordinate core frequently enter the toilet, lock the door and settle down to read the latest edition of *Viz*; toilet breaks have been known to last up to 30 or more minutes. Today Sparky is in the toilet, and has been for some time. Harry and Steve are taking turns to pass work to him (documents that cannot practically be collated) under the door. It is seen as a great joke by the group. The superordinates are situated in the main office engaged in the formal task.

In terms of legitimate spaces outwith strategies of surveillance, the toilet remains of prime importance. It is almost as if the 'body takes one to the toilet' rather than behaviour flowing from willed agency; in these terms 'special allowance' for absence is noted. Though this is to put the point crudely, surveillance of bodies is rarely absolute, yet remains at the centre of bureaucratic concern 'it is a fact worth stressing that the rationale of most, if not all, state (and other) bureaucracies, is to do with the surveillance and control of bodies' (Scott and Morgan 1993: 16).

Conclusion

The significance of empowering strategies has been demonstrated, largely through little-acknowledged oppositional or 'chaotic' bodily ritual and display within a particular military context. That these unfolded in a largely unremarkable 'everyday' (military) environment makes great demands on individuals attempting to understand their significance. Further, this underlines the tricky nature of theorising (and indeed more empirically oriented pursuits) that take as their starting point 'the body'. It remains a slippery concept, and it is hoped that in its own small way these accounts and accompanying interpretations may act to sensitise individuals keen to pursue similar 'embodied' lines of inquiry.

Throughout this chapter I have attempted to adopt a more 'embodied perspective' from a sociological stance, rather than a specific goal of furthering 'the sociology of the body' in its own right (Scott and Morgan 1993: 135). Here, work, gender and hierarchy intersect against the backdrop of a window of life course: 'The life course, for example, is a complexly embodied as well as a temporal trajectory' (Scott and Morgan 1993: 135).

Finally, these anecdotes have been relayed from the perspective of four apparently 'hard done to' airmen. In this respect they fit with a particular genre of story-telling, thus 'this kind of story is essentially one from the bottom up, the point of view of someone who would rather be anywhere else than on the field of battle or the parade ground, and for whom the main enemy is the superior officer or the Sergeant' (Morgan 1987: 23). There is no doubt that the interpretation of both the WO and the FS would be somewhat different!

Notes

1   See Cohen and Taylor (1992) on 'unreflective accommodation'. Similarly one might consider the irrevocable change that Goffman's work engenders within the context of everyday interaction (see e.g. Goffman 1963); can we ever walk down the street again without being acutely aware of the ritualised 'civil inattention' (see Taylor 1987)?

2   How might we begin to transform the significance of the body in these and other environments into substantive material? See Scott and Morgan (1993: 135–9) for a discussion of varying research strategies in this respect.

3   Of course, the extent to which institutions assume control over body and mind varies. I am thinking here of the more extreme example of incarcerated 'hunger strikers'. Though the connection is somewhat tenuous, the body/autonomy link remains against the backdrop of a 'controlling' institution.

4   See Campbell (1996) with regard to the ways in which the body 'sets limits on agency'.

5   Though Ditton (1977) found it a useful place to write sociological fieldnotes.

References

Benstock, S. (1988) *The Private Self: theory and practice of women's autobiographical writings*, London: Routledge.

Bogdan, R. (1974) *Being Different, the Autobiography of Jane Fry*, London: Wiley.

Campbell, C. (1996) 'Detraditionalization, character and the limits to agency', in Heelas, P., Lash, S., Morris, P. (eds) *Detraditionalization*, Oxford: Blackwell.

Canaan, J. (1996) '"One thing leads to another": drinking fighting and working class masculinities', in An Ghaill, M. (ed.) *Understanding Masculinities*, Buckingham: Open University Press.

Cockburn, C. (1987) *Two Track Training: sex inequalities and the YTS*, London: Macmillan Education.

Cohen, S. and Taylor, L. (1992) *Escape Attempts*, 2nd edn, London: Routledge.

Connerton, P. (1989) *How Societies Remember*, Cambridge: Cambridge University Press.

Ditton, J. (1977) *Part Time Crime: an ethnography of fiddling and pilferage*, London: Macmillan.

Foucault, M. (1977) *Discipline and Punish*, Harmondsworth: Penguin.

Friedman, S. (1988) 'Women's autobiographical selves: theory and practice', in Benstock, S. (ed.) *The Private Self: theory and practice of women's autobiographical writings*, London: Routledge.

Gabriel, Y. (1995) 'The unmanaged organization: stories, fantasies and subjectivity', *Organization Studies* **16**, 3, 497–501.

Giddens, A. (1991) *Modernity and Self Identity*, Cambridge: Polity Press.

Goffman, E. (1963) *Behavior in Public Places: notes on the organisation of gatherings*, New York: Free Press.

Hockey, J. (1986) *Squaddies: portrait of a subculture*, Exeter: Exeter University Press.

Jay, P. (1984) *Being in the Text: self-representation from Wordsworth to Roland Barthes*, New York: Cornell University Press.

McNab, A. (1994) *Bravo Two Zero*, London: Bantam Press.

Mazur, A. and Keating, C. (1984) 'Military rank attainment of a west point class: effects of cadets' physical features', *American Journal of Sociology* **90**, 1, 125–50.

Morgan, D. (1987) '"It will make a man of you". Notes on national service, masculinity and autobiography', *Studies in Sexual Politics, no. 17*, Manchester: Department of Sociology.

Morgan, D. (1992) *Discovering Men*, London: Routledge.

Plummer, K. (1983) *Documents of Life*, London: George Allen and Unwin.

Pringle, R. (1989) *Secretaries Talk: sexuality, power and work*, London: Verso.

Ribbens, J. (1993) 'Fact of fictions? Aspects of the use of autobiographical writing in undergraduate sociology', *Sociology* **27**, 1, 81–92.

Scott, S. and Morgan, D. (eds) (1993) *Body Matters: essays on the sociology of the body*, London: Falmer Press.

Shilling, C. (1993) *The Body and Social Theory*, London: Sage.

Stanley, L. (1992) *The Auto/biographical I: the theory and practice of feminist auto/biography*, Manchester: Manchester University Press.

Stanley, L. (1993) *Breaking Out Again*, 2nd edn, London: Routledge.

Taylor, L. (1987) 'Interview with Laurie Taylor', in Mullan, B. (ed.) *Sociologists on Sociology*, London: Croom Helm.

Willetts, T. (1990) *The Canadian Militia: a heritage at risk*, Colorado: Conference of Defence Associations Institute.

Chapter 11

Natural for women, abnormal for men

Beliefs about pain and gender

Gillian A. Bendelow
and Simon J. Williams

As we have previously argued (Bendelow and Williams 1995a, 1995b), scientific medicine has reduced the experience of pain to an elaborate broadcasting system of signals, rather than seeing it as moulded and shaped by the individual and their particular socio-cultural milieux. Although pain lies at the intersection of biology and culture, making it an obvious topic for sociological investigation, scant attention has, until quite recently, been paid to understanding beliefs about pain within the study of health and illness, and associated domains such as the sociology of the body.

A major impediment to a more adequate conceptualisation of pain has been the manner in which it has been 'medicalised', resulting in the inevitable Cartesian split between body and mind. Consequently, the dominant conceptualisation of pain has focused upon sensation, with the subsequent inference that it is able to be rationally and objectively measured. Yet as well as being a medical 'problem', as we have emphasised, pain is also very much an everyday experience: one rooted in the lived structures of embodiment and the emotional modes of being and selfhood this involves. It is culture which provides the symbolic bridge between the brute materiality of disordered physiological processes and meaning-laden character of human significance (Kleinman 1988). Embodiment, as the existential basis of culture and the self (Csordas 1994), lies at the heart of these issues, transcending the stark divide between mind and body, biology and culture, reason and emotion. This chapter attempts to bring these theoretical issues to bear on an empirical study of pain and gender, illustrating how cultural responses are crucial to our understanding of pain and embodiment.

Pain and culture

Culture shapes not only the meanings and interpretation we attribute to pain, but also the responses to it which we fashion. It was the physician, Beecher (1959), who was one of the first to stress the impact of the cultural meaning of pain on its perception and response. He found that injured combat soldiers reported little or no pain associated with their wounds, despite serious tissue trauma. Having established that they were actually capable of feeling pain, he also observed that they did not appear to be in shock, and concluded that their perception of pain had been altered by the motivation of being able to return home.

Both social constructionists (see Nettleton 1992; Arney and Neill 1982) and medical anthropologists (for example Good et al. 1992; Helman 1990) have emphasised the cultural meanings and dimensions of pain and pain behaviour, thus extending the analysis of pain with regard to the following propositions:

1 Not all social or cultural groups respond to pain in the same way.
2 How people perceive and respond to pain, both in themselves and others, can be largely influenced by their cultural background.
3 How, and whether, people communicate their pain to health professionals and to others, can be influenced by cultural factors.

(Helman 1990: 158)

In stressing these issues, there is a need for a far more interpretative approach, one which, whilst recognising the crucially important role which social and cultural factors play, accords a far more active, critical and reflective role to individuals who draw upon their own lay knowledge and beliefs in shaping both their interpretation and response to pain. In this respect the study of pain beliefs builds upon an important tradition of sociological research into lay concepts of health and illness together with wider structural concerns regarding their social patterning according to factors such as class, age, gender and ethnicity. Whereas there have been the beginnings of sociological work on pain around social class (Kotarba 1983) and ethnicity (Zola 1966; Zbrowski 1952), other factors have been largely ignored.

The relationship between pain and gender has been a neglected topic, despite the fact that epidemiological evidence appears to repeat the pattern of sex differences in morbidity. For instance in the United States, women report a higher incidence of both temporary and persistent pain than men (see von Korff et al. 1988; Crooke et al. 1984), and more women than men seek treatment for chronic pain (Margolis et al. 1984; Helkimo 1976). The research which has taken place appears to be almost exclusively under the rubric of psychophysical investigation, where gender is not viewed as a variable of any significance (see Hardy et al. 1968; Spear 1966; Chapman and Jones 1944). A more detailed search of the recent psycho-medical literature on pain perception reveals something of a controversy over gender differences. Using a variety of noxious stimuli, such as heat, cold, shock and pressure, some studies confirm the no difference hypothesis (see Lawlis et al. 1984; Neri and Agazzani 1984). In contrast, other studies, using similar techniques, indicated that women have lower tolerances (Dubreil and Kohn 1986; Otto and Dougher 1985; Woodrow et al. 1977; Notermans and Tophoff 1967).

Although experimental pain forms the majority of research, it is an artificial and limited approach. Experimental pain is not equivalent to clinical pain, or to 'everyday' pain, and, as we know, individuals personalise their analysis of what they see around them; the process of perception is subjective and selective. When beliefs about pain are taken into account, a different picture emerges from the findings regarding pain thresholds. Attitude surveys concerned with analgesia conducted by drug companies repeatedly confirm the view of *both* sexes that women are much more able to cope with pain than men. For example, Nurofen (1989) carried out structured interviews of 531 married and heterosexual cohabiting couples over 18, from different areas of the UK. When asked to rate their pain threshold and that of their partner on a scale from very low to very high, there were no gender differences whatsoever. However, when respondents were asked the question: 'Do you believe that women are better able to tolerate pain than men?' 75 per cent of the sample (64 per cent of men and 86 per cent of women) said yes, 15 per cent (20 per cent men and 11 per cent women) thought 'both equally'; the same proportion said they did not know or did not answer and only 10 per cent (16 per cent men and 3 per cent women) said 'no'. The same question was asked in a similar cross-national study in the United

States (Squibb 1987) of 2,500 married/cohabiting couples. In this case, 82 per cent of the sample felt that the majority of respondents believed that females have a higher capacity to cope with pain.

Although the focus on thresholds appears to be the only issue concerning gender that has received much attention in 'scientific' pain research, more recently the influence of sociological theory within health and illness can be seen in accounting for sex differences in pain. A study by Feine *et al.* (1991) which is concerned with these differences retains the focus on experimental laboratory testing, but does acknowledge there may be complex factors involved:

> these differences may be due to sociological factors *which demand stoicism in males and allow expression of pain in females*, or they may be due to physiologic or anatomical differences between the sexes.
>
> (Feine *et al.* 1991: 255, our emphasis)

In her meta-analysis of sex differences in pain, Berkeley (1995) goes even further in the refutation of simplistic biological differences by considering that theories involving sex-roles and the cultural socialisation of males and females may constitute possible explanations. As we know from the vast amount of work that has been generated since the mid-1970s, a number of hypotheses have been advanced to account for the gender differences in morbidity and mortality. These are summarised here as follows:[1]

1 Biological aspects of illness risks, i.e. those arising directly from different reproductive functions and those linked to aspects of different female/male genetic constitutions.
2 Acquired risks of illness from gender roles such as associated stresses of lifestyles, sex-typed occupations, exposure to hazards at work or in the home, i.e. women have more illness than men because their assigned social roles are more stressful.
3 Different health and illness behaviours and concepts associated with masculinity and femininity, for instance women report more illness than men because it is culturally more acceptable for them to be ill; differential childhood socialisation leads males and females to differ in their perception, evaluation and response to symptoms.

4   Different diagnoses and treatments such as the way in which professional health practitioners view gender roles, gender differentiated access to health services.

In the analyses of questionnaire and interview data which follow, all these explanations can, in varying degrees, be seen to be invoked in accounts of gender and pain.

Researching pain and gender

The research described in this chapter attempted to use a phenomenological, sociological approach to beliefs about pain, using a combination of structured questionnaires, in-depth interviews and a sequence of visual images, in a random sample of attendees of a general practitioner (GP) surgery in north-west London (see Bendelow 1992). A total of 107 questionnaires were distributed to 107 men and women aged 18–65 of varying social class and ethnic origin, attending different surgeries. The largest ethnic group was identified as white British (sixty-five), but with substantial numbers of black British, white Irish, African Caribbean and 'mixed race'. As well as demographic data, the questionnaire examined experiences and definitions.

These deeper, more abstract notions of pain were explored through semi-structured interviews of their own experience with a sub-sample of twenty-two men and women, and also used a sequence of images and paintings to discuss the nature of pain. In particular, as regards this chapter, we look closely at the relationship between the role of gender and perceptions of pain and the implicit cultural assumptions about the ability of women and men to 'cope' with pain. The problematic in terms of this chapter is not *whether* women are able to 'cope' better, have higher or lower thresholds or whatever but *why* people hold these views and the explanations they use to support them. Here, we concentrate primarily on transcript analysis of the qualitative data elicited by the study in order to 'tease out' answers to these questions; answers which relate to the complex relationship between gender, emotions and embodiment.

Why do women 'cope' better?

In common with the attitude surveys mentioned earlier, two-thirds of the questionnaire sample (n = 107) and all of the interview sub-sample (n = 22) stressed the view that women were better able to 'cope' with pain than men. The relative informality of the interview provided an opportunity to examine in more depth why this opinion was so firmly held, also to explore what 'coping' means. Many of the men stressed that it was a popular belief or mythology, for example: 'It's difficult to say – one is brought up to think that women cope better with pain ... I think they have a bigger threshold – whether that's a purely subjective view' (male, aged 26); 'Oh, women are better at coping with pain. *Q: Why do you think that is?* It's er, sort of folklore but I think it's true' (male, aged 57).

> Well, that's the only reason I put it, it's a general belief – women have to go through labour so. . . . As far as I can gather it's just something in the make-up of women that's different to men . . . but whether it's something you can scientifically prove, I don't know. . . . It might be one of those myths – like strength. A man is supposed to be stronger than a woman but women are stronger emotionally and can stand more pain.
>
> (male, aged 33)

Childbirth was portrayed as the ultimate painful experience, especially by the men in the sample. For instance, despite his personal experience over five years of malignant tumours resulting in amputations, a retired journalist still maintained that the worst possible pain he could imagine would be that of childbirth. He felt that in turn, women's ability to reproduce gave them a 'natural' advantage to cope with pain:

> My hunch is that it has to do with childbearing, I remember a sense of awe and fear even when [his son] was born – I could hear [his wife] shrieking and screaming from where I was in the hospital waiting room. There was a sense that I would never know that extreme of pain that she was undergoing.
> *Q: Would you say that now?*
> Yes I would, and I do think that many men do have that awe and the sense that this is the ultimate pain, that there can be no worse and of course we don't know and we can't know what childbearing is like. And there are many different attitudes towards the pain but as far as I can gather most women seem to feel it's worth it.

The view was repeatedly expressed by both women and men that the combination of female biology and the reproductive role served to equip girls and women with a 'natural' capacity to endure pain, not only physically, but also emotionally. This equation of woman with the 'natural' evokes the well-known distinction between public and private domains. Martin (1987), amongst others, has pointed out that women are intrinsically linked with the family, which is the location of bodily and 'lower' functions, whereas men are more readily associated with cultural, mental and 'higher' processes of the public world of paid work. This theme recurred frequently in connection with beliefs about pain and was articulated by all the respondents in some form:

> I think partly because women are more in touch with their feelings and they have certain yardsticks, not just having babies but periods, things happening to their bodies that they aren't in control of so they think about their bodies more and they learn to live with discomfort, I suppose. Most people find periods uncomfortable if not painful, and the same about pregnancy – some women enjoy being pregnant but others find it mildly irritating and uncomfortable. Even things like breast feeding – when do men ever experience anything like having cracked nipples but still carrying on with it – things like that. I think women just have more contact with their *natural biological part* and they are just more inclined to think about it and analyse it and not just complain about it which I think, well in my experience, is what men do, really. They're not really interested in the causes of pain or sort of in seeing themselves in relation to the pain, but they think of it as an outside irritant that's got to be dealt *with*.
>
> (female, aged 36)

> I suppose one naturally expects women within the course of a healthy life to be involved with pain but not men on the whole – unless they get hit with hammers.
>
> (male, aged 40)

> I wouldn't think it's a learnt thing, I think it is an actual biological difference. Although there might be women who are brought up to – well be beaten all the time, they might get used to it, like battered wives or something.
>
> (male, aged 21)

As in the open-ended questionnaire data, the interview revealed sophisticated explanations of pain and gender ranging from the biological to the socio-cultural frameworks. Although many explanations began with a biological basis, they often led in to role expectations:

> Women are made to suffer pain because we have periods and childbirth. Whatever happens, women end up bringing up children, we just don't have the 'privilege' of giving in to pain and sickness.
>
> (female, aged 39)

> I think that women cope better or have to cope better, well I think they have to because a man can go off to bed if he's feeling ill but a woman has still got the kids there or they're not really allowed to be ill – they don't think, she still has to get the jobs done – the kids are screaming for attention they don't really understand that Mum's not well 'cos if Dad's not well he'd be in bed . . . so I'd have to say that possibly it's worse for a woman, physically and mentally probably because they're not allowed to show it. The man only has to provide the earnings, well in a lot of cases the woman has to provide money too . . . so women suffer more – it's a man's world really in that respect.
>
> (male, aged 26)

> I think women have a very strong sense of responsibility. I suspect that's developed by society, that's what they're expected to be but also some of it is inborn and that the propensity is there because of the protection of children and the next generation. Human children take so long to grow up – you have to be responsible for them a long time – so women tend to put their pain on one side while they get on with being responsible so in fact the needs of other people override the need to experience your own pain – I think particularly emotional pain but physical pain, too.
>
> (female, aged 42)

The theme of gendered 'socialisation' was interwoven throughout the explanations and leads to a rather more sophisticated understanding of responses to pain which include not only physical but also emotional 'limits of tolerance', which are in turn contextualised socio-culturally.

The conditioned stoicism of men

In contrast to the 'natural' biological capabilities of coping with pain attributed to women, it was felt that boys' emotional expression during childhood was actively discouraged. As a consequence, adult males felt an obligation to display stoicism. Subsequently, the experiences of many men and women are that for men pain of any sort is abnormal and outside their expectations, the net result being that they are less able to deal with it. One young woman, aged 18, had grown up in a household with some experience of 'role reversal' in that her mother worked full-time, and her step-father worked part-time and carried out most of the housework, and made the following observation:

> Men are not allowed socially to express pain as much they're supposed to be stronger. We're allowed to cry and they're not . . . although women have more breakdowns than men, men don't allow it to come out, they hide it until it's unbearable whereas a woman will usually say 'I can't cope' long before. It's hard to avoid the indoctrination – you know men are stronger, therefore they could stand pain more but if I think about it logically I don't really think that . . . women can cope with mental pain a lot better. My parents are divorced and I know that my father still cannot cope with that, with the pain associated with the divorce and the things around it whereas my mother has come to terms with it and is much more able to give. Obviously in her mind she has dealt with it and analysed it, done it to death really – worked it all out, why this happened and that happened. But as I said, it does depend on the person – I do have male friends who are extremely sensitive and very analytical. I'd say perhaps 40 per cent of my male friends are expressive and emotional whereas perhaps 90 per cent of my female friends are but you can't really say whether that's biological or society – in the social environment people think it's a sign of weakness to show pain but actually it's a sign of strength.

Another interviewee, a male artist, aged 43, lived in a household with some role reversal – his wife worked full-time as a doctor, whereas he worked from home and had taken the major role in raising their two sons. He described a recent incident in which his

younger son, aged 9, had fallen over and cracked his skull. During
the visit to casualty, the boy wept continuously and profusely and
was very upset. Despite his claims that his own gender did not pre-
clude his ability to 'mother' his children, when recounting the
incident, this man expressed the view, albeit apologetically, that he
had felt his son to be making too much fuss and expected him to
be 'tougher'. He also admitted that he would not have had the same
expectations of a girl, and indeed would not expect a female child
to have such an accident in the first place.

This phenomenon of the 'macho' conditioning of boys
throughout childhood was a recurrent theme for many of the
respondents, for example:

> I think a woman would be more likely to seek help than a
> man would because I don't think a man would accept that
> there's anything wrong with them. Women would be the more
> sensible and the men would be more stubborn. It's *a form of
> brainwashing*, it's just − like at school you see a boy in the
> corner crying for his mum, but for a girl it wasn't the same
> − the boy is a sissy or whatever, with the girl *it's a form of
> brainwashing*, you don't even realise it like − boys it's all action
> men and guns and you know, they're taught to be tough
> where girls have all little dolls and things to dress up . . . you're
> not allowed to show your feelings, you're not meant to but
> why shouldn't you? It's just not accepted.
>
> (male, aged 29)

> I think women of a certain age are ready to consider the pain
> of childbirth − they know about it. Maybe a 4 year old seeing
> a woman on TV biting and screaming doesn't know what's
> going on, but by age 8 they see, they learn, they hear and grad-
> ually the psychological resistance builds up. I think that men are
> − historically they've been in a position of strength − muscular
> power, all that sort of thing . . . but . . . feel vulnerable when
> in pain and therefore that vulnerability can be exacerbated by
> the fact that they are feeling pain . . . 'why should I feel that −
> why me when I'm so strong, I am a man' . . . and the doubt
> and vulnerability goes on for a while. Conversely you could get
> someone who doesn't feel that at all . . . I was thinking about
> the reactions of a girl child and a boy child to blood, as a result
> of a cut and I would generally imagine that the girl it would

be 'Oh, I'm bleeding' but the macho act of the young boy
would be 'I've got a cut but I'm all right – I've got a plaster,
look at my scar'. Not that I don't think that girls could act like
that but the conditioning of boys to be macho is very strong.

(male, aged 23)

The negative effects of this 'conditioning' were perceived and
acknowledged by both men and women in this study. As the
quotes demonstrate, whilst all the interviewees acknowledged
the existence in some form or other of 'emotional' pain, physical
pain in the form of acute, readily observable symptoms, elicited
more legitimacy, sympathy and respect. Men, however, were more
likely to separate out the two, to ascribe a 'hierarchy of
respectability' to different types of pain, and were more reluctant
to consider emotional pain as 'real' pain. Women, in contrast,
although making similar distinctions, tended to operate with more
holistic, integrated, notions of pain, finding it easier to blur, if not
collapse the boundaries. So although emotional 'stoicism' to the
point of repression is encouraged as a masculine trait, it is actually double-edged as it leaves men ill equipped in terms of 'coping':

When I was working as a midwife we always reckoned that
if it was men who had the babies the birthrate would drop in
negative proportions!
Q: So why do you think women do cope better?
Well, we're brought up that way – a lot of that is
nature/nurture sort of stuff but at the same time we're brought
up to be allowed to express it – big boys don't cry and all
that sort of thing whereas girls are allowed to cry, they are
allowed to express their pain – it's probably just as well because
I think women do go through much more pain – emotionally – they're more likely to address it and deal with it rather
than – men are more likely to repress it and it comes out in
aggression . . .
Q: What do you mean by the nature/nurture stuff?
Well it starts at Day 1 really . . . there are very clear differences in the way that boys and girls behave and develop but
what is often superimposed upon that is what is acceptable
and what isn't acceptable. I've never had a child so I don't
have first hand experience but the children I've been around
– the damage that parents can do to kids, telling them that

they cannot, will not behave in a certain way – it's enormous. Well, it's partly parents and partly peer pressure but I really don't know – I think they definitely develop differently. Yet you see men, when faced with severe pain, go totally to pieces in a way that women don't, usually.

(female, aged 27)

In your childhood you're not brought up in a vacuum, like you see in problem pages in women's magazines, letters from mothers – 'I'm worried about my son, he's timid, he likes cooking and things – is he gay?' In other words you're only allowed to be sincere and sensitive if you admit to being gay, being like a woman. In this society, even men who are aware of it and don't like it, have to obey the rules – it's so drilled into you from childhood, you just can't escape it – to admit to being as sensitive as a woman, it's very difficult to overcome those social barriers. The more artistic – artists are allowed to be expressive, sensitive whereas scientific people have to be rational and sensible all the time. It is odd to see a man cry. I don't think there's anything bad about it, it's just that it's so rare. Maybe if a woman was brought up in the same way – you mustn't cry, go and play football instead . . . women themselves, even the most feministic, still go sort of helpless – oh please – sidle up and get what they want – I'm sure that happens to the best of us.

(female, aged 33)

These accounts raise an important contradiction in relation to the process of conceptualisation in that although beliefs about pain may transcend the mind–body divide, dualistic frameworks are employed in order to explain the complexities so that dichotomies of masculine/feminine, culture/nature, reason and emotion are evoked again and again.

Expressing pain: benefits and costs

The patterning of 'pain coping' by gender can be seen as ambivalent in terms of the 'costs' and 'benefits' it entails. We have seen how the data demonstrate these ambiguities for men, but the apparently superior capacity of women for 'pain-coping' is also double-edged:

Women are more prone to depressions, they're more prone to things sort of swamping over them, they indulge in it, stay at home all day and eat – um let me think, well men get looked after by their women-folk. Women have to sort of strive and get on with it, whatever whereas men can indulge themselves more. Women are actually stronger, they don't have illnesses so much. . . . When you think of individuals, I've got an aunt who whinges about the slightest pain, she's in pain all the time. It sort of goes this way and that. You get the sense of thinking that men will try and battle it out and don't take a painkiller at the first sign whereas women will. On the flip side of that women are more practical, they won't accept pain – it goes this way and that. If a woman's got pain and lots of kids she has to hang on and look after them. As a boy I was always told that the good Indian suffers in quiet.

(male, aged 23)

The assumption that they may be able to 'cope' better may lead to the expectation that they can put up with more pain, that their pain does not need to be taken so seriously, as in the case a 30-year-old woman whose career as a concert pianist had been ruined and her life severely disrupted by the misdiagnosing of a brain tumour for two years as depression. This tendency to minimise women's symptoms was perceived across both public and private worlds:

It's easier to be a man but maybe that's because I am a man and that's the way I've been led to think. I can only see it personally . . . I do think the one thing with pain, when it's your mum or whatever you do find yourself thinking she can cope with it. The impression that I get is that women aren't supposed to feel pain. Now I would, but as a kid I never felt any sympathy whatsoever, I didn't really understand.

(male, aged 29)

I think from my experience both being a nurse and a patient, doctors are much more likely to tell men what's going on, what's involved, especially when it's something surgical when it may be related to the workings of the combustion engine whereas they will assume that women are ignorant about the functioning of their body. Also often they don't relate very well to women, if you've got male/female, lay person/doctor and very often a class difference as well, and really being able to communicate with a female patient who maybe hasn't had a lot of education they find very difficult and they assume a lack of education much more.

(female, aged 28)

The issue of *legitimacy* is extremely important within the sociology of health, illness and suffering and being taken seriously was not perceived solely as a gender issue. Men and women in the study felt that the colour of their skin or being working class meant they were either ignored or not given information:

I think there's a big ethnocentric thing about pain as well. I know that people would say, and supposedly quite astute intellectuals, that it's not just a racist thing, but that women in Victorian times were used to their offspring dying. That because infant mortality rates were high that it wasn't that painful and I hear the same arguments about the families in India . . . that women there would be used to it and I think that's absolute shit, because it demeans the whole relationship of one human being to another.

(male, aged 33)

I'm very working-class in my relationship to doctors, I'm beholden to them but I don't trust them, and I do a lot of exploration of myself. God knows what would happen if I were really ill because I think the service we're retaining now in the NHS [National Health Service] isn't good enough. Back in the 60's my husband's mother, one of the first wave of black women from the West Indies, she complained of pain; she was ignored and ended up having cancer of the ovaries and she died. OK, everyone's got their own collection of horror tales but there are too many of them, from people I know and in my working life, to just dismiss it. I think accessibility to healthcare is becoming more and more dependent on money. If you've got the money you can 'buy off' the pain to the extent of the information you obtain and the quality of service you receive.

(female, aged 37)

As these quotes clearly testify, lay pain beliefs mirror the broader debates on social inequalities in health, particularly relating to 'women's lot' in life:

> Yes, women cope better with pain but should they have to? The 'we're here to suffer-type-thing'. The collection of women I've seen suffering in my lifetime is enormous – maybe my eyes are attuned to women – much more enormous than the pain I've seen men suffer. I've seen women, black women particularly, but white woman too, in enormous amounts of pain and just living with it.
>
> (female, aged 37)

Social 'fate' or biological 'destiny'; the relationship between gender and pain is both complex and contradictory, as we deliberate in the final discussion.

Discussion and conclusion

Pain is never the sole creation of our anatomy and physiology. Rather, it emerges only at 'the intersection of bodies, minds and cultures' (Morris 1991: 1). As well as being a medical 'problem', pain is an everyday experience and whilst the medical voice is a valid one, other voices, especially those of the subject, are often lost in 'the neglected encounter between pain and meaning' (Morris 1991: 2). As we have argued, an *embodied* approach to pain as an ongoing structure of lived experience is able to transcend many former dichotomous modes of western thought, thereby reconciling mind with body, biology with culture, reason with emotion, and championing the (biographical) voice of the 'lifeworld' over the dominant (dispassionate) voice of medicine.

People in pain need to find *meaning* and legitimacy for their symptoms, however inappropriate or anti-therapeutic this may seem from an orthodox biomedical viewpoint. We have argued that the field of pain perception has traditionally been dominated by the scientific somatico-technical approach, resulting in parallel divides between mind and body, emotion and sensation, and a 'faulty-machine' model of embodiment. Rather than merely reducing pain to a physiological 'symptom', it must be therefore seen as culturally shaped by an individual's worldview, requiring an approach which encapsulates its physical and emotional, biological and cultural, even spiritual and existential dimensions.

As the findings of our study suggest, issues of gender mesh closely with these arguments. Although we would emphasise that our sample is limited in terms of sweeping generalisations and represents the views of a socially mixed, multi-racial, inner-city community, there are resonances with larger surveys. A particularly striking feature of our study was the strongly gendered notion of men's and women's ability to 'cope' with pain. Whilst findings from experimental research suggest that women have lower pain thresholds, our study suggests a very different picture; one in which, irrespective of gender, women, rather than men, are seen to have a culturally endowed 'superior' endurance. These views, as we have seen, appeared to be underpinned by biological principles, yet still embraced socio-cultural issues such as gendered roles and differential patterns of childhood socialisation. The salient point here seems to be that female hormonal and reproductive functioning, together with the role of motherhood, were strongly linked to the capacity for emotion management, thus equipping girls and women with a 'natural' capacity to endure pain lacking in boys and men.

Again, the links between female bodies and emotions become apparent here as male socialisation is seen to actively discourage men from being allowed to express pain, whether physical or emotional. For males, pain is much more obviously a state of 'abnormality', making their bodies *dys*-appear, in contrast to the 'natural' expectation of females. Coping capacities, for women, are seen to encompass affective as well as sensory components, through more integrated notions of the 'mindful' body. These assumptions about female coping are, in turn, linked to wider structural divisions, particularly the public and the private domains, in which women, historically, have been tied to the domestic sphere and more readily associated with the 'natural' world of 'lower' bodily functions such as childbirth and menstruation. By comparison, men are more involved in the public world of culture and 'higher' mental process. As Martin comments; 'it is no accident that so-called "natural" facts about women, in the form of claims about biology, are often used to justify social stratification based on gender' (1987: 17).

Thus, emotion work is equated with women's work, including their perceived capacity to 'cope' with pain, and their greater readiness to talk about feelings generally. Feminist psychologists have also emphasised that female childhood socialisation encourages caring for others and the development of imagination and empathy for human pain, suffering and distress (Ruddick 1990; Gilligan 1982). In addition, women's ontological security and sense of identity may be less threatened by the admission of being in pain than is the case for men, for whom the psychological structure of masculinity is predisposed to inhibit the admission of vulnerability.

To conclude, we would suggest that, despite the so-called 'natural' assumptions made about female biology, the attribution to men and women of differential capacities for experiencing, expressing, understanding and responding to pain is primarily linked to gender-differentiated processes of socialisation and emotion management. This, in turn, draws attention to the various ways in which the experience of embodiment may be different for boys and girls (Young 1990; Martin 1987). Physical experience of the body, in other words, is modified by the social categories through which it is known. All theories about its care, its lifespan, its abilities, its functions, its ability to withstand pain, emanate from a culturally processed and located idea of the (gendered) body. Pain, as we have argued, lies at the heart of these matters. In the immortal words of one of our (male) respondents: 'Women have more *awareness* – a more intimate and responsible instinct to their biology – all we do is shave!'.

Note

1 There is an enormous literature on gender differences in health and illness; for an overview of these hypotheses, see Verbrugge (1985).

References

Arney, W. and Neill, J. (1982) 'The location of pain in natural childbirth: natural childbirth and the transformation of obstetrics', *Sociology of Health and Illness* **4**, 1–24.

Beecher, H. (1959) *Measurement of Subjective Responses*, New York: Oxford University Press.

Bendelow, G. (1992) 'Gender differences in pain: towards a phenomenological approach', unpublished PhD thesis, Institute of Education, University of London.

Bendelow, G. and Williams, S.J. (1995a) 'Transcending the dualisms: towards a sociology of pain', *Sociology of Health and Illness* **17**, 2, 139–65.

Bendelow, G. and Williams, S.J. (1995b) 'Pain and the mind–body dualism: a sociological approach', *Body and Society* **1**, 2, 83–102.

Berkeley, K. (1995) 'Sex differences in pain', *Behavioural and Brain Sciences* **35**, 1–46.

Chapman, W. and Jones, C. (1944) 'Variations in cutaneous and visceral pain sensitivity in normal subjects', *Journal of Clinical Investigation* **23**, 81–91.

Crooke, J., Rideout, E., Browne, G. (1984) 'The prevalence of pain complaints in a general population', *Pain* **18**, 299–314.

Csordas, T. (1994) *Embodiment and Experience: the existential ground of culture and self*, Cambridge: Cambridge University Press.

Dubreuil, D. and Kohn, P. (1986) 'Reactivity and response to pain', *Personality and Individual Differences* **7**, 907–9.

Feine, J., Bushnell, M., Miron, D., Duncan, G. (1991) 'Sex differences in the perception of noxious heat stimuli', *Pain* **44**, 3, 255–63.

Gilligan, C. (1982) *In a Different Voice: psychological theory and women's development*. Cambridge, MA: Harvard University Press.

Good, M., Brodwin, D., Good, B., Kleinman, A. (1992) *Pain as Human Experience: an anthropological perspective*, Berkeley: University of California Press.

Hardy, J., Woolf, H., Goddell, H. (1968) *Pain Sensations and Reactions*, New York: Hafner.

Helkimo, M. (1976) 'Epidemiological surveys of dysfunction of the masticatory system', *Oral Science Review*, **7**, 54–69.

Helman, C. (1990) *Culture Health and Illness: an introduction for health professionals*, Bristol: John Wright.

Kleinman, A. (1988) *The Illness Narratives: suffering, healing and the human condition*, New York: Basic Books.

Kotarba, J. (1983) *Chronic Pain: its social dimensions*, Beverley Hills, CA: Sage.

Lawlis, G., Achterberg, J., Kenner, L., Kopetz, K. (1984) 'Ethnic and sex differences in response to clinical and induced pain in chronic spinal pain patients', *Spine* **9**, 751–4.

Margolis, R., Zinny, G., Miller, D., Taylor, J. (1984) 'Internists and the chronic pain patient', *Pain* **20**, 151–6.

Martin, E. (1987) *The Woman in the Body*, Milton Keynes: Open University Press.

Morris, D. (1991) *The Culture of Pain*, Berkeley: University of California Press.

Neri, M. and Agazzani, E. (1984) 'Ageing and right–left asymmetry in experimental pain measurement', *Pain* **19**, 43–8.

Nettleton, S. (1992) *Power, Pain and Dentistry*, Buckingham: Open University Press.

Notermans, S. and Tophoff, M. (1967) 'Sex differences in pain tolerance and pain apperception', *Psychiatria, Neurologia, Neurochirurgia, Journal of the Netherlands Society of Psychiatry and Neurology* **70**, 23–9.

Nurofen (1989) *Pain Relief Study*, London: King's Fund.

Otto, M., Dougher, M. (1985) 'Sex differences and personality factors in responsivity to pain', *Perceptual and Motor Skills* **61**, 383–90.

Ruddick, S. (1990) *Maternal Thinking*, London: Women's Press.

Spear, E.G. (1966) 'An examination of some psychological theories of pain', *British Journal of Medical Psychology* **39**, 349–55.

Squibb (1987) *Survey of Mild-Moderate Pain amongst North American Men and Women*, Bristol-Myers, British Library.

Verbrugge, L. (1985) 'Gender and health: an update on hypothesis and evidence', *Journal of Health and Social Behaviour* **26**, 156–82.

von Korff, M., Dworkin, S., Le Resche, L., Kruger, A. (1988) 'An epidemiologic comparison of pain complaints', *Pain* **32**, 173–83.

Woodrow, K., Friedman, G., Siegelaub, A., Cohen, M. (1977) 'Pain tolerance: differences according to age, sex and race', *Psychosomatic Medicine* **34**, 548–55.

Young, I. (1990) *Throwing Like a Girl and Other Essays*, Bloomington, IN: Indiana University Press.

Zbrowski, M. (1952) 'Cultural components in response to pain', *Journal of Social Issues* **8**, 16–30.

Zola, I. (1966) 'Culture and symptoms: an analysis of patient's presenting complaints', *American Sociological Review* **31**, 615–30.

Chapter 12

Embodied obligation

The female body and health surveillance

Alexandra Howson

At some stage in their life course, most women will be asked when they had their last cervical smear, and subsequently offered one. *Reluctance* to participate may be an initial response:[1] 'one day I got a letter asking me to go to the doctors to have a smear. And I thought, damn cheek, I'm no going for no smear' (Margaret).

A range of responses are engendered by women who have different understandings about the purpose and implications of a cervical smear. For instance, it may be perceived as a *routine procedure*: 'I went for my first smear and I really thought it was par for the course. You just knew you had to go and get a smear test and that was it' (Ann). It may be seen as an explicit means of *detecting* cancer: 'I thought they were checking you for something like they check to see if there's anything there. I knew it was related to cervical cancer' (Ivy). Or it may be seen as a means of *preventing* cancer: 'I knew everything about it, I knew it was to prevent cervical cancer or if they had the information to catch it in time and clear it up' (Carol).

The cervical smear may also be seen as part of a package of health *entitlements* and as a way of acquiring *information* about one's own body: 'I just took it as part of what you get' (Fiona). 'I thought this was very necessary, this needs to get done' (Linda).

Despite the variety of initial responses to this request, invitation or injunction to have a smear, many women comply and either make an appointment to have a smear, or give permission for a smear to be taken at the time the request is made. Cervical screening has developed in the latter half of the twentieth century as a form of secondary prevention based on the identification of precancerous cells.[2] It is generally represented as a safe, simple procedure with high levels of success, where success is typically measured both in terms of lower mortality rates (Hakama 1982) and the restoration of 'abnormal' cells to a status of agreed 'normality' (Posner 1991). However, rather than securing conditions of certainty, the experience of screening participation can produce considerable anxiety and ambiguity, thereby creating a contradiction between its benefit for populations and the 'trouble' produced for individuals (G. Rose 1985), particularly in relation to one's sense of embodiment.

This chapter takes as its starting point the observation that prevention strategies, such as cervical screening, exemplify what Turner (1987: 217) terms the 'Foucault paradox'. In contemporary capitalist societies, citizenship may be underpinned by welfare systems which provide a greater degree of equality of opportunity in relation to healthcare. Where health is increasingly perceived as a desirable, though limited resource, the state is also required to provide a correspondingly greater degree of control over its populations. In this respect, citizenship is broadly considered as a series of individual rights and entitlements, therefore, the paradox is that the provision of citizenship, of which health is an aspect, entails greater surveillance and social regulation by quasi-governmental organisations and agencies.

Drawing upon the legacy of Foucault (1979, 1973) sociology has noted the historical transformation towards new forms of governance through strategies such as public health (Lupton 1995) and welfare policy (Hewitt 1983). This work has been concerned, in particular, with the nature of self-surveillance and its implications for social regulation and identity formation (Armstrong 1995). Amongst the achievements of this work has been the extent to which a variety of forms of healthcare have been identified as forms of governance, such as prevention (for instance, Bunton 1992; Crawford 1980, 1979). However, this approach has largely been concerned with the body and practices of surveillance, thereby foreclosing the possibility of examining embodied experience or, alternatively put, the transformation of such practices through local, embodied knowledges. This analytical oversight has produced two additional consequences. First, the body and embodiment are conflated in ways which make it difficult to identify resistance, where resistance is defined as social action. Second, the sharp focus upon surveillance obscures wider issues of governance which exist in relation to prevention, particularly the tensions between social democratic forms of citizenship as well as those associated with liberalism or neo-liberalism.

In what follows, I examine these statements by presenting material drawn from a case study of cervical screening. I use this to explore the negotiated experience of cervical screening participation and examine the 'trouble' of prevention as a facet of embodiment. First, I briefly outline conventional approaches to cervical screening and their failure to see such participation as embodied experience, in part through their adoption of a normative position in which compliance is assumed. Second, I discuss aspects of the 'surveillance literature' which operate slippages between 'the body' and embodiment. My intention here is not to deny the significant contributions this literature has made to sociological inquiry around the body, but to point more clearly to its analytical potential. I will demonstrate this through a discussion of how, in the context of cervical screening participation, women represent themselves as embodied agents in ways which express obligation. I place analytical emphasis upon the concept of embodiment as a medium of transformation, through which women simultaneously embrace and adopt a critical position towards screening. In doing so, I argue that obligation can be seen as embodied, in ways which highlight notions of citizenship which need to be addressed in relation to issues of surveillance.

Participation and compliance

Recurrent themes in the technical, policy and social science literature regarding cervical screening include a consensus around the ways in which success has been measured; issues of organisation and delivery; the role of personal choice in addressing cervical screening participation; and, more recently, the way in which issues of risk are increasingly mobilised to secure and sustain female participation in cervical screening. Published literature between 1960 and 1990 emphasises a strong statistical association between participation in cervical screening and mortality decline (for instance, Boyes et al. 1961). It has been argued that this association is particularly marked for areas of Scotland, British Columbia and the Nordic countries, and has been linked to good population coverage (Hakama 1982). Furthermore, research has highlighted that a high proportion of women with cervical cancer have never had a smear test (Paterson et al. 1982), and that women who are screened have a low incidence of cervical cancer (Chamberlain 1984). Generally, these data have been used to emphasise the need for systematic cervical screening, and to address the uptake of screening by women (Nathoo 1988), which is consistently perceived as inadequate (Doyle 1991).

Rates of participation and non-participation have been a significant concern which has largely focused on the relationship between screening uptake (for instance, Schwartz *et al.* 1989) and women's knowledge, beliefs and attitudes towards screening (McKie 1993; Savage and MacPherson 1983). There is a broad bifurcation in this literature between rational choice models of health behaviour and liberal feminist approaches to healthcare. However, in both approaches, there is a tendency to assume that given specified forms of information, women will make 'informed' choices and comply with the information with which they are presented. With few exceptions (for instance, Foltz and Kelsey 1978), the adequacy of the expert knowledge embedded within cervical screening is taken-for-granted, whilst the way it is shared is criticised. Nevertheless, women are expected to respond to cervical screening initiatives by participating. Furthermore, assumptions of compliance are at times framed, in expert and media discourse, by reference to the domestic and family obligations which women are perceived to have, which disease is seen to disrupt. For instance, in the mid-1980s, Dr John Davidson, head of the British Medical Association (BMA) Scientific Division was quoted as saying: 'This disease has a major impact on families and children. We are talking about premature death. . . . We have the technology to deal with it now' (*Guardian* 8 October 1986: 2).

Within such statements lies an assumption that women *ought* to be concerned with prevention, not only in order to secure their own health, but also in order to maintain their obligations to others. Compliance is the preferred outcome within much of this literature, although it is articulated through appeal to both personal choice and authoritarian models of participation.

The difficulties of securing mass population participation are emphasised over ambiguities in the processing and interpretation of cervical smears. These ambiguities are certainly acknowledged in conventional approaches (for instance, Wilkinson *et al.* 1990), nevertheless it is assumed they will be overcome by the provision of information which in turn may help women to make decisions about their health and treatment (Posner and Vessey 1988). However, placing emphasis on language and information as a source of empowerment also comes close to identifying women as responsible for their own health and having a duty to participate in screening (Singleton 1995). Hence empowerment in conventional approaches to cervical screening has potential to slip, in ways which reinforce assumptions of both social duty and compliance. Indeed, empowerment in this framework is only identified if expressed *through* participation, and is, therefore, equivalent in meaning to compliance. Furthermore, conventional approaches emphasise the significance of knowledge in securing participation yet fail to locate knowledge production in relation to embodied experience, thus perpetuating a mind/body dualism.

Regulated bodies in sociology

In contrast, Foucault's work has been used to examine how techniques of surveillance in the twentieth century have created new knowledges and orthodoxies in and around the body (for instance, Nettleton 1992). For instance, the development of clinical medicine, as a new form of knowledge, emerged from the birth of the clinic, as a particular kind of social space in which new practices were engendered (Armstrong 1983). In this space, practices were institutionalised and knowledge made systematic, in ways which established control over the body. Foucault is seen as important because of the way in which he placed the body as central to the development of medical epistemology. In addition, sociologists have used Foucault's work to address more directly the body's 'absent presence' in sociological theory and undercut the abstractions which are seen as part of the sociological project (most obviously, Turner 1984). In particular, Foucault's work has provided a means of conceptualising the emergence of the individuated, autonomous self, created by surveillance and self-surveillance (Foucault 1988). By providing a framework for sociological exploration both of those practices which constitute the body, and those which contribute to the constitution of self, by inviting individuals to govern themselves, Foucault has been used by sociologists and feminist theorists as a way of reinstating the commensurability of mind and body (for extended discussion of the latter, see Deveux 1994).

Some of the clearest statements in this regard can be found in the sociology of health and illness. The work of Armstrong (1983), Nettleton (1992) and Arney and Bergen (1984) have all contributed to a way of examining the relationship between the body and society, regulation and surveillance. Such work has focused on practices and perceptions which have shaped medical knowledge, which in turn have established a regulatory imperative towards 'health' (Lupton 1995). Health, in this work, is conceptualised as a new social value (Crawford 1984) which is governed by notions of social duty (Herzlich and Pierret 1987). Prevention is seen as critical to this regulatory imperative and has provided much of the substance around which debate has ensued. According to Foucault (1979), practices and knowledges of surveillance, through population observation and monitoring, regulate the phenomena they constitute. Surveillance here is seen as a form of social organisation which establishes a degree of enclosure or confines people to certain conceptual categories, in ways which ensure they internalise power/knowledge (Nettleton 1992). However, individuals are not coerced by the state to behave according to norms which it establishes. On the contrary, practices of surveillance, for instance through public health (Lupton 1995) or welfare policies (see for instance, Hewitt 1983), encourage individuals to observe and monitor their own behaviour, through the operation of disciplinary power. Foucault (1979) also, therefore, refers to self-surveillance, through which individuals come to behave in particular, specified ways. It is this lighter mode of 'liberal governance' (N. Rose 1990) which has drawn so much attention from sociologists and feminist theorists (for instance, Sawicki 1991; Bordo 1989).

Power/knowledge is drawn upon in order to conceptualise the relationship between the body and governance. The advantage which is attributed to power/knowledge is that power is seen to be exercised in ways which produce knowledges. Hence the body is discursively produced through the exercise of power, constituted through particular discourses. Effectively, power/knowledge underpins processes through which the self creates itself as an object, thus implying a more fluid notion of subjectivity. For instance, as patients become partners in medical culture (Armstrong 1984) through, for instance, preventive programmes, they draw on medical discourse to articulate their experiences, and engage in a dialogue with medical culture, in ways which reinforce their recruitment to the management of their own bodies. The conceptual utility of power/knowledge allows, indeed urges, a detailed focus on local practices, or the 'meticulous observation of detail' (Foucault 1979: 141), and their location within discourse. This emphasis on minutiae has the effect of shifting analysis from interest-led developments in medical knowledge, such as that associated with social constructionism, to the practices through which such interests are engendered. Such a methodological gesture has the effect of locating both medical developments, such as public health and prevention, and the body, in terms of outcomes and effects, rather than as either the consequences of technological imperatives or as a pre-social stable entity. This avoids locating medical practice and knowledge within relations of domination, and interjects a critique of Enlightenment reason and liberal humanism, in which the accumulation of scientific knowledge is linked to notions of progress.

However, there are tensions in Foucault's use of power/ knowledge in relation to surveillance which are reproduced in the marriage between the sociology of the body and the sociology of health and illness. This tension occurs in the slippage between reference to regulatory power and disciplinary power, and the analytical use to which the notion of the 'Panopticon' is put. This is used to signal a shift towards self-surveillance as a key mode of governance in late modernity, but is itself, surely, a centralised form of power. Disciplinary mechanisms, through which individuals are drawn into surveillance, transform subjects through the new actions and thoughts which are engendered, in which surveillance effectively reconfigures individuals 'through their constant and pervasive observation' (Foucault 1979: 71). Yet, the concept of the Panopticon which Foucault mobilises as an image of a softer version of power, also encapsulates a notion of centralised knowledge. It is precisely the idea of centralised knowledge and juridical power of which Foucault is critical, particularly through discussion of a shift *towards* self-surveillance *from* surveillance.

The analytical shift from surveillance towards self-surveillance as a process in which subjects come to locate themselves as active participants and knowledgeable subjects has been the focus of attention from sociologists of the body and health. Subjects within this logic are separated, individualised, made socially visible and offered technologies, such as the toothbrush drill (Nettleton 1988) or foetal monitoring (Arney 1982), which have the effect of normalisation, because of their increasingly widespread use and the expansion of their deployment in new social locations, such as the health centre. Normalisation, through disciplinary power, subjects individuals to monitoring and locates them within deviations based on probabilistic distributions (Armstrong 1995). Hence, disciplinary power conceptualises the ways in which institutionalised disciplines look at bodies, describe and assess them, and how the application of such power is met with 'multiple resistances'. It is significant, however, that whilst this approach, with the exception of Arney (1982), draws attention to the conceptual utility of disciplinary power, it appears unable to identify the 'multiple resistances' which such power is said to engender. This is because of the tendency to focus on *practices* of surveillance rather than the *experiences* of self-surveillance. Consequently, any sense of the resistances which power/knowledge are said to produce are obscured.[3]

There are, therefore, considerable tensions in Foucault's discussion of surveillance and self-surveillance, and their subsequent development in the sociology of the body, and of health. We see this most clearly when sociology uses the concept of disciplinary power to address social action and suggest that individuals become active participants in the monitoring of their bodies and in the production of health. The focus on self-surveillance is filtered through discussions of medical discourse, practices and techniques, and draws attention to practices of self. However, whilst this work details the development of surveillance and its relationship to power/knowledge, it does so on the basis of observations made about changes in medical *practice*. These observations are, in turn, a consequence of merging the notions of both the clinical gaze and the Panopticon to produce a more unified analytical framework than is warranted (Osborne 1992). Consequently, it fails to demonstrate those practices as *experiences* of self-surveillance, and thereby reproduces a dualism between the body and embodiment and a somewhat disembodied approach to those issues of the body which it has addressed.

In addition, this work has not explicitly addressed the gendered nature of power, nor the relationship of gendered bodies to regulating processes. With few exceptions (Holland *et al.* 1994; Bordo 1989), sociological work on surveillance has failed to address the specificities of the regulation of female bodies, or how regulation creates specific identities for female subjects. There is, certainly, an inference within Nettleton's (1991) work that female subjects are differentially marked out as mothers and guardians of children's teeth within preventive dental discourse (see also Graham 1979). Armstrong (1983) also alludes to this as he addresses female subjects as carers in the community, but neither place gender as a central category in their work, and are, therefore, unable to demonstrate the internalisation or negotiation of the identities attributed to them. It is this (re)negotiation to which I now turn in the following section.

The embodiment of obligation

In what follows, I wish to demonstrate how one's sense of embodiment mediates the experience of cervical screening participation.[4] For some women, the experience of cervical screening involved pain, discomfort and bleeding and they were made acutely conscious of their cervix both within this frame, and through the process of reflection which I asked of them in the interview context. Hence the experience of cervical screening was both fractured and contested, and the sense of embodiment articulated in the accounts which follow supports the notion of the body as a site of transformation and negotiation, particularly in relation to perceived boundaries between wellness and sickness (for a discussion of these shifting boundaries see de Swaan 1990). A common theme running through the experiences presented here was the way in which obligation to participate in cervical screening was constructed, perceived and manifest, and the significance of embodiment in the process of (re)interpretation. Cervical screening was seen as something in which women were obliged to participate, identified as: 'an *everyday thing*' (Carol TU 59–60); 'something which *just had to be done*' (Sheila TU 26–27); 'something that women *get used to*' (Julie TU 61–62); 'something that women *should go and get done*' (Rose TU 97–99).

Below I address two instances of obligation articulated in women's accounts of their experiences of cervical screening, which I describe in terms of regulated femininity and, drawing on Gilligan (1982), an 'ethic of care'.[5]

Regulated femininity and responsible citizenship

Cervical screening was seen by some women as a routine procedure associated with femininity, with part of being/becoming a woman. For instance, Mary (aged 39) associated her understanding of smear tests as part of a 'common knowledge' which certain women would have: 'Women that have been ... sort of ... on the Pill, or had children, or things like that should go for smear tests' (Mary TU 52–53). Mary links cervical screening here to both sexual activity and reproduction. Susan (aged 36) makes similar connections. Her previous contact with health services was minimal and she had participated in screening since the age of 16 in the context of family planning. Susan elaborated on the notion of 'common knowledge' and commented that she would make her daughter go for smear tests 'as soon as she is old enough'. When asked to explain what she meant by 'old enough', she said:

> I don't know ... eh ... to be perfectly honest with you. I mean, they're no really fully developed are they, at even 12. I don't know what age they start doing smears on them ... I think maybe ... it depends how mature they are ... I would say maybe 15 or 16. Because, I mean, it could be lying there, and they would catch it in time or whatever. I think maybe 15 or 16 they should have ... because obviously they're having their period at that age and so surely they should be able to have a smear by that time as well. Just as I say with Lisa, I would definitely get her a smear test and that when she's old enough to have it done, you know? I would never let her say, 'I'm no going'. If I had to drag her, I would drag her.
> (Susan: TU 126–127; 214–215)

Susan alludes here to a sense of the female body as one which undergoes transition, but in ways which invite regulation. This normative view of femininity as regulated was further supported by statements referring to the initiation of young women into femininity. For Fiona (aged 33), for instance, screening was also seen as something which should be part of the education of growing up as a girl, linked to learning about menstruation, sexuality and reproduction. Furthermore, she identified the nature of women's participation in terms of whether they were good or negligent citizens:

> I think everybody from the age of maybe ... oh, when you start having sex. I think that girls should be more aware. Like at school when they get talks about periods and things, I think they should be taught about cancer smears as part of growing up. I think I wasn't very good, if I'd thought about it, to me, it was just a nuisance, getting a smear. I thought it was uncomfortable and an embarrassment. I think you should start it early, but I think you should continue them on. No woman wants to have them, but I think you should have them more often.
> (Fiona: TU 80–81).

The obligation to attend for a smear test and the examinations and treatment which an abnormality engendered clearly implied a compliance which could be linked to routine interventions which regulated female bodies. The smear test was also seen as a gender marker. Cervical screening for these women symbolised transitions to adult femininity represented by the onset of menstruation, initiation into sexual activity or pregnancy. This form of obligation could also be seen as a form of self-surveillance ('starting early, keeping regular, going often') and was considered important by women who did go regularly for smears, or who claimed that they would do so in the future.

Obligation could therefore be read as a cultural expression of normative femininity, in which the latter, as a public understanding of responsibility, is incorporated into the world of private conduct. Thus women who did not participate in screening were perceived by those who did so, as negligent citizens, and moreover, sometimes perceived as unliberated and out of tune with their bodies. For instance, as Linda (37) reflected on her first smear experience, she struggled to present a picture of herself in terms of responsibility. She tried to discount her feelings of discomfort as she talked about her experience. She did not, for instance, remember feeling embarrassed, but acknowledged that embarrassment might have manifest itself in ways which she would not, in retrospect, recognise. She says:

Linda Extract 1: TU 14–15

01   I didn't really feel too bad about it.
02   I thought this was very necessary,
03   this needs to get done and I gauged my reaction
04   in contrast to other women
05   I know women who actively avoid going for smears
06   and some who I suspect might have never gone for smears at all
07   because they just find it too embarrassing, and I just find that so . . .
08   I suppose I think that's nonsense.
09   I feel sad – that's a terrible way to feel.
10   It's a shame.

This extract is framed by a discourse of responsible citizenship, where Linda perceives participation in screening in terms of necessity [01–04], and 'choosing' to participate represents rational action.

She presents herself as an 'informed' woman and implies that women who participate in screening know that this is best for their bodies and health, and have been freed from constraints of femininity which make it difficult for women to subject their bodies to examination or discussion [08–10]. Indeed she expresses sadness and presents a normative femininity which is open to scrutiny, which does not get embarrassed under a medical gaze since this is a gaze which has 'seen it all before'. The understanding of femininity which Linda presents here is one which is rational and calculative, a regulated, yet self-possessed femininity, through which she actively constrains expressions of irrationality, such as embarrassment. Both the rationalisation of the female body and a logic of surveillance are reinforced where the importance of the individual in the production and reproduction of self-governance is emphasised.

Responsible citizenship was also articulated in other ways. For instance, one young woman suggested that having smears ought to be 'like giving blood', a distinctly public minded form of behaviour. Chris (aged 21) perceived cervical screening as taboo and that it ought be 'detabooised' and become even more routine through, for instance, advertising.

Chris Extract I: TU 334–342

01 I don't know if it's regular practice here to offer smears
02 when you reach a certain age.
03 Maybe it depends on what doctor you go to.
04 I don't know. But I think it's a good thing,
05 if you come to a certain age.
06 I suppose maybe you should lower the age now, because, definitely,
07 people are having sex younger now than they did do
08 and maybe they should lower that age to 17. Maybe even 16.
09 I suppose it's going to be a bit of an ordeal
10 for someone who's a bit younger – going for a smear –
11 but it should become a common thing, like
12 going to give blood . . . to have your smear, it's an important thing.
13 Probably I don't think it's talked about enough.
14 It's like a taboo subject.
15 So the more taboo it is,
16 the more apprehensive people are going to be doing it.

This extract places cervical screening participation in a more authoritarian or social democratic discourse of responsible citizenship in which cervical screening is seen as something which should become a social norm [09–12]. This stands in contrast to the neoliberal versions of citizenship articulated above, with their emphasis on notions of personal choice. For Chris, as a young woman negotiating her sexual identity in the context of a recent sexual relationship, screening for cervical cancer was also part of a wider set of social taboos which she perceived as requiring redress [13–16]. She draws links between the personal and the public as a means of increasing participation and consequently locates notions of responsibility in the public domain. For Chris, bringing the private conduct associated with screening into public discussion, operates as a normalising strategy which places emphasis on social norms. Furthermore, this extract draws attention to the 'technologies of citizenship' (N. Rose 1990) such as advertising, which regulate the private sphere through the production and dissemination of social norms.

The accounts presented here draw on a sense of responsible citizenship articulated through the embodied experiences of cervical screening. Despite considerable ambiguities, anxieties and ambivalences, many women see themselves as moral agents who, by placing their own bodies under surveillance, also meet social expectations, or exercise social duty through the expression of what they see as rational action.

Negotiating surveillance and care

I'm going for smears, I'm doing everything I can.

(Diane, TU 85–86)

Obligation was expressed by some women in relation to a perceived regimen of self-care and watchfulness over other women. For instance, an obligation to inform and persuade friends and kin of the necessity of screening features strongly in some accounts. Mary recounted how she responded to a sister and a friend who were requested to attend for a cervical smear. The following narrative extract illustrates how Mary places emphasis on the way in which this vigilance is expressed.

Mary Extract 3: TU 48–49 'The Persuasion'

01   . . . a couple of years ago she says to me
02   – they've sent me a thing for a smear.
03   I'm not going and opening my legs – she says.
04   And that's the sort of attitude she had,
05   and I said I think you'd better be going.
06   But I never made any comment that
07   I had problems or anything like that.
08   Some women, as I say, they say it's embarrassing.
09   I've a friend who actually came with me when I went for a
     smear
10   and the nurse was saying about what's up with these women
11   who just won't come for a smear?
12   And I says her out there won't come.
13   Well she got nabbed for an appointment and she had . . .
14   well she did go.
15   To me, they just don't bother.
16   I think it's a thing you should . . .

Mary first introduces her sister as non-compliant [01–03], and
indeed appeals to 'privacy' to ground her non-compliance. Mary's
own critical voice is embedded within this story and she actively
obscures her own struggle to deal with the ambiguities in her own
experiences of screening [05–07]. She acknowledges the reluctance
of other women to participate and the way in which women appeal
to 'embarrassment', as a means of explaining their non-participation
[08–11]. Despite her own struggles however, Mary presents her own
participation in terms of obligation. Her reference to her sister
[01–03], her friend [09] and the nurse's observation about women
who do not participate [10–11], all draw boundaries around her own
identity as a woman who has acknowledged her social obligations
and those women who have failed to do so. The nurse's reference to
'these' women especially operates as an identity marker which alerts
us to Mary's consideration of her own sense of embodiment.

   In recalling her response to her sister, with whom Mary no
longer has contact, she is clear that she considers the best course
of action for her is to have a smear. Yet she immediately qualifies
this definitive statement with reference to her own experience
[06–07], which was characterised by a series of abnormal smears,
examinations, normal smears and treatment. Yet she alerted neither

her sister nor her friend to this complex experience and indeed submerged it in a positive statement of the necessity of screening. This indicates a certain ambivalence on the part of Mary. In her reference to her friend, Mary is more belligerent. She reveals to the nurse taking her smear that her friend falls into that category of women who 'avoid' having smears. She is therefore exposed as a 'defaulter', deviant, an outsider. Mary felt justified in providing the nurse with this information and may have done so on the assumption that the nurse would then approach her friend and 'nab her for an appointment', thus providing no means of avoidance [13]. Therefore, not only health professionals participate in the opportunistic screening of which many women complain. Indeed, some women themselves may participate in this watchfulness over other women through a sense of obligation to reveal to kin and friends ways of maintaining health and preventing disease, and in doing so, appeal to an authoritarian discourse of citizenship.

A sense of watchfulness was also evoked by some women in relation to the care they received in their experience of screening, and the way in which nurses in particular tried to provide information from which women might make decisions. For some women, this was perceived as 'care', whilst for others it was perceived as counter-productive. For instance, Julie suggested the 'cosy, all women' atmosphere of health centres and colposcopy clinics undermined the clinical context in a way which was unhelpful for her, precisely because of the way she was expected to make decisions and, therefore, deal with their consequences. Kathleen echoed this sentiment. She was full of praise for the way in which she had been reassured and her anxieties had been addressed by both her general practitioner and the clinic. However, such reassurance could also be counter-productive. For instance, Kathleen said:

> perhaps they collude with you in underestimating the impact of having somebody . . . having gone through this panic that you've got cancer, and just having that physical assault – and it is one – it's so . . . *minimised*. And there's this big notion that it's all preventive and that it's wonderful. And you think, yeah, that's great, but it actually minimises the bit that says this is frightening. It's traumatic and an assault on your body.
>
> (Kathleen TU 48–49)

Obligation to participate in response to watchfulness is expressed here in ways which draw on neo-liberal notions of information and choice. The provision of information under the rubric of 'care' is part of a number of changes in the delivery of prevention which is meant to be inclusive, and invite individuals to participate in the maintenance of their own health (see Armstrong 1984 for a discussion of this point). Kathleen's response to information sharing and reassurance is to drawn attention to the potential this creates for a disembodied experience, in a way which may also undercut participation. In contrast, some women expressed a sense of increased vigilance in relation to their own screening participation, associated with the identification of the impact of the experience of others upon them, or the ways in which their experience impacted on other women. For instance, Fiona links her own experience of participating in screening with her sister's abnormal smear.

> My sister had a smear test that was abnormal and then the whole family went out, and all my friends went out and got appointments to get smears taken, even folk that wouldn't normally ... every one of them, they panicked, thinking cancer. I think that's all it takes really, just a fright. Somebody that you know anyway, and that's you alerted. I do remember anyway my mum and my sisters going.
> (Fiona: TU 91–92).

A sense of vulnerable embodiment is being drawn upon here as a source of connection with other women. Fiona draws links between her sister's embodied experience and that of other women in her family to underpin her own sense of obligation. Hence, the care expressed here articulates a sense of embodied understanding which secures participation on the basis of contingency, rather than 'personal choice'.

Embodiment, obligation and citizenship

In this chapter I have presented material which describes the nego-tiated character of participation in forms of surveillance, such as cervical screening. Prevention, as an expression of surveillance, whilst administered through the state, is not done so coercively to ensure widespread compliance, nevertheless, compliance is an implicit objective, as my earlier discussion of the technical and policy literature indicates. However, women's 'compliance' with cervical screening participation should not be seen merely as an expression of either coercion or disempowerment. In many cases, both obligation and critical engagement coexisted in ways which undermine liberal feminist arguments which position women as disempowered by their experiences of cervical screening (McKie 1993; Posner 1991). Indeed, obligation should be seen as a more complex expression of self-governance, through which women express a sense of moral agency which emerges from an active, embodied engagement with the process of screening. Cervical screening participation provides a space in which women are active participants as moral agents in relation to both self and others. Such action is supported by prevention as a 'helpful discourse' (Foucault 1988), which read through gendered embodiment, can also be seen as an 'ethic of care' (Gilligan 1982).

As feminist discussions of embodied experience and issues of health indicate (Ruzek 1978; Ehrenreich and English 1974), notions of entitlement, empowerment and choice have been central to the challenges women have posed to medical culture (see Hastie *et al.* 1995 for a recent overview). Yet the pursuit of autonomy and empowerment can imply a need to overcome one's embodiment in order to subject one's body to scrutiny, as Linda's reference to embarrassment illustrates, in a way which positions female embodiment as irrational. It can also imply a need to draw upon embodiment, as a source of authenticity, to challenge medical culture. I suggest that both positions reinforce a mind and body dichotomy which requires reintegration in order to become autonomous, and concomitantly, empowered. The material I have presented in this chapter poses an alternative position, which is that the screening experiences articulated by women should not necessarily be regarded as disembodied, and therefore, disempowering. Rather, I draw upon the notion of embodiment as a medium of transformation through which experiences are transformed and articulated. Hence, the articulation of obligation expresses a sense of embodiment which, in turn, can be linked to at least three notions of contemporary citizenship.

First, some women appeal to neo-liberal notions of choice, autonomy and entitlement in their interpretation of their experience. Increasingly, individuals are implicitly and explicitly encouraged to engage in what Nikolas Rose (1990) has termed 'liberal governance', as the language of choice and the market enters the organisation and delivery of healthcare. For instance, the boundaries between the public and the private have been reordered through the introduction of quotas and targets. Within this framework, citizenship is expressed through active self-maintenance and notions of choice and entitlement. The liberal, autonomous individual is encouraged, and indeed, is obliged, to take up social entitlements such as that represented by cervical screening. The autonomous individual, as both reflexive citizen and consumer, is obliged to be aware of her embodied experience and 'become skilled at translating embodiment into medical discourse' (Greco 1993: 361) in ways which express a sense of personal choice but, nonetheless, meet the demands of a broader agenda.

Whilst a neo-liberal notion of choice is mobilised in women's accounts of their screening experiences, this is elsewhere modified by other expressions of responsible citizenship. The experience of cervical screening as a routine feature of regulated femininity, appeals to a more authoritarian version of social obligation. This should not be read as merely the internalisation of normative authority, but rather, as an expression of both a social duty and the embrace of social entitlement, through which women place themselves as part of a moral community. Here female embodiment can be seen as a site of transformation in which responsibility is both required and reinforced through the logic of surveillance. Responsible citizenship, however, can also be understood as an ethic of care, which emerges through statements about the role women take, not only in relation to self-care, but also in relation to their watchfulness over other women. The concern displayed by some women for others who form part of their social network, draws attention to a notion of relational citizenship (I.M. Young 1990; Gilligan 1982).

Conclusion

The body has been central to sociological inquiry in relation to contemporary regulation and surveillance. Prevention has emerged as a notable substantive area in which these discussions have taken place, and in this chapter, I have presented cervical screening, as an instance of surveillance, for review. The emergence and development of cervical screening is characterised by a range of enduringly contested knowledges across various sites, including medicine, social science and public discourse, in which compliance emerged and remains a crucial concern.

I have used the notion of embodiment to examine and highlight one aspect of the experience of cervical screening, which supports a view of screening as a form of regulation in which individuals are obliged to participate in specified ways. Whilst neo-liberal notions of obligation arise in these accounts in ways which support arguments about the emergence of lifestyle and liberal governance as characteristic of health in late modernity, this is by no means the only way in which notions of obligation are expressed. I have also identified authoritarian notions of social duty and a sense of care in these accounts and I have suggested that these point to a sense of citizenship as a product of the experience of screening. However, the sense of embodiment articulated by women suggests that we should not see this *only* in terms of the internalisation of disciplinary techniques. Whilst women expected to subject themselves to medical surveillance, as the data suggests, at the same time, they developed a critical response to their experience. Hence, obligation expresses local – *embodied* – knowledges which are the consequence of negotiation and reflection.

The expansion and shift in the nature of surveillance continues to be a critical theme within Foucauldian sociology, particularly that associated with issues of health and prevention, yet the material I have presented here suggests that focus on 'the body' obscures those local experiences with which sociology, feminism and Foucault have ostensibly been concerned. In contrast, the notion of embodiment, or 'thinking through the body' (Grosz 1994; Caddick 1986), as a mode of local transformation, reveals previously obscured aspects of surveillance, such as obligation. Therefore, surveillance must be examined *in relation* to citizenship, not as distinct from it, in order that the paradoxes embedded within prevention can more clearly be seen.

Notes

1　The data presented here are taken from interviews with twenty-four participants in cervical screening, collected as part of a case study of cervical screening funded by an ESRC Research Studentship.

2　The nomenclature used to describe changes in cervical cells has been subject to considerable and contentious debate in the technical literature. In practice, 'precancerous' is one of many terms used to describe changes in cervical cells which indicate the potential for the development of cancer. It is this potential which is under surveillance and which is subject to further examination and intervention.

3 For discussion of resistances in relation to welfare surveillance see Bloor and McIntosh (1990).

4 I use embodiment to refer to a dialectical process between embodied experience and the language available to articulate such experience. Hence, the notion of embodiment refers to a process of transformation and mediation in which embodied experience is authentic and articulated through cultural categories. This notion draws on work by Merleau-Ponty (1962), Gadow (1992) and Shilling (1993), but Marshall (1996) also provides valuable discussion with specific reference to feminist concerns. My analysis of interview data, as a means of tapping into 'embodiment', draws on the work of K. Young (1989).

5 In my presentation of interview data, I use TU to refer to units of text in the original transcription. Elsewhere, I present data in numbered lines which allow me to refer to specific phrases in my discussion of the data.

References

Armstrong, D. (1983) *The Political Anatomy of the Body*, Cambridge: Cambridge University Press.

Armstrong, D. (1984) 'The patient's view', *Social Science and Medicine* **18**, 9, 737–44.

Armstrong, D. (1995) 'The rise of surveillance medicine', *Sociology of Health and Illness* **17**, 3, 393–404.

Arney, W.R. (1982) *Power and the Profession of Obstetrics*, London: University of Chicago Press.

Arney, W.R. and Bergen, B.J. (1984) *Medicine and the Management of Living*, Chicago: Chicago University Press.

Bloor, M. and McIntosh, J. (1990) 'Surveillance and concealment: a comparison of techniques of client resistance in therapeutic communities and health visiting', in Cunningham-Burley, S. and McKeganey, N. (eds) *Readings in Medical Sociology*, London: Routledge.

Bordo, S. (1989) 'The body and the reproduction of femininity: a feminist appropriation of Foucault', in Jaggar, A. and Bordo, S. (eds) *Gender/Body/Knowledge*, New Brunswick: Rutgers University Press.

Boyes, D.A., Fidler, H.K., Lock, D.R. (1961) 'Significance of in situ carcinoma of the uterine cervix', *British Medical Journal* 1, 203–5.

Bunton, R. (1992) 'More than a woolly jumper: health promotion as social regulation', *Critical Social Policy* **3**, 2, 4–11.

Caddick, A. (1986) 'Feminism and the body', *Arena* **74**, 60–90.

Chamberlain, J. (1984) 'Failures of the cervical cytology screening programme', *British Medical Journal* **289**, 853–4.

Crawford, R. (1979) 'Individual responsibility and health politics in the 1970s', in Reveroy, S. and Rosner, D. (eds) *Health Care in America*, Philadelphia, PA: Temple University Press.

Crawford, R. (1980) 'Healthism and the medicalisation of everyday life', *International Journal of Health Services*, **10**, 3, 365–83.

Crawford, R. (1984) 'A cultural account of "health": control, release and the social body', in McKinlay, J.B. (ed.) *Issues in the Political Economy of Health*, London: Tavistock.

de Swaan, A. (1990) *The Management of Normality*, London: Routledge.

Deveux, M. (1994) 'Feminism and empowerment: a critical reading of Foucault', *Feminist Studies* **20**, 2, 223–47.

Doyle, Y. (1991) 'A survey of the cervical screening service in a London district, including reasons for non-attendance, ethnic responses and views on the quality of service', *Social Science and Medicine* **32**, 8, 953–7.

Ehrenreich, B. and English, D. (1974) *Complaints and Disorders: the sexual politics of sickness*, London: Compendium.

Foltz, A.M. and Kelsey, J.L. (1978) 'The annual pap smear test: a dubious policy success', *Millbank Quarterly* **56**, 426–62.

Foucault, M. (1979) *Discipline and Punish: the birth of the prison*, Harmondsworth: Penguin.

Foucault, M. (1986 [1973]) *The Birth of the Clinic: an archaeology of medical perception*, London: Routledge.

Foucault, M. (1988 [1986]) *The History of Sexuality: the care of the self volume 3*, New York: Vintage Books.

Gadow, S. (1992) 'Existential ecology: the human/natural world', *Social Science and Medicine* **35**, 4, 597–602.

Gilligan, C. (1982) *In a Different Voice*, Cambridge, MA: Harvard University Press.

Graham, H. (1979) 'Prevention and health: every mother's business', in Harris, C. (ed.) *The Sociology of the Family: new directions for Britain*, Sociological Review Monograph, Keele: University of Keele.

Greco, M. (1993) 'Psychosomatic subjects and the "duty to be well": personal agency within medical rationality', *Economy and Society* **22**, 3, 357–72.

Grosz, E. (1994) *Volatile Bodies*, Bloomington IN: Indiana University Press.

Hakama, M. (1982) 'Trends in the incidence of cervical cancer in the Nordic countries', in Magnus, K. (ed.) *Trends in Cancer: causes and practical implications*, Washington, DC: Hemisphere.

Hastie, S., Porch, S., Brown, L. (1995) 'Doing it ourselves: promoting women's health as feminist action', in Griffin, G. (ed.) *Feminist Activism in the 1990s*, London: Taylor and Francis.

Herzlich, C. and Pierret, J. (1987) *Illness and Self in Society*, trans. E. Forster, Baltimore, MD: Johns Hopkins University Press.

Hewitt, M. (1983) 'Biopolitics and social policy: Foucault's account of welfare', *Theory, Culture and Society* **2**, 67–84.

Holland, J., Ramazanoglu, C., Sharpe, S., Thomson, R. (1994) 'Power and desire: the embodiment of female sexuality', *Feminist Review* **46**, 21–38.

Lupton, D. (1995) *The Imperative of Health*, London: Sage.

McKie, L. (1993) 'Women's views of the cervical smear test: implications for nursing practice – women who have not had a smear test', *Journal of Advanced Nursing* **18**, 972–9.

Marshall, H. (1996) 'Our bodies ourselves: why we should add old fashioned empirical phenomenology to the new theories of the body', *Women's Studies International Forum* **19**, 3, 253–65.

Merleau-Ponty, M. (1962) *Phenomenology of Perception*, London: Routledge and Kegan Paul.

Nathoo, V. (1988) 'Investigation of non-responders at a cervical cancer screening clinic in Manchester', *British Medical Journal* **296**, 1041–2.

Nettleton, S. (1988) 'Protecting a vulnerable margin: towards an analysis of how the mouth came to be separated from the body', *Sociology of Health and Illness* **10**, 2, 156–69.

Nettleton, S. (1991) 'Wisdom, diligence and teeth; discursive practices and the creation of mothers', *Sociology of Health and Illness* **13**, 1, 98–111.

Nettleton, S. (1992) *Power, Pain and Dentistry*, Buckingham: Open University Press.

Nicoll, P., Narayan, K.V., Paterson, J.G. (1991) 'Cervical cancer screening: women's knowledge, attitudes and preferences', *Health Bulletin* **49**, 3, 184–90.

Osborne, T (1992) 'Medicine and epistemology: Michel Foucault and the liberality of clinical reason', *History of the Human Sciences* **5**, 2, 63–93.

Paterson, M.E.L., Peel, K.R., Joslin, C.A.F. (1982) 'Cervical smear histories of 500 women with invasive cervical cancer in Yorkshire', *British Medical Journal* **289**, 896–8.

Posner, T. (1991) 'What's in a smear? Cervical screening, medical signs and metaphors', *Science as Culture* **2**, 2, 167–87.

Posner, T. and Vessey, M. (1988) *The Patient's View*, London: King's Fund.

Rose, G. (1985) 'Sick individuals and sick populations', *International Journal of Epidemiology* **14**, 32–8.

Rose, N. (1990) *Governing the Soul: the shaping of the private self*, London: Routledge.

Ruzek, S. (1978) *The Women's Health Movement: feminist alternatives to medical control*, New York: Praeger.

Savage, W. and McPherson, A. (1983) 'Cervical cytology', in McPherson, A. and Anderson, A. (eds) *Women's Problems in General Practice*, Oxford: Oxford University Press.

Sawicki, J. (1991) *Disciplining Foucault: feminism, power and the body*, London: Routledge.

Schwartz, M., Savage, W., George, J., Emohare, L. (1989) 'Women's knowledge and experience of cervical screening: a failure of health education and medical organisation', *Community Medicine* **11**, 279–89.

Shilling, C. (1993) *The Body and Social Theory*, London: Sage.

Singleton, V. (1995) 'Networking constructions of gender and constructing gender networks: considering definitions of woman in the British Cervical Screening Programme', in Grint, K. and Gill, R. (eds) *The Gender–Technology Relation*, London: Taylor and Francis.

Turner, B.S. (1984) *The Body and Society*, Oxford: Blackwell.

Turner, B.S. (1995 [1987]) *Medical Power and Social Knowledge*, London: Sage.

Wilkinson, S., Jones, J.M., McBride, J. (1990) 'Anxiety caused by abnormal result of a cervical smear test: a controlled trial', *British Medical Journal* **300**, 440.

Young, I.M. (1990) *Justice and the Politics of Difference*, Princeton, NJ: Princeton University Press.

Young, K. (1989) 'Narrative embodiments: enclaves of the self in the realm of medicine', in Shotter, J. and Gergen, K.J. (eds) *Texts of Identity*, London: Sage.

Part IV

Ageing

Chapter 13

The sight of age

Bill Bytheway and Julia Johnson

In the course of our daily lives, most of us who are living a mainstream life in contemporary Britain use the mirror. It may be a mindless automatic routine but it does serve as a kind of confirmation of who we are and 'how we are doing'. The mirror provides us with an opportunity to 'talk to ourselves'. We may have little time or inclination to reflect upon the more psychological aspects of how we relate to this mirrored self, but there is little doubt that, if nothing else, we routinely check our appearance with how we will appear when we move from the privacy of the bathroom into the public arena. Normally, this attention will focus upon various aspects of personal grooming but, over time and in the course of these everyday deliberations, we will occasionally reflect upon age and upon what is expected and appropriate for someone of our age.

This concern with appearance and with the mirrored image is lifelong and remains a continuing concern as we grow older (Öberg 1996; Thompson *et al.* 1990). It is part of what Cole has called 'the appraisal of living' (1992: xviii). Focusing more on the collective experience of ageing, Turner (1995: 253) argues that within 'ongoing interactions of everyday life', signs of ageing become a topic of comparisons and the basis of 'interpersonal monitoring of transformations of bodies'. The visual signs of age, like the weather, is a universal topic of everyday conversation between adults. What then, in anticipation of ordinary social interaction, does the older person make of the sight of the mirrored self?

In this chapter we discuss some of the issues that widely available images of later life raise. In particular we focus upon how age might be recognised and how older people might interpret these images. Although this question should be addressed directly through interview-based research, it is also important that the processes of production and dissemination, and the content of such images should be closely analysed and discussed.

A note on method

Given the huge variety and quantity of media images, it is expensive and difficult to obtain systematic representative samples. One method which is more than adequate, given a non-existent research budget, is to simply include what readily comes to hand. Rather than chase after what may be interesting sources, it is better to focus on the mundane images that become available in the course of other activities. The analysis that follows includes some images that will be familiar to others who have worked in gerontology, but we also include images from birthday cards and magazines on sale in a local newsagency and images acquired whilst one of us undertook a course on cartooning. Our simple objective has been to collect and analyse a broad range of familiar and readily available images.

The mask of age

Since it was first discussed by Featherstone and Hepworth in 1988, there has been a widespread and growing interest in the concept of 'the mask of age'. They argue that there is a view of ageing that assumes that old age is a mask which 'conceals the essential identity of the person beneath' (1988: 148). To support this argument they cite one of the clearest and most well-known examples. Morton Puner's book *To the Good Long Life*, written in 1974, was a set text for the influential Open University course 'An Ageing Population'. On the very first page, Puner begins his positive account of later life with the question 'what does it feel like to be old?' He cites the answer of the writer, J.B. Priestley:

> It is as though, walking down Shaftesbury Avenue as a fairly young man, I was suddenly kidnapped, rushed into a theatre and made to don the grey hair, the wrinkles and the other attributes of age, then wheeled on stage. Behind the appearance of age I am the same person, with the same thoughts, as when I was younger.
>
> (Puner 1978: 7)

In this statement, a very clear distinction is being drawn between two conflicting images. One image is built around the word 'same' and is characterised by an unchanging identity and a comprehensive denial of change: 'I may look older but I'm still the same person'. The other is that conveyed, explicitly, by reference to two familiar signs of old age: grey hair and wrinkles. Priestley indicates that these are two of several 'attributes of age'. Imagining himself being wheeled on stage (the implicit loss of autonomy and mobility are of course two further attributes of age), he felt that he would be presenting a standard image of what it is to be old, that the audience would think of him only as 'an old man'. This is not dissimilar to the claim that prejudice follows when it is disability or skin colour that is seen not the person (Hervey 1992: 81; Goffman 1963).

In drawing attention to this idea of a mask, Featherstone and Hepworth were mounting a sociological argument which related as much to the power of popular stereotypes as to self-image. Somewhat obliquely they introduce the concept of the mask in the following way:

> The perpetual tension between social categories based on generalisations about ageing and the actual personal experience of ageing in its diversity is of constant concern and increasingly so for those who work with older people. In recognition of this tension some writers find it easier to describe the ageing process as a mask or disguise which, like some trick of the make-up artist's craft, conceals, layer after layer, the timeless human personality beneath.
>
> (Featherstone and Hepworth 1990: 254)

The opening sentences of Puner's book are indeed a good example of this strategy. After quoting Priestley's observation, Puner continues:

> In word and study, the data are consistent: Most people over 70 are secretly young, disguised in old skin. The ageing and the old don't think of themselves as ageing and old and don't see themselves as others do. . . . Both sexes would rather not have too many mirrors around. But underneath that ageing skin and body, both may feel as alive as ever, and with a strong need to celebrate life.
>
> (Puner 1978: 7)

In other words, since it no longer reflects the 'true' image of people over 70 but only what others see, the mirror is obsolete.

The primary concern of Featherstone and Hepworth is to study and understand the many different ways in which images are constructed and interpreted – not least by those such as Morton Puner who work with, or write for, older people. Featherstone and Hepworth do not promote 'the mask' as representing some kind of truth about image and age. Rather they suggest it is an idea that helps in the interpretation of mirror images.

In practice, however, the image in the mirror may not be seen as others would see it. Featherstone and Hepworth distinguish between the idea that 'the ageing process' is a mask that conceals 'the enduring and more youthful self' and the fact that some older people attempt to mask the ageing process through cosmetic disguise (Woodward 1991; Sontag 1978) and through routine grooming and dress (Williams 1990: 71).

However, in considering how the mirror image might be seen, some may not feel the need to disguise or conceal it. Dennis Bromley has suggested that when an older person looks in the mirror, it is not the present image that is seen but rather that of a younger self (Open University 1995). Gerald Scarfe, the cartoonist, agrees:

> Do we know our own face? Few of us examine it in great detail. Possibly the only time we see our face is in the bathroom in the morning trying it out in the mirror. . . . We may, because we haven't really looked for years, see ourselves in a time warp. We take for granted the image before us without recognising how we are changing, ageing. It was a great revelation to many when they first saw themselves on video. That unfamiliar view from the back or from the side. Who is that old fogey with the saggy jowls? Oh my God! It's me.
>
> (Scarfe 1993: 16)

In his view what we see is the ageless public image that we have sustained for years and which the early morning routine is intended to reproduce. For him – the cartoonist – the mask, far from being the body concealing the inner self, is the decoration and cosmetic composing of the body that replaces its early morning reality: 'We wear a mask to hide our true self – we try to present the face we would like people to see' (Scarfe 1993: 37).

The inner self, far from being possessed of a more beautiful, more youthful image, is uglier. Just as Puner believes that a positive reality exists beneath layers of ageing skin, so Scarfe is convinced that there is a less attractive truth: 'The artist's job is to capture the true character of the face behind the mask. The caricaturist should leap for the jugular with a snarl, tearing away the sophistication and affectation and arriving at the bare bones' (ibid.).

How then do older people view their own mirror image. At the age of 65 years, Barbara Macdonald co-authored a book on ageism and women (Macdonald and Rich 1984). The book's cover includes a photographic portrait of her and the following is her description of what she sees in this photograph:

> My hair is grey, white at the temples, with only a little of the red cast of earlier years showing through. My face is wrinkled and deeply lined. Straight lines have formed on the upper lip as though I had spent many years with my mouth pursed. This has always puzzled me and I wonder what years those were and why I can't remember them. My face has deep lines that extend from each side of the nose down the face past the corners of my mouth. My forehead is wide, and the lines across my forehead and between my eyes are there to testify that I was often puzzled and bewildered for long periods of time about what was taking place in my life. My cheekbones are high and become more noticeably so as my face is drawn further and further down. My chin is small for such a large head and below the chin the skin hangs in a loose vertical fold from my chin all the way down my neck, where it meets a horizontal scar.
>
> (Macdonald and Rich 1984: 13–14)

It is not difficult to imagine Macdonald examining her mirror image literally as she writes this account. She compares what she sees with what she remembers of distant mirror images ('the red cast of earlier years'). She tries to explain what she sees through reference to what she has survived ('puzzlement' and 'bewilderment'). She acknowledges the impact of biological ageing ('as my face is drawn further and further down').

What is important for the present argument is that she does not suggest in the above description that her mirror image is in some way masking her real self. Rather she accepts that this is how she appears to others, and endeavours to explain the origin of the more distinctive characteristics of this image. But, a little further on, she comments: 'I see my arm with the skin hanging loosely from my forearm and cannot believe that it is really my own. It seems disconnected from me; it is someone else's, it is the arm of an old woman' (Macdonald and Rich 1984: 14).

So she too feels disconnected from the image that her body presents. She interprets the sight of her arm to be that of an old woman, not her own.

The basic question underlying this chapter is how do we recognise age in the sight of our bodies? How do we come to address the disarming question: is this me or is this an old person? How can health promotion construct an image with which older people can identify, that is not primarily delusionary?

Interpreting the image

To be able to interpret an image as that of someone who is old, we need a well-developed sense of what constitutes the image of an old person. How is the face, the arm or the body recognised to be that of age rather than self, an image to be denied?

It is when Priestley lists grey hair and wrinkles as being among the attributes of age; when Scarfe sees his 'saggy jowls' on the video; and when Macdonald uses words from the vocabulary of ageism ('grey', 'wrinkled') to describe her image – and then refers to some of the physiological signs that are commonly associated with age (the deep lines on her face and the loose skin beneath her chin) – it is when this vocabulary is used to disaggregate the image, to isolate the various symbolic elements, that we are able to recognise the image of age.

This deconstruction of the image is spelt out clearly in the training of cartoonists. Brendan Akhurst (1995), writing for a correspondence course on illustration and cartoons, comments: 'Wrinkles, loss of, or grey, hair, reduced distance between nose and chin because of loss of teeth, sunspots, glasses, stooped backs, bowed legs, gnarled fingers . . . old people have so much to offer' (1995: 18).

The five worked examples he offers his trainee cartoonists include all these features. In addition, it is easy to identify in these examples other physical attributes of age such as fleshy jowls, and double or absent chins.

In part, the skill of the cartoonist lies in the ability to draw and caricature the ageing body. As Akhurst indicates, it is not difficult to break this down into a series of symbolic elements. It is convenient that wrinkles are easily represented by simple lines and sunspots by spots. Age is also conveyed, however, by various appendages and contextual signifiers which confirm age. Akhurst's five examples also include walking sticks and outdated clothing styles such as long-johns, mortar boards, bow-ties and hair-pins.

A cartoon by Peter Clarke published in the *Guardian* (13 March 1997) portrays John Major and an unnamed woman. He has sawn off one leg of her zimmer frame. She is dressed in an ill-fitting cardigan, and is wearing zip-up slippers. There is nothing about her face, legs or hands, however, to indicate age, that this is someone dependent upon 'old age care'. The same drawn body, differently dressed and without the frame, could have been used to represent a teenager. What this indicates is that in this instance old age is represented not by the caricaturing of the ageing body but rather by dress and mobility aids.

Unlike Scarfe's cartoons, this and Akhurst's examples are not in any sense portraits of real people. Rather, as in the case of ageist birthday cards, they are empty, featureless bodies (like mannekins or skeletons), exhibiting, or dressed up in, a selection of the standard signs of age. Because the viewer of the cartoon is expected to understand this, the image can be interpreted solely in stereotypical terms. Regarding the caricaturing of real people, Scarfe has commented:

> How is the mask stripped away and a true portrait achieved? . . . A caricaturist creates a super-extension of the face and character. He creates a surreal image which convinces the viewer that is how the person really looks, although he knows it to be impossible.
>
> (Scarfe 1993: 44)

Just as the viewer can recognise the cartoon to be of John Major and can be convinced that, although a surreal image, it is how he 'really looks, although I know it to be impossible', so the viewer can look at the woman in Clarke's cartoon, or one of Akhurst's examples, and think: 'Ah, this is how an old woman really looks, although I know it to be impossible'.

The construction of the image of age

Macdonald and Rich (1984) make no direct comment on the design of the cover of their book. Macdonald's photograph, reinforced by the book's title *Look Me in the Eye*, is however a direct challenge to the reader. Much of the book is concerned with the invisibility of older women: how they are 'not seen', not even in the women's movement (1984: 40–1). In much the same way the well-known poem 'Kate' challenges the nurses:

> What do you see nurses
> What do you see?
> Are you thinking
> when you are looking at me
> A crabbit old woman
> not very wise,
> So open your eyes nurses,
> Open and see,
> Not a crabbit old woman
> look closer – see Me.

(Liddiard and Carver 1978: ix–x)

Unlike John Major, however, Barbara Macdonald's is not a familiar media image. Rather the image on the cover of the book might be described as 'indisputably that of an old woman'. Setting aside the fact that the words 'Old Women', part of the subtitle of the book, are printed on her forehead, how is it possible to claim that this designation is 'indisputable'?

Featherstone and Hepworth (1990: 252) suggest that the immediacy and facticity of photographic images makes them appear real and self-evident. All you have to do is point the camera and press the button: what you see is what you get. But the image evokes more than just the reality before the camera. Turner (1995: 252) argues that mass photography has led to the standardisation of images of ageing and that this was nowhere more apparent than in the humanist-realist photography of the famous 1955 *Family of Man* exhibition at the national Museum of Modern Art, New York. Planned by Edward Steichen, he collected over two million photographs and selected 503 to be included: 'It was conceived as a mirror of the universal elements and emotions of the everydayness of life – as a mirror of the essential oneness of mankind throughout the world' (Steichen 1955: 4). Hervey (1992: 55) however, has suggested that, in neglecting disabled people, it offered a selective and positive image of an unproblematic and noble post-war world.

Likewise, Featherstone and Hepworth warn that photographs and other representations, 'are only able to function within a symbolic order' (1990: 252). What they mean by this is that we only recognise an image to be one of age if it includes certain key elements. This is precisely what J.B. Priestley and Barbara Macdonald were able to do. Both recognised in their own mirror image, the various elements of the – to them – familiar image of age.

One abundant source of such images that is readily available to older people are the magazines that are targeted on them and available for purchase in high-street newsagents (Featherstone and Hepworth 1995). YOURS magazine is a good example. The only indication that it is intended for older people – other than its content – is the front-cover slogan 'Keeping YOU young-at-heart'. The March 1997 edition contained 82 large advertisements (each over a quarter of a page in size) and more than 250 smaller advertisements. Many of these include the image of an older person or persons. The products advertised include: cereals, housing, residential care, clothing, hearing aids, finance and insurance, health foods, heating panels, musical cassettes, shopping trolleys, poetry competitions, cosmetics, insurance, orthopaedic aids, funeral plans, footwear, gardening equipment, bedding, wigs, catalogues, chair lifts, bath lifts, armchairs and electric scooters.

One two-page advertisement feature for home and gardening equipment includes a photograph of a bespectacled, grey-haired man using a long-handled gripper. Unnamed, he represents both the potential purchaser of the gripper and the readers of the magazine. Turning the page, there is a photograph of 'YOURS reader Mrs Hilda Alderman', knitting for the magazine's Age in Action Week. In the same vein, the first feature in the magazine is a two-page spread entitled 'All About You'. This includes photographs of four other readers.

There is a certain distinction in these features and advertisements between images of 'the young old' and 'the old old'. For example, an armchair advertisement includes a colour photograph of an elegant, fashionably dressed woman with coiffured hair and earrings, looking relaxed and seemingly oblivious to the photographer. Similarly, most of the finance and insurance advertisements are future-oriented, often portraying couples, in one case having a picnic in the countryside and enjoying fruit and wine. Often clothes and other appendages to the body such as hearing aids are advertised through the use of ordinary photographic models, leaving the sceptic uncertain as to whether the implication is that age is irrelevant or the product is being associated with the 'attractiveness' of youth.

In contrast to these 'young-old' images in which age seems under- or down-played, other, usually smaller, advertisements include black and white drawings of women in armchairs or on stairlifts, dressed in pleated skirts and cardigans, wearing spectacles and looking stiffly at the viewer. These images are reminiscent of those of the cartoonists who use dress and aids to signify age.

Regardless of chronological age, all these advertisements typically portray 'satisfied customers', people using the products and posing somewhat self-consciously or implausibly for the photographer or the artist. The priority of the advertisers in these examples appears to be that of creating an image of utility and satisfaction rather than one of reality. Nevertheless they also generate, collectively, an image of a certain market, defined if not labelled by age (Sawchuk 1995). Potentially these advertisements are not only setting new trends in consumption, but also influencing the ways in which their consumers will present themselves in public.

Associating age with dependency

Issued free with this edition of YOURS magazine is a further magazine called Tender Loving Care. This has been created 'to help home carers everywhere'. The introductory editorial echoes the claim of YOURS magazine to be 'Britain's favourite magazine for retired people' and then turns its focus on 'home carers – especially those who are getting on a bit'. The front cover includes a couple hugging and this, one presumes, is intended to convey a universal image of loving care. Both are smiling and white-haired, but otherwise there are no other clear interpretative clues and no reference to age.

Inside the magazine the first feature is 'Meet the Carers' and four case studies are featured. Two concern the parents of carers. The first gave up her job to care for her mother and her mother-in-law: 'It is very demanding and I do feel that because I have cared for two elderly people for ten years I have saved the

Government a great deal of money'. The second begins: 'Caring for an infirm and elderly parent is a full-time job'. The carer herself is quoted: 'Being a carer for elderly parents is very demanding . . . I think it's very important that elderly people are well looked after when they are weak'. On the letters page, a letter begins: 'I have just been through the turmoil of getting an elderly friend with no relations into a residential home'. A feature on adapting the home begins: 'Many homes can be adapted to make life easier for an elderly or disabled person'.

These items, referenced to the dependency of 'elderly' people, are interspersed with photographic images. One shows a couple in their seventies and the woman comments: 'Being old and not so good on one's feet is the biggest problem when caring for someone else'. Another, illustrating care products, shows two young uniformed care assistants helping a patient up out of a wheelchair, and another shows the entertainer, Max Bygraves, kneeling beside Irene Finch, a resident of a Methodist Home for the Aged.

These images are similar in composition to many that appear in professional care magazines. In Johnson and Bytheway (1997) we present an analysis of 270 photographic images of care relationships published between 1978 and 1994 in a successful magazine directed at professional carers. The criteria for selection were that a photograph featured an older person and a younger person and they were directly linked to an article concerning paid care. We identified four types of images. The first and least common was the 'teacher shot'. Here the younger person had a teacher-like or supervisory position in relation to one or several older people. 'Portrait shots' resembled traditional family portraits, typically including smiles and gestures of affection. 'Caring for shots' focused on various tasks such as cleaning, delivering and dressing. The most common was the fourth: the 'caring about image'. Here the relationship was portrayed as more intimate and symmetrical: two people talking and demonstrating a degree of mutual affection.

The magazine included a statement indicating that, unless otherwise stated, photographs were taken from library stock and many included, in small print, the label 'posed by models'. This provides clear confirmation that, in this particular instance, 'mass photography' was reproducing standard images of care relationships. As with the advertisements for new kinds of products in DIY magazines for example, this professional care magazine has bombarded readers throughout the 1980s and 1990s with repeated photographic examples of the same kind of image: each a slight variation on a familiar theme. Many of these illustrations had captions that directly associated the older person with being 'elderly' and 'dependent'; for example 'Money matters: elderly people are often unaware of the choice they have if they are unexpectedly discharged into care'. All four types of image portray the older person as 'passive, controlled and dependent'. Rather than document the reality of care, they represent models for care practice.

These two magazines are targeted on different sections of the care market, one on older carers who read *YOURS* magazine, the other on paid carers typically employed by local authority social services or by private care agencies. Both illustrate how the concepts and imagery of 'old age' and 'elderly people' are constructed in a way that sets them apart from 'carers' and from other images of adulthood. In constructing an image of the care relationship, an unambiguous distinction is drawn between carer and cared-for. Many informal carers are themselves of pensionable age (Arber and Ginn 1990) and this is well illustrated by the initiative of *YOURS* magazine. One suspects that the same is true of paid carers. Even so, in the development of a new commercial market and in the promotion of good care practice, it is essential that clear distinctions are maintained. In this respect, the word 'elderly' and other unambiguous allusions to age are associated with the recipient of care. They are portrayed as indisputably old, the essential image of age, and as dependent upon their carers. Indeed, as the disability movement has argued, the fact of being cared for confers dependency (Morris 1991).

Discussion

The standard – universal – human face is disaggregated through a simple vocabulary: mouth, nose, eyes, ears, etc. Children are taught to draw the human face by drawing each of these elements in turn, and in time the more serious artists among us begin to develop particular skills in depicting each. In this way we all learn to recognise a 'good' drawing of the human face, one which can be adjudged a 'good likeness'. This is all the more remarkable given that the drawing itself is no more than a patterning of lines upon a blank sheet of paper.

In a similar way, the symbols of age are represented by a number of symbolic features, each associated with a particular word: bent, grey, wrinkle, bald, zimmer, spectacles. The trainee cartoonist develops his or her skills in drawing these elements and the public learns to routinely recognise and interpret this same imagery and vocabulary.

This analysis has suggested that there are three broad strategies available for the construction of the image of age. In order that an image is recognised as being that of age, at least one has to be adopted. The first is to focus attention upon the body and, in particular, the various signifiers of age. Wrinkles are perhaps the most obvious. The second is to attach to the person a set of appendages which represent age and, in this instance, the most obvious is possibly the zimmer frame. The third is to portray the person in a relationship with others, a relation which reflects an age difference and a state of dependency.

Having settled upon a certain strategy, a decision may follow about whether the image is intended to represent the distinctive consequences of age or the irrelevance of age. If the former, then the message is clear: because of age (as represented by the image), this (difficulties in hearing or whatever) follows. If the latter, the message is equally clear: despite age (represented now only by such inconsequential signifiers as grey or white hair), this (holidays in the Caribbean or whatever) is still possible.

Whatever the overall strategy, the construction and dissemination of a particular image can have a number of consequences. The intention may be that a section of the population will identify with it and act upon the associated message. What this analysis suggests is that a certain reality is constructed in the image, and people are then persuaded to play the part. An inevitable consequence of this is that the repeated dissemination of a particular kind of image will generate a distinctive vocabulary, and that this inevitably will become the stuff of new stereotypes.

It might be argued that mass campaigns to change popular attitudes and behaviours have to draw upon stereotypes. Success depends upon successful targeting and this depends upon recognising popular beliefs about social identities. The concept of 'stereotypes' may have negative connotations, may be an unacceptable representation of reality, but may yet be part of the grammar of mass communication. Be that as it may, the construction and dissemination of images of age, linked to age-specific target groups, can only promote increased age-consciousness and age-sensitivity and thereby the negative aspects of an ageist culture (Bytheway 1995).

Regardless of whether it is white-haired couples striding up mountains, women in cardigans hanging on to zimmer frames, or 'frail old ladies' being looked after with tender loving care, older people are being set apart as people who are 'different from us'. When we see these images of 'them', when we look in the mirror and see the same signs of age, when we talk – and hear talk – of wrinklies, woopies, or old fogeys, then our future health and well-being is immediately being undermined.

References

Akhurst, R. (1995) *British Freelance Cartoonist's and Illustrator's Course, Tutorial 3*, Weybridge: Morris College of Journalism.

Arber, S. and Ginn, J. (1990) 'The meaning of informal care: gender and the contribution of elderly people', *Ageing and Society* **10**, 4, 429–54.

Bytheway, B. (1995) *Ageism*, Buckingham: Open University Press.

Cole, T.R. (1992) *The Journey of Life: a cultural history of ageing in America*, Cambridge: Cambridge University Press.

Featherstone, M. and Hepworth, M. (1988) 'Ageing and old age: reflections on the postmodern life course', in Bytheway, B., Keil, T., Allatt, P., Bryman, A. (eds) *Becoming and Being Old*, London: Sage.

Featherstone, M. and Hepworth, M. (1990) 'Images of ageing', in Bond, J. and Coleman, P. (eds) *Ageing in Society: an introduction to social gerontology*, London: Sage.

Featherstone, M. and Hepworth, M. (1995) 'Images of positive ageing: a case study of *Retirement Choice* magazine', in Featherstone, M. and Wernick, A. (eds) *Images of Ageing: cultural representations of later life*, London: Routledge.

Goffman, E. (1963) *Stigma: notes on the management of spoiled identity*, Englewood Cliffs, NJ: Prentice Hall.

Hervey, D. (1992) *The Creatures that Time Forgot: photography and disability imagery*, London: Routledge.

Johnson, J. and Bytheway, B. (1997) 'Illustrating care: images of care relationships with older people', in Jamieson, A., Harper, S., Victor, C. (eds) *Critical Approaches to Ageing and Later Life*, Buckingham: Open University Press.

Liddiard, P. and Carver, V. (1978) *An Ageing Population*, London: Hodder and Stoughton.

Macdonald, B. and Rich, C. (1984) *Look Me in the Eye, Old Women: ageing and ageism*, London: The Women's Press.

Morris, J. (1991) *Pride Against Prejudice*, London: The Women's Press.

Öberg, P. (1996) 'The absent body – a social gerontological paradox', *Ageing and Society* **16**, 6, 701–19.

Open University (1995) *An Ageing Society* (K256), audio cassette 5, Milton Keynes: Open University.

Puner, M. (1978) *To the Good Long Life: what we know about growing old*, London: Macmillan.

Sawchuk, K.A. (1995) 'From gloom to boom: age, identity and target marketing', in Featherstone, M. and Wernick, A. (eds) *Images of Ageing: cultural representations of later life*, London: Routledge.

Scarfe, G. (1993) *Scarface*, London: Sinclair-Stevenson.

Sontag, S. (1978) *On Photography*, London: Allen Lane.

Steichen, E. (1955) *The Family of Man*, New York: Museum of Modern Art.

Thompson, P., Itzin, C., Abendstern, M. (1990) *I Don't Feel Old: understanding the experience of later life*, Oxford: Oxford University Press.

Turner, B.S. (1995) 'Ageing and identity: some reflections on the somatization of the self', in Featherstone, M. and Wernick, A. (eds) *Images of Ageing: cultural representations of later life*, London: Routledge.

Williams, R. (1990) *A Protestant Legacy: attitudes to death and illness among older Aberdonians*, Oxford: Clarendon Press.

Woodward, K. (1991) *Ageing and its Discontents: Freud and other fictions*, Bloomington, IN: University of Indiana.

Chapter 14

'Growing old gracefully' as opposed to 'mutton dressed as lamb'

The social construction of recognising older women

Eileen Fairhurst

Changes in physical appearance are part of physical ageing so that as individuals grow older they may lose height or their skin becomes wrinkled. Some men may go bald and some women may develop facial hair. From a physiological standpoint, human ageing is a process whereby a body develops and then declines and the attendant physical changes are explicable in such terms. Thus, loss of height results from atrophy of the discs between spinal vertebrae and skin changes from the disappearance of subcutaneous fat which alters the elasticity of the skin. Such physiological matters tend to be carried over into the realm of the social; growing older is seen as a period of decline.

It is worth noting the evaluative connotations of this term 'decline' for in nature decay is amoral. Indeed, decay can be socially constructed as positive rather than negative so that in the former usage decay may be valued. For instance, meat, especially game, is left to hang before being eaten and vintage port is laid down. Both these practices are intended to improve flavour with age. Identifying these two distinctive notions of decay enables me to suggest that the evaluative connotations of decline which underpin a physiological notion of ageing is using science to warrant a social conception of ageing. The object of these varying definitions of decay is the body and, specifically, how changes in that material mass are interpreted. In this chapter I intend to focus on the ways in which middle-aged men and women portray the implications of physical aspects of growing older and how these are socially constructed. I shall then go on to show how ideas about physical attractiveness are used by these women and men to assess and confer meaning onto their own ageing process.

We do not need to look very far to recognise that a woman's physical appearance may be used to sell newspapers or almost any commodity one cares to name. Nor can we quibble with the notion that society tends to define women in terms of their physical appearance. From this it is a short step to assert that a women's physical appearance is the pivot of her identity *qua* female. Stannard (1977) argues that women's equation with beauty is consciously purveyed by men in an attempt to emphasise women's dependency upon them. Both de Beauvior (1972, cited in Posner 1975) and Sontag (1972) take this relationship between women and physical attractiveness a step further by contending that, since attractiveness is synonymous with youth, growing older is particularly traumatic for women compared with men. Indeed, Sontag refers to the 'double standard of ageing'. Arguably, a more optimistic view of female ageing is offered by Greer (1992). She contends that, as long as women take control of their health by questioning assumed 'truths', then the menopause promises freedom and, thereby, 'serenity and power'. As she exhorts,

> Only when a woman ceases the fretful struggle to *be* beautiful can she turn her gaze outward, find the beautiful and feed upon it. She can at least transcend the body that was what other people principally valued her for, and be set free both from their expectations and her own capitulation to them.
>
> (Greer 1992: 378)

The alleged traumatic repercussions of supposed loss of physical attractiveness with age is especially apparent in some writing on the menopause. The argument goes that, since the menopause signals onset of old age, then those women who endow their physical appearance with importance will have difficulty coping with the menopause. (Oliver 1977; van Keep and Kellerhals 1975).[1]

It is certainly the case that when oestrogen therapy was first marketed in the United States, one of its alleged benefits was its ability to keep women looking young by alleviating or preventing wrinkles. Moreover, a linkage was often made between youth and femininity. Wilson, one of the pioneers of oestrogen therapy, called his book *Feminine Forever* (1966). He and his wife (Wilson and Wilson 1963) called for oestrogen for women from puberty to the grave in order for them to retain their youthful appearance. Since those heady days such claims have been scrutinised by clinicians.

Not only are the effects of oestrogen therapy restricted to control-ling the vasomotor responses such as hot flushes and alleviating vaginal dryness but also much more serious doubts have been raised about use of oestrogen therapy and its association with carcinoma of the breast and endometrium. See, for example, *The Lancet* (1977, 1975) and Dewhurst (1976).

Indeed, there is still no consensus about the relationship between breast cancer and hormone replacement therapy (HRT). A large study began in early 1998 to address this matter. The national breast screening service for women over the age of 50 is being used as the study group.

This focus on HRT as a way of enabling women to 'manage/cope with' the menopause hinges on bodily changes associated with declining ovarian activity. Feminists have argued that, as such, this is a further example of medicalisation of women's health and results in the construction of the menopause as a 'disease' (for an examination of this see Klein and Dumble 1994). The theme of the menopause as 'disease' can be traced back to earlier medical writing. Tilt, the Victorian gynaecologist, called the menopause 'the dodging time' when a constellation of 'diseases of the change of life' were to be expected. In particular they were characterised by 'nervous diseases' which could be controlled by either sedation or blood letting, 'Nature's own sedative' (for two historical exam-inations of the menopause see Fairhurst 1979 and Wilbush 1979).

Although the material on which the chapter is based came from a study of women's experience of the menopause, that is not my main focus here.[2] All I do want to say about that is that the way women interpreted physical feelings was more in terms of their idea about their own normality rather than matters such as supposed loss of physical attractiveness or the menopause signalling old age (see, for example, Fairhurst and Lightup 1981a, 1981b; Fairhurst 1980; Fairhurst and Lightup 1980).

It is perhaps worth pointing out that few women and men had heard about the apparent beneficial effects of oestrogen therapy as a 'youth pill'. Some of those who had used experience of friends who sought oestrogen therapy to retain a youthful appearance as a cautionary tale of going against nature. Such women were claimed to have had nervous breakdowns upon stopping oestrogen therapy.

It would be naive to suggest that the dominant cultural image of women as individuals who should retain their youth is without foundation; after all grey hairs are said to be distinguished on men but women are advised to 'wash the grey away'. A note of sociological caution, however, needs to be injected here. One difficulty with that literature which advances the equation of women and youth is the specific view propounded of the notion of social role. Referring particularly to the way in which some women are portrayed in studies of ageing, Beeson (1975) identifies the structural-functional perspective on role as predominant. She cogently argues that one consequence of this is that dominant social values are mistakenly assumed to be synonymous with subjective experience. Such a view might be called the 'oversocialised conception of women'. As I now go on to show, though women are aware of the linkage of youth with attractiveness, the ways in which they orient to this aspect of cultural knowledge varies according to the meaning they place on growing older.

'Growing old gracefully' as opposed to 'mutton dressed as lamb'

The connection between youth, attractiveness and chronological age is conveyed in the phrases 'growing old gracefully' and 'mutton dressed as lamb'. In the latter, a sharp contrast is made between old age and youth. The metaphor rests on the idea that lamb is a tastier meat than mutton, which is tougher because of age, and the former is more highly valued then the latter. 'Gracefully' is an adjective frequently used in relation to actions and, when applied to growing older, implies the idea of process with an attendant change in action over time. Sociologically these two phrases are typifications used to describe individuals. When people interviewed used these typifications they often went on to relate them to ideas about 'being' or 'acting your age'. In this way, individuals see particular types of action as linked to specific categories. As Atkinson (1973) has argued, age and ageing rather than being 'biological facts' to be confirmed by reference to a birth certificate are socially constructed phenomena. He showed how certain forms of action are taken to be appropriately tied to a particular life stage. Phrases such as 'act your age' convey the idea of action appropriate to a particular life-stage.

All women and men interviewed were aware that at their stage of life the physical manifestation of ageing such as wrinkling of the skin, greying hair or weight changes were likely to occur. The specific ways in which middle-aged individuals attend to these matters are the keys to assigning people to the categories of either 'mutton dressed as lamb' or 'growing old gracefully'. Men and women described as 'mutton dressed as lamb' had hair or clothes inappropriate for their stage of life.

The recognition of 'mutton dressed as lamb' was relatively easy for women and men. A constellation of features constituted 'mutton dressed as lamb' and permutations were selected so that any one description did not tally exactly with another. In this way, 'mutton dressed as lamb' covered a set of family resemblances (Heritage 1981). The presence of any one of inappropriate clothes, hair, make-up or jewellery was sufficient for people to know 'mutton dressed as lamb' when seen.

For this woman, as for many others, emphasis was placed on teenage clothes.

> She usually has those 'pretty, pretty dresses' as I call them – those teenage ones that only teenagers can get away with and she'll have a particularly revolting colour. As I say it's usually a teenage dress which you know is a teenage dress. I mean if you're a proper women you know what sort of clothes suit you and what don't but I think there is nothing worse.

Others were more florid in their descriptions and a number of factors were combined in their description:

> Looking at her face she's in her 50s say or late 40s and she's got a lot of excessive jewellery on and very, very heavy make-up and pencil type skirts and slits and big – high, you know, really big high heels. That to me is mutton dressed as lamb.

Though men were more likely to associate women, than their own sex, with 'mutton dressed as lamb', they did not see concern with physical attractiveness and physical appearance as being the prerogative of women alone. Typically, men did not think it was incumbent upon women to try to look young any more than this was so for men. Indeed, it was beyond their comprehension and a futile exercise for either sex to embark upon such a path. A few men differentiated between themselves and women by stressing that women, but not themselves, should attempt 'to look young'.

Despite the exclusively gender based underpinning of Sontag's (1972) idea of the double standard of ageing, concern with physical appearance may cross-cut gender. There is other research which also leads to a re-examination of this thesis. Hepworth and Featherstone (1982: 53) have indicated that during the 1970s the media 'has helped to push a new, more positive and youthful image of middle age into prominence: one which extols the benefits of body maintenance and care for appearance'. They suggested that the new image of middle age is one whereby 'the battle against ageing . . . becomes a social duty' (ibid.: 95). Though the men in our study did see physical appearance as an issue applicable to themselves, they did not see it as a social duty. Strenuous attempts to retain a youthful appearance warranted derision, encapsulated by the phrase, 'they must be puddled'.[3]

The way in which women and men expressed a concern for physical appearance was in terms of 'making the best of yourself' rather than striving to remain looking youthful and this was applicable to the opposite sex, irrespective of gender. Making the 'best of yourself' called for 'smartness' and adapting the fashion to oneself – dowdiness and Crimplene dresses for women or denims for men were definitely inappropriate. Moreover, making the best of yourself had ramifications for psychological well-being and morale. 'If you look good, you feel good'. To make the 'best of yourself' enabled the identification as 'growing old gracefully'.

Making the 'best of yourself', however, could not be an untrammelled indulgence for ideas existed about the lengths to which it was acceptable to go. It was possible to go 'too far' and to try 'too hard'. Both women and men, but especially the former, pointed to the way their children controlled the limits, beyond which it was acceptable to go. Children were relied upon by parents to adjudicate how well they had made the best of themselves. The acknowledgement of the place of children in identifying the boundaries of 'making the best of yourself' adds to Atkinson's (1973) ideas about 'stages of life'. In contrast to that Parsonian framework on socialisation which theorises it in terms of a one-way process from parents to children, categories of 'stages of life' illuminate the data here. Children call upon typification of appropriate dress for specific life stages in order to inform parents of their transgression of the acceptable.

This taken-for-granted aspect of intergenerational relationships has entered popular culture. A pervasive source of humour in the television programme *Absolutely Fabulous* is the relationship between Edina, 'the ageing hippie', and Saffron, her serious, unfrivolous teenage daughter. It is precisely the reversal of the typification 'acting your age' in the two characters that is the source of so much amusement. Thus, Edina, not her teenage daughter, is the one concerned with 'having fun' and clothes, whereas Saffron is depicted as the serious person unconcerned with typical teenager pursuits.

There is a fine line between 'making the best of yourself' and style of appearance. To err and to end up on the wrong side of the boundary would lead to being seen as 'mutton dressed as lamb'. Colour of a women's hair is potentially problematic in relation to this matter. Dyeing hair is inappropriate but tinting or rinsing (excluding blue rinsing) is acceptable. It is interesting that dyed hair carries the connotation of harshness much more than rinsing or tinting. The subtle distinctions made between dyeing and rinsing are drawn out in this woman's views:

> I had my own hair dyed up to last year but gollywog black − I never had mine like that. Although I was jet black as a little girl, as I got older it went brown so, therefore, it was tinted brown. But you see them with this 'gollywog' black hair and nobody but nobody has gollywog black hair over 40 and I think that looks awful . . . I think you should grow old gracefully but still do the best for yourself.

We can see the way in which she ties colour of hair to a particular phase of life. According to her, people over 40 do not have jet black hair and its presence implies they have gone 'too far'.

The interpretation placed upon hair colour was one area where gender-based distinctions were apparent. Though men followed the distinction between dyeing and rinsing in relation to women and shared the notions of acceptability of rinsing, when referring to their own sex, qualifications came into play. Male attempts to retain hair colour by dyeing was not advocated but it did not warrant necessarily the same dismissal as for women. Dyeing of men's hair was acceptable because it could make them 'feel happy' or 'good'.

That making the 'best of yourself' was an appropriate endeavour suggests that it is not the supposed loss of physical attractiveness *per se* which middle-aged individuals are bothered by but rather seeking to avoid the pejorative connotations of 'mutton dressed as lamb'.

Physical attractiveness and the meaning of growing older

So far I have described what the notions of 'growing old gracefully' and 'mutton dressed as lamb' convey to some middle-aged women and men. I now want to turn to how they identified the consequences of physical attractiveness for the meaning of growing older. When talking about growing older, people clustered their thoughts around three main themes: first, the inevitability of ageing, second, a fear of old age; and third, a separation of the self and the body.[4]

The inevitability of ageing

For most of the people in our study, growing older was an inevitable feature of life. Given that, reference was often made to 'letting nature take its course' when considering physical attractiveness and retention of youth. For these individuals, 'making the best of yourself' provided an opportunity not to interfere in the course of nature but, at the same time, to grow 'old gracefully'. This notion of 'growing old gracefully' may be tinged with an air of resignation (Hepworth and Featherstone 1982) and the acceptance of growing older is captured in this man's reflection: 'I'm generally one of those people who accepts things and I tend to, hope anyway, to look at things practically. I don't have theories about anything. I look at a thing and I say well, that's the situation'. Nevertheless, whilst the man was resigned to growing older, at the same time, he saw himself as normally being a person who 'accepts his lot'.

Prominent as notions were about the inevitability of growing older and its acceptance, they did not serve to totally pervade its experience for individuals often went on to stress that 'you're as old as you feel' or 'it's all in the mind'. Such comments imply a distinction between the mind and the body – a matter which will be returned to subsequently.

In the late 1970s the Health Education Council ran an 'anti-slob' campaign which was specifically directed at middle-aged men. Its emphasis was on keeping healthy by keeping active. An additional benefit was said to be that men would look and feel younger. There is a way which this campaign was part of the attempt to build a new image of middle age which questioned the inevitability of old age (Hepworth and Featherstone 1982). Elements of this campaign appear to have impinged upon some of the men in the study. Thus:

> I don't know whether looking young really worries me. Keeping active yes. I don't worry too much about whether I'm looking older. I don't know whether I've aged a lot in the same way as some people have. I haven't gone bald or anything like that. Of course, perhaps I haven't had a lot of worry. Keeping active and healthy, yes.

This man, and others who expressed similar views, stressed the importance of physical activity for its benefits to health rather than to their appearance. Nor was activity seen as something which would stave off old age for that was inevitable.

Fear of old age

Though growing older had compensations for women and men, the thoughts of being old were disquieting.[5] There was a noticeable difference, however, in the language used by women and men when talking about being old. None of the men identified it as something to be feared but a few women did. Furthermore, all of these women emphasised that they tried to look young. As one women put it when relating an incident at work:

> I was bending down to pick something up and one of the cutters said 'such a body is looking at your back – ogling at you'. So I said, 'that's all right. You can do as much as you want because there won't be much ogling in a bit'. That was my feeling of getting older.

These women were particularly concerned with how their hair looked, controlling their weight and carefully attending to make-up and clothes. They wanted to 'grow old gracefully' rather than be 'mutton dressed as lamb'. It would be difficult to claim from this, however, that their expressed fear of old age was causally connected to loss of physical attractiveness. The matter was not so straightforward. As important as physical attractiveness was to these women, it was not so much its supposed loss which worried them but rather the pictures conjured up by the term 'old age'. These pictures were embedded in their assessments of present or previous life experience which had little to do with physical attractiveness.

The biblical maxim of a lifespan being three score years and ten had a powerful resonance for many women and men. While the attainment of age 50 was perceived as placing them nearer to the end of their allotted lifespan, for the woman who talked about a fear of old age, it had specific significance. Death of a spouse heralded the possibility of a lonely old age. Similarly, earlier memories of a parent looking in the newspaper and noting the death of a contemporary were brought back. The salience of such memories were increased when women realised, upon the death of their own contemporaries, that they were now in a similar stage of life.

One woman's graphic portrayal of her tiredness pervaded her fears about old age.

> I'm very conscious of getting older . . . I don't really want to be old. I'd like to put the clock back to stop at about 40 and stop there because, although I enjoyed the children when they were little, at 40 I was enjoying my job. I was on top of the world. I was full of bounce . . . I'm a bit afraid of it now I'm over 50. I can see 60 coming so close now and I really feel that's very old . . . I can see retirement coming and, although my husband says we'll go round the world and we're going to do all sorts of things, my fear is that by the time we are old enough to do these things, because we haven't got to do jobs, we shan't be young enough to enjoy them . . . I'm a bit afraid that I will deteriorate very quickly when I get older.

She believed her lack of bounce was related to her tiredness which she associated with her menopause:

> I'm a bit afraid that that's [tiredness] going to stay with me and, in fact, increase. I'll get tired and tired. And that really frightens me. I can't bear to think of not being well . . . I don't mind being old if I'm well. I'm frightened of being old and being a drag, being down and being miserable. I don't want to be like that. I'm frightened of being like that.

This women's formulation of her fear of old age rested on her comparisons between her present and previous feelings. She now felt constantly tired and believed this had implications for her future old age. Although she and her husband had made plans for their retirement, she used her current experiences to assess the likely realisation of these plans. She considered that, if she were still tired, she would not be able to enjoy her retirement. In addition, the prospective nature of her view of old age is apparent. Her present feeling of tiredness was employed to trace out a plausible scenario of her old age: a possible increase in tiredness would be accompanied by deterioration and culminate in her identification as 'a drag'.

Separation of the self and the body

I earlier noted references made by women and men to ideas about 'you're as old as you feel' and 'it's all in the mind'. Such phrases embrace the common sense notions we have of growing older being more than a biological matter. Over and above this there were some women and men who made a different linkage between the biological/non-biological split and the meaning of growing older. Such individuals distinguished between the physical body and self: the two were seen as two separate entities.[6]

Lest it be thought I am suggesting that this mind/body separateness refers to distinct ontological entities, let me emphasise that these boundaries are constructed in, and through, language usage. Language is not the conduit for the revelation of the mind. On the contrary, distinctions between mind and body are contextually produced. The earlier reference to Greer's (1992: 378) view of the menopause enabling women to 'transcend their bodies' is of relevance here. From a conventional feminist perspective one might applaud Greer's optimism and exhortations but theoretical problematic issues are raised about mind/body dualism precisely because of the underpinning epistemological view. (For a more explicitly ethnomethodological analysis of women's experiences of bodily changes, emotions and the menopause, see Fairhurst, 1998.)

Those individuals making the distinction in their discourse between the body and the self differentiated between physical alterations in appearance or functioning and the self which was more enduring.[7] Thus, while the body is subject to change with the passing of time, the self, if not totally untouched, is less likely to be affected by such chronological issues. As one man suggested: 'I think you'll find yourself that you reach a stage where you don't grow any older inside. Outside you do but you're perpetually 28 or something or whatever it may be – wherever you stop'.

One ramification of making a distinction between the self and the body in terms of it is 'still me despite physical changes' is that awareness of becoming older rests on the significance attached to specific events. In these instances matters such as episodes of illness; viewing certain events as bench-marks; or the response of others serve to confer meaning onto growing older.

Illness suffered by an individual, especially coronaries by men, reminds them that such illness is often age associated. Heart disease is more common among older than younger individuals. Having ill-health and its relationship to the meaning of growing older may also impinge upon those who do not suffer it. One woman not only pinpointed the shock from her husband's recent accident as accounting for her awareness of growing older but also believed it had 'aged' her ten years.

Just as Roth's (1963) notion of bench-marks has proved useful in the analysis of patient careers so does it have an application to the way people assess their movement towards getting older. In doing so they made comparisons with their own grandparents whom they had always pictured as old. Just as Crawford (1981) reports, though, being a grandparent was not seen as synonymous with being old but being older. For others, reaching the age 50 was in their own words 'a milestone' and many reported upon having birthday parties or receiving more cards than usual to mark this occasion. The extent to which chronological age could be partitioned off from the self is indicated here: 'I feel a young 50 but I don't feel old. I feel as young as I was 20 or 30 years ago . . . I'm glad nobody sent me a card with 50 on it, otherwise I would have felt old'.

Reflection upon previous life was a feature of some men's accounts of growing older. For them, the realisation that 'you are not what you thought you were going to be' acted as a bench-mark for the evaluation of their own path of ageing.

We are all familiar with ideas, upon seeing somebody after some time, about remarks being made like 'I didn't recognise you – you've changed so much'. For those who distinguish between the self and the physical body, physical ageing may be acknowledged but they do not recognise the ageing of the self. Others, however, may not make such distinctions. Incidents may be vividly recounted of an individual's perception not being shared by others as this extract illustrates:

> Young is in the mind not in the body really . . . I think perhaps I mean physical 50. You know the anatomy, the body part, the wrinkles and the lines and losing my teeth which I've only just done and I hate it. I've only just had them out you see. And your hair is going grey. It's still me in here, you know, so when I realise that I'm going grey I think, well, so what? Let it go grey. Don't try and hide it. It's silly . . . but it does affect you, the actual biological growing old. It does. It affects you in weird, funny ways.
>
> One instance actually shocked me rather. We'd been to see my oldest son and his wife. We went to this garden centre and she got me a plant. We went to the counter and there was this young boy behind the counter, well the same age as my youngest son. . . . I asked a question and he answered my daughter-in-law. I felt terrible because it was as if I wasn't there, you know. And of course, I thought well naturally he's not going to look at me. He's going to look at a young girl; but I felt terrible because it was me who asked the question. It was me who wanted the answer and I'm still a person, albeit a 50-year-old person. I am still a person and to be ignored and to be talked and passed over upset me more than I thought it would until you realise that you've lost something, that something's gone. The bloom of youth is gone you know and you've lost it and if you walk about with a young girl you tend to be pushed, well not pushed but mentally pushed out. I understand it, don't get me wrong. I understand it because I've been young and it's happened to me. But when it means that you're the person in the background you cry a little inside because as I said before I am still me inside here. I haven't altered to myself and then you realise that you have altered physically and that upset me, it really did. But on the other hand, another way it doesn't upset me is that when I'm at work and meet men of my age I am talking on the same level because all this jousting, the sexual bit, those sexual overtones have gone now. I don't have to do that anymore. There's no to-ing and fro-ing that there used to be. So that's gone and you find that you can have a conversation with a man it means

exactly what it is – a conversation and you can be friends. So in a way that perhaps compensates.

How individuals make physically available, through their talk, the distinction between the self and the body is demonstrated here. This woman acknowledged the physical trappings of getting older but she did not see herself as growing older. It was only when the garden centre assistant directed his answer to her daughter-in-law rather than to her that the meaning of growing older was brought home to her. In this instance, growing older meant the possibility of being ignored as a person in her own right and being treated as if she were not present. In this way there are parallels with handicapped people's accounts of their talk being deflected via a third person and encapsulated in the phrase, 'Does he take sugar?'

Before concluding, a more general comment on sexuality, gender, physical changes and ageing is warranted. The focus of my study has been solely on heterosexual partners. There is a growing corpus of knowledge on ageing amongst gay males. Pickstone's (1996) examination of this theme suggests that there may be differences between heterosexual and gay males about the interpretation of bodily changes and their relationship to ageing. The store set on retention of physical attractiveness and the importance assigned to its loss conforms more to the conventional wisdom of this being a concern for women rather than men. As Pickstone (1996: 3) notes the idea of 'accelerated ageing' in light of the gay community's 'emphasis on youth' means that 'gay men are considered middle-aged and elderly by other gay men at an earlier age, than heterosexual men in the general community'. Pickstone, however, cautions against an assumed homogeneity of experience by emphasising Bennett and Thompson's (1991) point that, since gay men tend to exist in both a gay community and the wider society, ageing experiences in both worlds require study (cited in Pickstone 1996: 3).

A feature of some studies of HIV has been its implications for the meaning of ageing amongst gay men. Tyson's (1993) ethnography of a Body Positive organisation sheds some light on this matter. He argues that, as a diagnosis of HIV-positive is a life-threatening condition, it poses a 'threat to self'. Tyson demonstrates that, consequently such gay men are confronted with the biographical task of coming to terms with their past and future. In this sense, Atkinson's (1973) idea of a 'normal natural order' to the lifespan cannot be achieved. Such biographical work, however, is not applicable to older men and intravenous drug-users. Interestingly, then, chronological age in terms of number of years lived, its quantity, remains a 'master status' for older gay men.

Conclusion

I have had two purposes in this chapter: to contribute to the debate about gender-located underpinnings of physical attraction and to relate this to how people talk about growing older. My emphasis has been on talk as a topic for analysis in its own right so that the experience of bodily changes, at a particular stage of life, have been situated in language usage.

For the middle-aged individuals studied, the typifications of 'growing old gracefully' and 'mutton dressed as lamb', which connote ideas about changing physical appearance with chronological age, have salience. By pinpointing how women and men orient to these descriptive categories, I have been able to show that physical attractiveness is not the exclusive concern of women. Both women and men believe they should make the 'best of themselves'. I would suggest this has implications for the ways in which gender is claimed to operate. When the orientations of both women and men are sought on the issue of physical attractiveness, a different picture emerges. On the basis of the material presented here the implications of physical attractiveness are not confined only to women. Moreover, examinations of ageing amongst gay males suggests that the relationship between physical attraction and ageing is just as complex amongst homosexuals as heterosexuals.

The uses to which middle-aged individuals may put the ramifications of physical attractiveness is related to the meaning conferred upon growing older. While those women who stressed they tried to keep 'looking young' also feared old age, their articulation of these fears owed little, if anything, to a supposed loss of physical attractiveness. Their expressed fears hinged upon their prospective image of old age. For those women and men who distinguished between their self and body, changes in physical appearance were recognised but the realisation that others did not necessarily share one's view of the self as enduring was problematic. Growing older, though, entailed for most an inevitable matter, part of the natural ordering of a lifetime and, as such, called for acceptance rather than something to be fought against.

Acknowledgements

This chapter is a revised version of a paper originally given at the 1982 BSA Annual Conference. I should like to acknowledge the financial support of Ciba-Geigy and SSRC (grant number HR6156) for this research. Roger Lightup worked with me on the study and I should like to acknowledge his contribution to it.

Notes

1   Although Deutsch (1945) explicitly associated loss of beauty with the menopause she paradoxically argued that beautiful women developed the ability to protect themselves against this supposed loss of physical attractiveness.

2   The purpose of the study was to discern how women, themselves, interpreted physical and other changes which occur in midlife. Tape-recorded, thematic interviews were conducted with two small groups of women: eighteen attending a menopause clinic at a hospital and sixteen 'well women' randomly selected from the age-sex registers of two general practices. The criteria for inclusion in the study were age 50 and married. In order to incorporate the role of significant others in assessments made by women, where appropriate spouses were also interviewed. In all twenty-four men were interviewed. The interviews were conducted separately but concurrently in women's own homes. Although the data do not allow generalisations to be made, I have used them for teaching on Women and Health courses. From the response I have had from women attending these courses, it is apparent that the data do have salience to women's experiences of the 'change of life'.

3   Such notions question the mental stability of men taking this course of action. There is an interesting gender distinction here. A cultural stereotype exists that menopausal women are likely to be mentally unstable and this may be used to account for middle-aged women's actions. In the case of men, however, it would seem that accusations of mental stability rather than being general are much more specific.

4   In identifying these themes I am not suggesting they are mutually exclusive. My use of them is to portray the kind of issues which individuals focus on when seeking to understand growing older.

5   In particular, a feeling of greater confidence with increasing age was noted by both women and men.

6   This distinction between the body and the self is characteristic of western medical practice. See, for example, Manning and Fabrega (1973) and Balogh (1981).

7   Jerrome (1981) also notes this distinction between the self and the body where she notes its implications for the significance of friendship among older women.

References

Atkinson, M.A. (1973) 'Formulating lifetimes: the normally ordered properties of some life cycle properties', unpublished MA (Econ.) thesis, University of Manchester.

Balogh, R.W. (1981) 'Grounding the alienation of self and body: a critical, phenomenological analysis of the patient in western medicine', *Sociology of Health and Illness* **3**, 2, 188–206.

Beeson, D. (1975) 'Women in studies of ageing: a critique and a suggestion', *Social Problems* **23**, 1, 52–8.

Bennett, K. and Thompson, N. (1991) *Accelerated Ageing and More Homosexuality*, Birmingham, NY: Haworth Press.

Crawford, M. (1981), 'Not disengaged: grandparents in literature and reality, an empirical study in role satisfaction', *Sociological Review* **29**, 3, 499–520.

de Beauvoir, S. (1972) 'Joie de vivre: on sexuality and old age', *Harper's Magazine* January.

Deutsch, H. (1945) *The Psychology of Women*, 2 vols, New York: Grune and Strattan.

Dewhurst, C.J. (1976) 'The effects of oestrogen replacement therapy on the risk of cancer during the post-menopausal years', in Campbell, S. (ed.) *The Management of the Menopause and Post-Menopausal Years*, Baltimore, MD: University Park Press.

Fairhurst, E. (1979) 'Historical trends in the management of the climacteric', *Mums' Magazine* 15 July, 21–5.

Fairhurst, E. (1980) *A Preliminary Study of the Meaning of the End of the Reproductive Cycle in Women*, Final Report to the SSRC on grant number HR6156.

Fairhurst, E. (1998) 'Suffering, emotion and pain: towards a sociological understanding', in Carter, B. (ed.) *Dimensions and Perspectives on Pain*, London: Arnold.

Fairhurst, E. and Lightup, R. (1980) 'Being menopausal: women and medical treatment', paper presented to the BSA Medical Sociology Group Conference, York, September.

Fairhurst, E. and Lightup, R. (1981a) 'The notion of normality and the interpretation of physiological events: the case of the menopause', paper presented to the Third International Congress on the Menopause, Ostend, June.

Fairhurst, E. and Lightup, R. (1981b) 'The menopause: trauma on the road to serenity?', paper presented to the *Women in Later Life Conference*, London, June.

Greer, G. (1992) *The Change: women, ageing and the menopause*, New York: Knopf.

Hepworth, M. and Featherstone, M. (1982) *Surviving Middle Age*, Oxford: Blackwell.

Heritage, J. (1981) 'Aspects of the flexibilities of language use', *Sociology* **12**, 1, 79–103.

Jerrome, D. (1981) 'The significance of friendship for women in later life', *Ageing and Society* **1**, 2, 175–97.

Klein, R. and Dumble, L. (1994) 'Disempowering midlife women: the science and politics of hormone replacement therapy (H.R.T.)', *Women's Studies International Forum* **17**, 4, 327–43.

Lancet, The (1975) 'Eternal youth: editorial', *The Lancet* **1**, 1282–3.

Lancet, The (1977) 'Hormone replacement therapy and endometrial cancer: editorial', *The Lancet* 12 March, 577–8.

Manning, P. and Fabrega, H. (1973) 'The experience of self and body: health and illness in the Chipas highlands', in Psathas, G. (ed.) *Phenomenological Sociology*, New York: Wiley.

Oliver, R. (1977) 'Women's hidden agenda: menopause', paper presented to the American Psychological Association 85th Annual Convention, San Francisco, August.

Pickstone, T. (1996) 'The problematics of gay men and ageing', unpublished manuscript, Department of Health Care Studies, Manchester Metropolitan University.

Posner, J. (1975) 'Dirty old women: Buck Brown's cartoons', *Canadian Review of Sociology and Anthropology* **12**, 4, 471–3.

Roth, J. (1963) *Timetables*, Indianapolis, IN: Bobbs-Merrill.

Sontag, S. (1972) 'The double standard of ageing', *Saturday Review*, 23 September, 29–38.

Stannard, U. (1977) 'The mask of beauty', in Gornick, V. and Moran, B. (eds) *Women in Sexist Society*, New York: Basic Books.

Tilt, E. (1883) *The Change of Life in Health and Disease,* Philadelphia: P. Blakiston, Son & Co.

Tyson, P. (1993) 'A study of counselling and support', MPhil thesis, University of Manchester.

Van Keep, P. and Kellerhals, J.M. (1975) 'The ageing women', *Acta Obstetricia et Gynecologica Scandinavica* Supplement 51: 17–27.

Wilbush, J. (1979) 'La menespausie: the birth of a syndrome', *Maturitas* **1**, 145–51.

Wilson, R.A. (1966) *Feminine Forever*, New York: Evans.

Wilson, R.A. and Wilson, T.A. (1963) 'The fate of nontreated menopausal women: a plea for the maintenance of adequate oestrogen from puberty to the grave', *Journal of the American Geriatrics Society* **22**, 183–5.

Chapter 15

The male menopause
Lay accounts and the cultural reconstruction of midlife

Mike Hepworth and Mike Featherstone

The male menopause, along with the associated terms, the menopause and the midlife crisis, has its origins in medical and academic
discourses. All three terms have made their way into popular
discourses with the mass media, in particular since the 1970s,
playing a key role in circulating both expert and lay accounts to
wider publics. In this sense it is possible to regard all three terms
as part of a progressive medicalisation of ageing and intervention
of expertise into everyday life.

Eyebrows are now no longer raised when the male menopause
is cited as an explanation for male behaviour in midlife, nor is the
male menopause the subject of the dismissive humour of twenty
years ago (Hepworth and Featherstone 1982). Over the last two
decades the male menopause has attained a greater legitimacy and
social acceptability, and can be understood as part of a set of terms
drawn upon to diagnose midlife problems. This terminology has
become acceptable within consumer culture and circulates in newspapers, magazines, advice books, radio and television programmes,
government health education literature and, more recently, the
Internet, in which various expert and lay accounts are drawn
together to construct a public discourse.

All three terms occupy an ambiguous space between assumptions
of a 'natural' set of bodily and experiential changes in midlife,
which require little attention, intervention and treatment (seen as
part of 'normal ageing' in which bodily decline should be
approached with stoicism) and the sense that this normal is
somehow pathological, that intervention is necessary if we are to
sustain the plateau of youthful vitality and well-being throughout
the life course. Here the mediation of the consumer marketplace
has become important with the 'you can have it all' philosophy;

a strong individualistic message in which the self, body and sex life are seen as flexible and capable of being refashioned (see Featherstone 1982; Featherstone and Hepworth 1982).

It should be added that this expanding market has been bolstered by the fact that the post-war 'baby-boom' generation is now well into their late forties and fifties and, as a particularly large cohort, has always been able to exercise a significant impact upon the consumer market and cultural change (as was the case in the 1960s with the 'sixties generation'). They are also the first cohort from which significant numbers entered higher education and therefore one would expect this to be the basis for a greater receptivity, not only to the various medicalised and expert definitions of these 'conditions', but also as the basis for the construction of oppositional accounts which circulate in the public sphere (e.g. feminist accounts critical of the medicalisation of the menopause which will be discussed below). These processes along with the emergence of increasing variability and flexibility of working lives, family structures and lifestyles have led to an undermining of the more orderly life course (Castells 1996; Featherstone and Hepworth 1986). We now see greater variability and complexity in the life course with a weakening of universal age-related transitions and status passages within institutional structures such as work and the family. In effect there has been a de-institutionalisation of the life course. Hence there is a greater insecurity and the sense within consumer culture that the life course, like one's lifestyle, should be regarded as less a question of fate and more a matter of individual responsibility and construction (Beck 1992). The middle classes in particular, are part of an expanding market for information from all quarters, about how-to-do-it, how-to-live-it, how-to-avoid-it, and are encouraged to maximise and speed-up, to get more out of life, at the same time as the conditions for achieving these goals are more precarious. For those who are deep into the middle years, the problem-and-solution literature which circulates around conditions such as the menopause, male menopause and midlife crisis, may well gain increasing relevance.

This process of the amplification, legitimation and institutionalisation of a new social problem can be illustrated with reference to the history of the midlife crisis. The term seems to have first been used by Elliot Jacques, a psychologist, in an article 'Death and the mid-life crisis' published in 1965. Its circulation was confined to academic life until the early 1970s, when it was taken up by journalists writing feature articles in the 'quality' press. The term then migrated to tabloid newspapers and magazine articles, along with occasional discussions in television chat shows. An important factor in this process was the emergence of networks of new cultural intermediaries working in the media, who had not only good connections with academic life, but also good international connections, and a sense of the expanding global audience for popularised accounts of intellectual, expert and scientific knowledge. Hence popular books, magazine and newspaper features and television programmes were produced and reworked by journalists, as the concept rapidly moved between the United States, Britain, Germany and other countries. (There are interesting parallels here with the circulation of the term 'postmodernism' in the 1970s and 1980s: see Featherstone 1991). The emergence of various formal and informal networks (more recently bolstered by advances in information technology such as the Internet) means that new information can be transmitted rapidly, both within societies (between various media sectors and market segments) and across them. It is therefore possible to detect a series of ripple or wave effects, as the latest stories are taken up by journalists and cultural intermediaries, whose frame of reference and reference group is constantly being enlarged.

It is possible to understand phenomena such as the midlife crisis through social problems theory. The process of the development of a social problem involves a number of stages. First, the identification, of a particular condition as a social problem by cultural, moral or scientific entrepreneurs. Second, the taking up of the problem by journalists and cultural intermediaries who circulate accounts in the popular media and public sphere as the problem becomes legitimised. Third, the attempts to demand and build institutionalised responses and modes of treatment for the problem. This entails the involvement of government and other agencies to institutionalise the training of professional experts who provide diagnosis and treatment. If this stage has been reached and the condition gains acceptance and legitimacy from the public, the grounds have been laid for the problem or condition to become normalised.

In the case of the midlife crisis the process was less clear cut but it could be seen to be in operation when evidence started to emerge from two sources. First, the appearance of letters in newspaper and magazine agony columns from the wives of middle age men with problems, asking if their husbands' distress was a result of the midlife crisis. This was coupled with the response from agony aunts endorsing and legitimising the condition and suggesting various strategies of treatment. Second, a further stage occurred in the United States when the midlife crisis started to appear as a legitimate condition in course material designed for the training of nurses (for examples of both processes see Featherstone and Hepworth 1986, 1982; Hepworth and Featherstone 1982).

For the process to be fully working, then, we would expect to have evidence from lay accounts that the wider public had accepted and normalised the condition. Such evidence can be found in the letters and interviews with ordinary men and women who use the term, or are searching or considering it as a useful vocabulary of motive. Further evidence was provided by a Gallup poll survey in 1992 which found that over two-thirds of middle-aged men in the UK believed that there was some indefinable phenomenon called the 'midlife crisis'. Furthermore, it stated that over half of the sample thought they had experienced a midlife crisis, or were actually having one, at some point between the ages of 40 and 60 (Neustatter 1996: 80).

Yet when we look more closely at what people mean by the midlife crisis, we find a good deal of confusion, a confusion which is not alleviated by media, academic, expert and medical accounts. Some definitions of the condition present it as a psychological developmental crisis triggered by inbuilt mechanisms in the life course, something which is both universal and occurs at a specific age (e.g. Levinson 1978; and the best-selling *Passages: predictable crises of adult life* by Gail Sheehy 1976). Others present it as a vague catch-all term related to the pressures of modern life and the ageing body. Yet others, and this is particularly true of treatment in the popular media and lay accounts in letters to magazines and newspapers, see it as related to, or indistinguishable from, the male menopause. Hence there is a process of abrupt juxtaposition of the midlife crisis, seen as an existential and psychological crisis of midlife, with concepts such as the male menopause which are seen as much more grounded in biological processes. We therefore find a good deal of blurring between the midlife crisis and male menopause, which draws its impetus from the female menopause. Hence the confusion manifest in lay accounts is by no means surprising when the public is bombarded by conflicting advice from media and medical experts and cultural intermediaries on the one hand, along with proto-social movements and pressure groups (such as the women's movement) in the public sphere, on the other.

This blurring of the boundaries between the terms is furthered by the medical and cultural entrepreneurs who have a stake in the emergence and legitimation of new conditions such as the male menopause. Given the commercialisation of the menopause since the late 1960s with the marketing of hormone replacement therapy (HRT), it is not surprising to find a similar interest in legitimising some form of male menopause, which is equally deserving of treatment. Hence a noticeable gender convergence between accounts of the menopause (feminine) and the male menopause (masculine) can be detected. In 1993, for example, Dr Aubrey Hill, a practising American physician, exemplified the common-sense knowledge of contemporary midlife when he pointed out that the terms 'andropause' (andro = Greek for man) and 'viropause' (vir = Latin for men) are used in association with the word 'pause' precisely 'to acknowledge the similarities of the ageing process in men and women. Many of us in the medical profession have begun to recognise that much of the ageing experience of the two sexes is similar' (Hill 1993: 3). The term is also used by Dr Malcolm Carruthers who runs a Harley Street 'Hormonal Healthcare Centre' in London. Carruthers argues that men experience similar symptoms to the female menopause, and that the 'viropause' can be treated with testosterone hormone replacement therapy (Neustatter 1996: 212; Vines 1993: 136).

At the same time important questions remain to be answered concerning the cultural reconstruction of male midlife and the perception of an experiential female/male convergence. In this chapter we argue that the answer can be found in the phrase that women frequently used in the past to describe the menopause: 'the change'. Explanation of the emergence and legitimisation and convergence of lay accounts of the male 'pause'/'change' from the 1960s to the present day can be found in broader changes in gender relations and the social status of men, and the influence of these changes on what it means to be a man, and in particular an ageing man, in contemporary western society. To borrow from C. Wright Mills (1959), the male menopause is a neat example of the way in which private troubles reflect public issues. For this reason any consideration of the male menopause inevitably requires reference to the history of the menopause as a women's issue and of the 'cultural intersections' (Gullette 1993) between menopause discourse and lay accounts of the male menopause.

Lay accounts do not just come into being or exist 'in themselves', they need modes of articulation and formulation. The gender convergence may exacerbate the sense of unease some men feel in midlife. But the articulation of this sense of unease needs the intervention of discourses and vocabularies of motive, in which experts are able to stitch together vague symptoms into a syndrome. Lay people, whether men or their wives or partners, may first encounter the term from a variety of sources (the media, friends or medical experts) and find the term serves as a useful catch-all concept to 'explain' and legitimise, the unease or problems they experience. In one sense, if it is an authorised and socially legitimatised 'condition' then an individual is given permission to suffer and is deserving of attention and treatment. Hence, as we have already suggested, lay accounts do not exist in a social vacuum but may be regarded as efforts to make sense of complex everyday experiences in terms of various set of images and vocabularies of motive; these are provided by a variety of sources, among which should be included medical experts, academics and a range of cultural intermediaries and journalists working in the media and advertising sectors. This chapter, then, will examine lay accounts of the male menopause in relation to alleged changes in conceptions of feminine and masculine identity and their realisation in the embodied experience of ageing, with a sensitivity to the mediated nature of these accounts.

Menopause/male menopause

The history of the male menopause is part of the history of the social construction and reconstruction of gender and gender relations from the mid-part of the nineteenth century. The concepts 'menopause' and 'male menopause' emerged in tandem in what was essentially a gendered biomedical discourse. The term 'menopause', originating in France, first came into medical usage in the late eighteenth century with the emergence of male medical specialists in 'women's problems' (Wilbush 1979). As a result of developments in a male-dominated medical science, 'menopause' gradually displaced the traditional everyday phrase 'change of life'. The displacement of lay terminology by a new scientific/technical system of classification was part of the trend which began in the eighteenth century of basing social distinctions between men and women on what were perceived to be essentially biological differences between men and women. These distinctions were legitimised, as Stephen Kern (1975) has shown, by the theory of evolution, and the new 'sciences' of humans which included anatomy, physiology and anthropometry or the comparative measurement of the proportions of human bodies. In particular, the increasing dominance of the theory of evolution in scientific thinking and its pervasive influence throughout the second half of the nineteenth century on politics, literature and the arts, and sociology was used to reinforce the patriarchal view already prevalent in western culture that men were destined by nature to assume an active initiatory role in social affairs whilst women were essentially passive and imitative (Dijkstra 1986). Visible 'evidence' to support this construction was provided by the perception of men's bodies as closed, self-contained and strong whilst the bodies of women were open, vulnerable, leaky and messy. In this construction of the 'natural' grounding of gender differentiation the female reproductive system was perceived to be the fundamental source of physical vulnerability and therefore inferiority. Feminine frailty was articulated in terms of the medicalisation of menstruation, pregnancy and the menopause (Martin 1989). In Stephen Kern's words:

> A recurring article of popular belief was that menstruation was the key to female temperament. This chronically bleeding wound was a sign of her unfinished state – a cyclical incapacitation which drained her vital energy and rendered her incapable of handling responsibilities that required uninterrupted health.
>
> (Kern 1975: 97–8)

Throughout the nineteenth century menstruation was regarded as a disease in the dominant strand of biomedical discourse. The female body was seen as a body 'in trouble' (Hughes and Witz 1997), a leaky, messy, bloody, troublesome body which should be confined to the private realm. The leaky body, as Margrit Shildrick has argued, is the body out of control: 'the very sign of fertility, the menses, has been regarded as women's inherent lack of control of the body and, by extension, of the self' (1997: 34). Her internal fluids are not contained within a strong masculine casing and it is perhaps for this reason that corsetry for women has often been portrayed in the form of armour encasing the soft and yielding body within (Kunzle 1982). In the feminist sociology of gender, women are often described as socially constrained through cultural constructions of their reproductive role, as more embodied than men, their bodies under less control. As Shildrick observes, 'sophisticated medical references to hormones, pre-menstrual tension, menopausal irritability ... are ... rooted in an essentialist view of women's bodies and women's nature' (1997: 12). The essentialist construction is one which involves a dualistic dichotomy between woman-body/man-mind. The central role given to reproduction as a bio-logical source of essential difference from the late eighteenth century relegated women to a second-class status. Sexual differentiation in the eighteenth century gave the 'uterus, vagina and above all the ovaries ... enormous consequence in the determination of female behaviour' (Shildrick 1997: 42).

Given the close association in western thinking between menstruation and reproductive femininity, it is hardly surprising that the cessation of menstruation became the most significant point of entry into middle age; what Gullette has described as a 'magic marker' (1997: 98). Walker writes:

> Menstruation is the only tangible evidence that most women have of the continuous cycle of fertility going on within the reproductive system. For most of human history, menstruation has been the only evidence everyone has had of women's reproductive potential.
>
> (Walker 1997: 28)

Yet it is also the case that the close association between men-struation, the menopause and the reproductive and maternal role of women in Victorian society inevitably resulted in a great deal of ambiguity. On the one hand menopause could be seen, especially by women, as a welcome 'change', as a positive biological process bringing in freedom, in an age before effective contraception, from debilitating childbirth and 'the curse' of menstruation. On the other hand the menopause could be seen as the first stage of the period of decline leading up to old age, a stage in life which was regarded in the Victorian period, as it is at the present time, as at best highly ambiguous. Ironically the menopause signalled the end of one disruptive bodily leakage only to replace it with another 'obscenity' (Nead 1992), the aged female body in a state of irreversible physi-cal dissolution resulting in the blurred lineaments of the femininity idealised in the artistic imaginings of the sanitised female nude. Such negative images existed in a state of tension with a series of much more positive images of old age as a highly desirable condition for those women who lived through the menopause, classic examples being the 'matron' and the grandmother or 'grannie' (Blaikie and

Hepworth 1997). In her sociological analysis of medical metaphors for menstruation and the menopause Emily Martin has noted that some nineteenth-century commentators 'regarded the period after menopause far more positively than it is being seen medically in our century, as a period of enhanced physical vigour and social renewal' (Martin 1989: 35; see also Featherstone and Hepworth 1985a, 1985b). It is the element of ambiguity inherent in cultural representations of ageing which contribute to the construction/reconstruction of both female and male midlife as a period of uncertainty and anxiety and generate the quest for meaningful accounts.

Although the ambiguities surrounding the menopause also extended to male middle age it is generally agreed that men had much less to lose in terms of social status as they grew older. In contrast to the weaker and more vulnerable feminine body, the site of transient beauty and sexual allure, the ideal male body was conceptualised as unitary, physically strong and slow to age: designed through the evolutionary process to cope with a lifetime's battle for survival in the public sphere. Because male bodies were seen as relatively unproblematic, untroubled by the host of disorders the female reproductive system was heir to, there was an absence of biomedical interest in the male reproductive system which was regarded until recently as an uncomplicated procreative force (Pfeffer 1985). Because of the inherent instability and vulnerability of the female reproductive system, and in particular the cessation of the ability to produce children in middle age, women were considered to age earlier than men, who did not lose their virility until well into old age. Whilst the ageing body in both genders was seen to be a body in decline, the menopause was widely regarded as the cause of an earlier decline in women than men. The ageing of men tended therefore to be considered much less problematic and as a consequence ageing male bodies tended not to be associated with powerlessness and decline. The visible signs of ageing in men – a tendency to put on weight around the abdomen, thinning hair, wrinkling skin – were less readily perceived as socially undesirable and often regarded, particularly in men of good social standing, as the signs of 'maturity', stability and achievement. The ridicule to which ageing men were sometimes exposed was tempered by respect for their power.

It is not surprising, therefore, that the discovery of hormones reinforced the dualistic biomedical model which separates out the female body from society and culture and defines the menopause in terms of 'natural' hormonal change. During the 1920s and 1930s 'oestrogen was established as a female sex hormone, it was none-theless *ovarian* oestrogen that became the quintessentially female hormone' (Wei Leng 1996: 33). According to this biomedical logic ovarian oestrogen was 'normal' and its absence, caused by the biomedical processes of ageing, was abnormal or pathological – a deficiency that should if possible be remedied.

But, as we have previously noted, underlying the dualistic model of female and male middle age as essentially different are signs of ambiguity, of a sense that female and male ageing are not neces-sarily as divergent as was imagined. Even during the Victorian period, the dominant model of divergence between women and men in middle age intersected with an alternative model of conver-gence. In her analysis of the cultural construction of midlife from the late nineteenth century through to the 1920s and 1930s, Gullette (1993) has shown how the concept of the menopause as the onset of decline in women is closely linked with the belief that a parallel decline can be detected and expected in the midlives of men. In the 1920s and 1930s popular guides to science and medicine associated hormonal change with physical decline in both women and men, a cultural convergence she describes as 'gender symmetry' (1993: 21). Both genders were regarded as subject to the influence of the hormonal body although in the case of men these processes were seen to be perhaps less transparent. In fiction it is no accident that Sir Arthur Conan Doyle's Sherlock Holmes story, 'The Creeping Man', first published in 1927, is about a distinguished professor who at the age of 61 falls in love with a young woman and injects himself with an anthropoid serum in an attempt to regain his youthful virility. The consequences, as the title indicates, are disastrous for the professor, who is biomedically transformed into an ape-like being:

> The real source lies, of course, in that untimely love affair which gave our impetuous Professor the idea that he could only gain his wish by turning himself into a younger man. When one tries to rise above Nature one is liable to fall below it. The highest type of man may revert to the animal if he leaves the straight road of destiny.
>
> (Conan Doyle 1965: 183)

The emergence of the belief that the ageing process produced a diminution of sex hormones in *both* women and men was, as

Conan Doyle's story suggests, commonplace in the fiction of the day. And hormonal decline was held accountable for physical and mental decline.

> One of the most striking phenomena is that literature ...
> began with some frequency to age its main characters into the
> middle years and beyond. ... Suddenly a host of characters
> in their forties or fifties or in some vague middle age began
> to appear and simultaneously decay. Many of the most striking
> and ultimately canonical of these were about men.
>
> (Gullette 1993: 27)

In addition to a 'host of popular novels', Gullette (1993: 27) cites examples from 'high' fiction which include Oscar Wilde's *Portrait of Dorian Gray* (1891); Henry James's *The Ambassadors* (1904); Thomas Mann's *Death in Venice* (trans. 1911); F. Scott Fitzgerald's *Tender is the Night* (1934); and Evelyn Waugh's *Brideshead Revisited* (1944). Gullette describes the cultural processes involved in the construction of the decline model of middle age as 'a kind of unconscious collaborative effort' which was 'constructing an imagined life course for men' (1993: 27). The novels bestowing 'subjective content' on the biomedical manuals of the day (ibid.: 28). Such images represent one strand of the intersecting cultural resource from which lay concepts of the male menopause are derived.

Nineteenth- and early-twentieth-century thinking on the menopause and the male menopause does not, therefore, reflect an uncomplicated binary distinction between male and female ageing but is a complex cultural construction reflecting divergent/ convergent notions of male and female ageing. Originating in the increasing interest in the ageing process in the Victorian period, the balance between convergence/divergence gradually began to swing towards the convergence which is regarded as characteristic of contemporary concepts of the male menopause. This shift in emphasis reflects, as we indicated earlier, changes in the status of men and women and in gender relations which have become more salient since the 1970s, and the development of a feminist critique of the divergent hormonal model of the menopause.

Feminist critics of the biomedical model urged the importance of cultural influences in constructing the female body in decline and the value of the subjective perspective as an important tool for rescuing women from the oppression of male science. In her highly successful handbook, *Women's Experience of Sex*, Sheila Kitzinger (1985) confronted the 'bad press' given to the menopause and advocated a women-centred approach which reflected the diversity of subjective experiences of 'the change'. A few years later Germaine Greer (1991) published a robust critique of the discourse of menopausal decline and a defence of the positive quality of a post-menopausal life freed from the tyranny of the reproductive body. Even more recently, developments in the 'discursive approach' as used, for example, by Yardley to designate 'the socially and linguistically mediated nature of human experience' (1997: 1) have sharpened the sociological critique of the biomedical nature of the menopause.

According to this perspective, biological changes such as the cessation of menstruation cannot be ignored because they are an integral feature of the material life – the condition of embodiment – but biology does not have an existence independent from human social and cultural activities. The 'material-discursive' (Yardley 1997) perspective regards embodied existence, the biomedical, as an 'intrinsic and vital part of the shared socio-cultural experience upon which our systems of language and reality are based' (Yardley 1997: 9). Thus the biological changes which occur in the body can be apprehended only within the cultural framework that exists to give them meaning. Stories of the menopause and male menopause are examples of the resources available to individuals to articulate and explain their experiences – physical and emotional – to other people. The menopause, as a signpost of feminine middle age, requires a prior conception of the life course as having a beginning, a middle and an end. This story of the human life of 'three score years and seven' comes to human beings ready-made with a series of sub-divisions or 'stages' all of which have their 'entrances and their exits'. Whilst the basis for the model of the 'ages of man' and the complementary 'ages of woman' is clearly biological (birth, infancy, childhood, youth, adulthood, middle adulthood, old age, death), their cultural elaboration is indispensable to an understanding of the meaning of the human life course. In Yardley's words:

> discourse analysis does not deny the scientific analysis of physiological functioning – it simply emphasises that biomedical entities are not simple facts, since the definition, character, meaning, and implications of these phenomena are fundamentally shaped by socio-cultural practices and preoccupations.
> (Yardley 1997: 9)

An excellent example of the interplay between the biological, the cultural, and social is found in Philipa Rothfield's (1997) analysis of 'menopausal embodiment'. Grounding her observations in her own experience of pregnancy – both pregnancy and menopause are 'culturally and biomedically defined in relation to notions of reproductive femininity' (1997: 35) – Rothfield describes the menopause as indisputably 'body-centred' by which she means 'one of those experiences *seen* to be of the body' (ibid.: 49, n. 2) as distinct from those things which are, in dualistic thinking, seen to be things of the mind. Adopting the phenomenological approach of Merleau-Ponty, she rejects the dualistic thinking which posits an essential separation between body and mind (hormones and psychological experience) and sets out to bring the two together in a processual conceptual framework which emphasises the flexibility and variability of experience. Whilst the menopause is an inevitable biological change for most of the women in the world who live long enough, it is not a universal experience with unified social and subjective meanings. The wide variations and ambiguities which exist are explained by the 'lived character' of hormonal changes (Rothfield 1997: 34).

Rothfield poses a number of phenomenological questions, two of which are particularly relevant to our discussion of the social construction of the male menopause: how do we come to know a condition such as menopause? Who is in a position to know? She asks:

> If we have a set of bodily experiences, when can we say that they are due to hormonal activities rather than something else? That is, when can an experience be attributed to hormonal causes? How do we know about menopause?
>
> (Rothfield 1997: 35)

Like Gullette, Rothfield regards the biomedical prioritisation of physical change as an appropriation of experience and subordination of women to science. A misleading imbalance of conceptual powers which results in an inadequate interpretation of the nature of the ageing process: 'A phenomenological perspective on menopause would refuse to polarise the physical and the psychological' (Rothfield 1997: 42). But unlike Gullette, Rothfield's critique refuses to prioritise the cultural: it is not a question of biology or culture, but biology *and* culture. Whilst hormonal activity is an integral and inescapable part of embodied experience, it does not necessarily cause the wide range of subjective and social experiences associated with the menopause. For the biological is essentially 'open-ended': open, that is, to a wide range of inter-pretations and meanings.

Accounting for the male menopause

Following the lines of analysis outlined above, it is not surprising to discover that there can never be only one story of menopause, one final authoritative version. What we do find are individualised stories of the menopause, shaped by historical and cultural forces and exhibiting certain social patterns, yet open to continuous rein-terpretation and reconstruction. We have seen that the 'materialist discourse'/phenomenological critique of the biomedical model of the menopause argues for an 'open-ended' model of biology. Attempts to understand the menopause do not require a decision in favour of *either* biology *or* culture. The issue is one of meaning and experience: 'the lived body'. But how do we know the body?

Any consideration of embodiment – the lived body – requires a look at the conceptualisation of external and internal states. For women the existence of biological change provided a basis on which to attribute alterations in emotional experience and behav-iour to biological changes taking place internally in the body. Because there is only the slightest evidence of comparable internal change in men, changes in emotions and behaviour are more easily attributable to external factors. But the task of the feminist critique has been to establish an external cause for the personal problems associated with the menopause, a line of thought which has opened up the cultural space for the accreditation of the male menopause. The more it is accepted that women's problems in midlife can be attributed to social and cultural factors, the more likely it is that male menopause will increase in credibility. To this can be added changing socio-economic pressures which are altering gender rela-tions and the concept of what it is to be a male and the increasing acceptance in an ageing society of the social construction of ageing/old age.

If we accept the validity of the sociological critique of the concep-tual weaknesses of a privileged biomedical model of the menopause then the absence of unambiguous biomedical evidence in favour of the existence of the male menopause ceases to be problematic. It is no longer a case of restricting the quest for evidence of hormonal changes *within* the physical body of the male but of looking at lay accounts of the lived experience of midlife for evidence of the changing experiences of midlife and their sources in contemporary society. Whilst biomedical interventions in the human body have a significant part to play in the cultural construction/reconstruction of the ageing process, it is essential to develop an understanding of these processes by way of a phenomenological perspective which attempts to explicate the interplay between body, self and society.

Our interest in the sociology of the male menopause began in the early 1970s when the first signs of a public interest in midlife were beginning to emerge in the UK. As part of our analysis of changing images of ageing we collected accounts of the male menopause from a number of non-biomedical sources: interviews with men and women 'in' midlife, accounts of the popular media, and fictional accounts which we juxtaposed with accounts in the biomedical and other professional literature. We also attended and presented papers at several international conferences on midlife and the menopause where we charted the outlines of a social constructionist approach to middle age as an emergent stage of life in the contemporary life course. We were particularly interested in looking for evidence of the intersections between lay and professional accounts in the social construction of midlife and in the role of consumer culture on the social construction of midlife (Featherstone and Hepworth 1985a, 1985b, 1982; Featherstone 1982; Hepworth and Featherstone 1982).

One of the key features of lay accounts of the male menopause is the sense of uncertainty they express concerning the body and the experience of ageing. Characteristically they are expressions of doubt and a quest for meaning. Research into lay accounts/theories of midlife tends to show that 'lay theorising has to accommodate both individual difference and exceptions to the rule' (Cunningham-Burley and Milburn 1995: 21). In-depth research in Scotland into health promotion in middle age amongst a group of men and women aged 45–59 indicates that the middle years are typically viewed as 'a period of uncertainty' (Cunningham-Burley and Milburn 1995: 1). Accounts of middle age display 'the dual process of certainty and uncertainty, constraints and control' underlying descriptions of health and illness. There is an awareness of the increasing possibility of sudden change in midlife and also of 'individual variation of the life course, such that generalisations are inappropriate and always subject to modification or rejection' (Cunningham–Burley and Milburn 1995: 5). Support for individualised accounts of the experience of midlife does not, however, require a total rejection of the broader cultural view that middle age is marked by the onset of a decline that challenges self-identity. Whilst, on the one hand, middle age is seen by male and female interviewees as essentially different and more difficult for women because of the menopause, there is, on the other hand, support for the notion that a convergence is taking place between the experiences of women and men:

> generalised statements tended to reflect . . . convergence of experience between men and women. There were two elements in this: ageing was a ubiquitous process affecting both men and women; respondents also identified elements of cultural change which led to a levelling of experience between men and women.
>
> (Cunningham–Burley and Milburn 1995: 21)

The impact of ageing tends to be seen as unrelated to gender. In particular convergence is seen as especially significant for the relationships between work and domestic roles. Yet at the same time the menopause is still seen by this group as the biological source of gender distinction in midlife. Amidst the uncertainties and vicissitudes surrounding the middle years, the menopause is seen as 'a biological certainty' (Cunningham–Burley and Milburn 1995: 27) and although it is occasionally mentioned by some women, the men in this study make no reference to the male menopause.

There is therefore considerable evidence of doubt in lay accounts concerning the nature and status of the male menopause. Whilst the recurring question in lay accounts is: 'Does the male menopause exist?' (*The Times* 11 January 1996) this is coupled with an absence of embarrassment in using the label and a sense that it describes a range of significant experiences. Although popular commentaries on the male menopause may be written with tongue in cheek (*Daily Record* 4 May 1994: 21) they all display an underlying sense of unease and concern. When questioned about the upsurge of interest in novels about male writers suffering from middle-aged anxiety, the novelist David Lodge, author of a novel on the male menopause, *Therapy* (1995), equated an interest in self-doubt with a general sense of social unease in Britain in the 1990s and the absence of the feel-good factor (Roberts 1995: 28).

In 1994 Sally Vincent, writing in the *Guardian Weekend*, asked rhetorically: 'Is there a male menopause?':

> Britain's leading agony uncle, Philip Hodson, has noticed that requests for his impotence leaflet outnumbered those for other male problems by ten to one. This might be a matter of the anxious man, like the bad workman blaming his tool, but it does suggest that something epidemic is afoot.
>
> (Vincent 1994: 20)

The question 'Is there a male menopause?' has been asked repeatedly over the last twenty years and provides evidence of a close interaction between the media and the age group 40–65. As the author Malcolm Bradbury observed in the *Sunday Times* in 1995, the male menopause is not new but the idea that middle age is psychologically significant 'seems to be growing speedily in general current' (1995: 8). He also referred to 'the borrowed menopause', stating in reference to gender issues that 'male problems are as meaningful as female' (ibid.).

Correspondents continue to write to newspaper agony aunts with the question 'Is there such a thing as the male menopause?' (*Daily Record* 9 January 1995). In 1995 the magazine for the 50+ age group, *O50*, reported 'a wave of interest in men's attitudes to physical, sexual and emotional well-being' (Davidson 1995: 32) and the male menopause as 'the experience of crisis can be real enough' (1995: 32). The years 45–60 produce a real sense of vulnerability in men and an awareness of health and other problems.

In 1993 Gail Sheehy's long article 'The unspeakable passage: is there a male menopause?', summarised the dilemma:

> menopause is actually a misnomer when applied to men. Their reproductive glands do not all shut down around that same age the way women's do. What happens to men is more gradual than menopause, and not universal. It also has nothing to do with fertility: a healthy proportion of men continue to have sufficient sperm to sire children well into old age. But although it isn't strictly a menopause, many older men do experience a lapse in virility that is not due entirely to the natural process of ageing.
>
> (Sheehy 1993: 72)

This pronouncement raises a number of pertinent questions. First, the problem of gradualness and point of entry: one of the key difficulties facing researchers into the menopause is that of determining with any accuracy the precise point at which it begins. Second, the male fertility question assumes a detailed knowledge of the male reproductive system which some critics (Pfeffer 1985) argue is absent. In Sheehy's view (and she writes as one of the most influential popular western writers on midlife), there is little positive biological evidence to support the existence of the male menopause but there is plenty of evidence that it is a lived experience of male midlife. It is, like the menopause, often described as a 'silent crisis': a series of experiences in search of a vocabulary. And the quest, as Gullette has observed, usually terminates in the language and imagery through which ageing is given meaning. Sheehy (1993: 118) goes on to ask if the cause of male menopause is not basically the ageing process which she describes as 'simply all the insults to the body that accrue with ageing'.

Published in an expensive glossy magazine, Sheehy's article is only one of several indications that analysis of the male menopause cannot take place outside the context of a society in which ageing into old age is perceived as problematic and in which relationships between men and women are undergoing significant changes. Contemporary discourses of menopausal man are an integral feature of the broader history of the ageing process. Biological ageing is accompanied by changes in social categorisation which have implications for the experience of self.

In September 1984 Scotland's most popular Sunday paper, the *Sunday Post*, described the 'awkward age' of men as the 'male menopause'. The advice column stressed that the symptoms can 'mimic the ailments many women suffer as they go through the awkward age – hot flushes, dizzy spells, chest pain, anxiety, headaches and loss of appetite'. The article also stressed that the male menopause was a 'problem of our modern age and that grandfather would not have recognised a midlife crisis if he'd met it walking down the street' (30 September 1984).

In the same year the magazine *Family Living* carried a feature article, 'Living with a menopausal male'. It described the typical problems as described above as a modern problem: 'We may have only put a name to it around 15 years ago, but we have always suffered from "midlife crisis"'. It's possibly more obvious than ever before, partly because we now recognise it for what it is'.

Both these articles agree that the term 'male menopause' is an appropriate one for defining the problems associated with male midlife and they also agree that it is a modern problem, related somehow to socio-economic change.

Convergence

During the ensuing period – from around 1985 to the present day – there are clear signs, as noted from the outset, that the discourse of the male menopause has been socially legitimised. There are also clear signs that the move towards convergence between the menopause and the male menopause, which is one strand in the cultural construction of midlife, has latterly become more salient. In his history of middle age in Britain in the twentieth century, Benson (1997) detects a gradual diminution of nineteenth-century discrimination between gender and class in attitudes towards middle age. Middle age during the twentieth century has, he argues, been subject to a process of homogenisation; it is increasingly associated with physical decay and the possibilities of combating and delaying decay in all social classes and in women and men alike. Benson detects a move towards what the *Guardian* (Vincent 1994) describes as a 'genderless' middle age.

In her work in the United States, Gullette has taken a similar line in the cultural analysis of the associations that are made between middle age and physical and psychological decline in recent times. She, too, argues that 'women and men are converging in their middle years' (1997: 139), locating the source of this change in the current tendency towards greater instability in the employment prospects of men aged 50+ which are ironically forcing them into the kind of retreat into the private sphere formerly reserved for women. As in the case of women in the past, men now look increasingly towards their private lives as a source of emotional support and self-validation. 'It is precisely . . . in the world of love and sexuality that the system exacerbates their "problem", offers men an explanation and a solution: "ageing" and its alleged anti-dotes' (Gullette 1997: 147).

Evidence of this change is found in the proliferation of midlife stories in fictional and non-fictional literature, and in cinema, TV and video. As we observed during the late 1970s, the proliferation and these images has been so great that terms like 'menopause', 'male menopause' and 'midlife crisis' rapidly passed into popular usage and became a characteristic shorthand term in lay accounts for denoting a wide range of experiences, especially a sense that life was in some way on the decline, during what are still loosely described as 'the middle years' (see Featherstone and Hepworth 1986, 1985a, 1985b, 1982). In Gullette's words: 'By now, midlife horror can be captured, in a poem, a scene, a single sentence – even a phrase. One of the best proofs that decline is dominant is that its most truncated shorthand is now meaningful' (1997: 163).

The essential point of Gullette's book is that convergence between female and male accounts is around an emphasis on the shared difficulties caused by the ageing body; the potential to entrap both men and women in a discourse of decline which is essentially ageist. But attempts to reconstruct the sexist boundary between male and female middle age will not do either gender any favours if the end result is to reinforce the view that ageing into old age is socially unacceptable and should be resisted to the end. The key problem for Gullette is what she regards as the predominantly negative influence of consumer culture. In the late 1990s she detects the persistence of a dangerous tendency towards consumer-oriented individualism and the prescription of remedies of ageing in the 'private sector of body control' (1997: 147). Whilst the ageing of the population and gender convergence offer an opportunity for a reconstruction of mid- and later life as a positive phase of the life course there is the ever-present danger that consumer culture will reinforce the stigma of ageing in the stimulation of the desire to promote youthfulness and the rejection of old age. For Gullette this process entails a movement from external cultural to internal subjective consciousness and a movement away from the feminist promise of social reconstruction towards the biomedical modification of the body. The desire to feel young is effectively internalised and expressed in terms of the 'entrance' into midlife as awareness of the onset of age as a profoundly unwelcome experience. The proliferation of stories about entrance (menopause, male menopause, midlife crisis) involves a 'confession of an internal event: that moment when a subject is forced to "recognise" simultaneously that he [*sic*] has suffered a loss and that this is what "no-longer-being-young" means' (Gullette 1997: 165), and it is at this point that convergence ceases to be cultural and reverts back to the biomedical model.

The parallel between the menopause as the cessation of reproductive productivity and the decline of productivity and their association with loss of meaning in a man is significant. The 'factory' metaphor detected in Emily Martin's (1989) analysis of the language of menopause is relevant here. The biological body is linked to society through the convergence of masculine and feminine productivity. Just as the menopausal woman is the non-producer of children so the menopausal man is a non-producer at work and in his sexual and social relationships. He has withdrawn into the non-productive world of self-involved disengagement. But to add to the ambiguities of midlife, the metaphor of biological decline at least provides for some individuals a justification for social disengagement. Specifically, it promises the relief of biomedical treatment. The words 'andropause' and 'viropause' reflect the search for a biomedical cause of social disengagement. There is an ironic turning of the tables here. Men, who invented the term menopause, medicalised it and allegedly imposed it on women (Greer 1991), are now looking for solutions to the problems of midlife in the chemical manipulation of their internal secretions and other forms of body modification.

The notion of hormone replacement for men further reinforces the view that the male menopause is a sexual issue: a problem of libido and its hormonal nature. Boost up the libido and all will be well. It has been argued that research suggests that injections of testosterone may provide some relief from osteoporosis and diminishing muscle strength. Asking the familiar question about the male menopause in *The Times* (11 January 1996), John Laurence used the term 'andropause' to distinguish the masculine condition from the menopause. Pointing to evidence of emotional difficulties experienced by men in midlife, he reported that 'the medical establishment now accepts that men, like women, undergo a menopause'. He described the advent of hormone supplement therapy for men in the shape of the 'Androderm patch' and the view that there was an increasing demand for it. His description is not without interest: 'Men with dead-end jobs or dull marriages may seek release from humdrum lives through a treatment already described as an elixir of youth'. A year earlier, the *Sunday Times* medical correspondent, Lois Rogers, had reported that hormone patches would be following American precedent and coming to Britain in 1996. Again, her juxtaposition of men and women is interesting: 'Advocates say the extra hormone dose from the patches, to be marketed under the name Androderm, will enable tired 50-year olds to keep pace with their HRT powered wives'.

Interestingly, this 'speed up' image is also evident in the representations of women under a 'natural' menopause without recourse to HRT. Gail Sheehy in her best-seller *The Silent Passage* (1995: 46), after giving a qualified 'yes' to the question 'is there a male menopause?' quotes Dr Penti Sitteri, co-director of the Reproductive Endocrinology Center at the University of California, San Francisco, as saying 'Sooner or later . . . virtually *all* men will have a male menopause'. But for their wives, the menopausal decline in oestrogen levels has the compensation of raising the ratio of testosterone to oestrogen, which according to Sheehy provides a biological basis to explain 'the widespread phenomenon of postmenopausal zest and the greater assertiveness recorded, cross-culturally, among postmenopausal women' (1995: 46). The message is clear: with or without HRT, post-menopausal women will experience a new 'zest' and assertiveness which puts pressure on their middle-aged male partners to keep up.

All of which brings us back to the problem of the nature of 'the change' for men. As Jeff Hearn (1995) has shown, the status of men has undergone a number of significant changes during the 1980s and 1990s. Amongst these he includes a gradual shift in the traditional sources of men's power in the physical strength of the body, patriarchal power over family life, changes in occupational structure which shift power towards the state, and industrial and commercial organisations which tend to be dominated by younger men. In addition to these negative influences on the traditional sources of male empowerment, there are what in some quarters are regarded as more positive trends towards the emergence of a relatively privileged generation of occupational pensioners whose tastes are catered for by consumer culture. For an advantaged and increasingly conspicuous minority there are the compensations of the power to purchase and to command goods and services in the retirement industry. There is therefore increasingly structural evidence that men in midlife are positioned between intersecting and conflicting social forces which destabilise the traditional 'ages of man' and create new hopes and fears. An important aspect of this process is the shift from physical to mental labour in a free market bringing a transition from ownership of the body to ownership of the mind. The experience of 'what it is to be a man' is changing in response to these pressures which are inevitably variable in their influence and ambiguous in their implications. In the words of Jeff Hearn the result is that men's power can be understood in a number of 'aged' ways. This may help to explain why age has such a contradictory significance for men. It may imply power at a common-sense, even emotional level, even though this is only part of the picture. The important issue is that age is constructed as a maker of power, or as a reference point of power, even when power is lacking.

(Hearn 1995: 102)

It is our contention that the experiences associated with the male menopause arise out of the ambiguities that now surround the male identity in western society; until recent times age has been 'a major source of power for men in this and many other societies' (Hearn 1995: 100). But, as we have noted, the situation is changing and these changes provide valuable evidence in support of the constructionist approach to ageing. In particular it affords insight into what Gullette (1997) has described as the 'cultural intersections' which constitute contemporary images of midlife and attitudes towards middle age. The most salient intersections include feminist critique of the biomedical model of the menopause, recent developments in the sociological analysis of the social construction of masculinity and femininity, and the increasing interest in the issue of 'embodiment' amongst sociologists of the body. As a significant element of changing attitudes to ageing, the male menopause is framed within the sociological analysis of the social construction of gender and the role of culture in shaping the lived experience of growing older in contemporary society. A number of recent authors have remarked on the absence of sociological analysis of male experiences of ageing (Benson 1997; Hearn 1995).

This chapter, which has been developed from previous comparative analyses of the histories of the menopause and male menopause, represents an attempt to highlight the cultural intersections which find subjective expression in lay accounts of distressing experiences during what are loosely defined as 'the middle years'. Indeed, it is our contention that the cultural imagery of the male menopause represents an effort to articulate a growing sense of awareness of the changing roles of men and relations between men and women. The historical development of the male menopause is culturally inseparable from the menopause. The two concepts emerged in tandem during the latter half of the nineteenth century in what was essentially a biomedical discourse. As biomedical accounts by 'experts' of the reasons for male difficulties in midlife these stories displayed contradictory tendencies towards convergence and divergence which continue to be evident in the present day. Because of the interplay between lay accounts of the embodied experience of the male menopause and those of the experts, along with the various representations of these accounts produced by journalists and cultural intermediaries in the popular media, it is not surprising to find that they reveal the tensions of the convergence and divergence to be found in the wider culture.

References

Beck, U. (1992) *The Risk Society*, London: Sage.

Benson, J. (1997) *Prime Time: the middle aged in twentieth century Britain*, London: Longman.

Blaikie, A. and Hepworth, M. (1997) 'Representations of old age in painting and photography', in Jamieson, A., Harper, S., Victor, C. (eds) *Critical Approaches to Ageing and Later Life*, Buckingham: Open University Press.

Bradbury, M. (1995) 'Stuck in the middle', *Sunday Times Culture* 9 April: 8–9.

Castells, M. (1996) *The Rise of the Network Society*, Oxford: Blackwell.

Conan Doyle, A. (1965 [1927]) 'The creeping man', in *The Case Book of Sherlock Holmes*, Harmondsworth: Penguin.

Cunningham-Burley, S. and Milburn, K. (1995) *Health Promotion and Middle Age*, Edinburgh: final report to Health Services and Public Health Research Committee, grant no. K/OPR/2/2/D64.

Davidson, N. (1995) 'Men, myths and mid-life', *O50* summer, 27: 32–5.

Dijkstra, B. (1986) *Idols of Perversity: fantasies of feminine evil in Fin-de-Siecle culture*, New York and Oxford: Oxford University Press.

Featherstone, M. (1982) 'The body in consumer culture', *Theory, Culture and Society* 1, 2, 18–33. Reprinted in Featherstone, M., Hepworth, M., Turner, B.S. (eds) (1991) *The Body: social process and cultural theory*, London: Sage.

Featherstone, M. (1991) *Consumer Culture and Postmodernism*, London: Sage.

Featherstone, M. and Hepworth, M. (1982) 'Ageing and inequality: consumer culture and the new middle age', in Robbins, D., Caldwell, C., Day, G., Jones, K., Rose, H. (eds) *Rethinking Social Inequality*, Aldershot: Gower.

Featherstone, M. and Hepworth, M. (1985a) 'The male menopause: lifestyle and sexuality', *Maturitas* 7, 235–46.

Featherstone, M. and Hepworth, M. (1985b) 'The history of the male menopause 1948–1936', *Maturitas* 7, 249–57.

Featherstone, M. and Hepworth, M. (1986) 'New lifestyles for old age?', in Phillipson, C., Bernard, M., Strang, P. (eds) *Dependency and Independency in Old Age*, London: Croom Helm.

Featherstone, M. and Hepworth, M. (1991) 'The mask of ageing and the postmodern life course', in Featherstone, M., Hepworth, M., Turner, B.S. (eds) *The Body: social process and cultural theory*, London: Sage.

Greer, G. (1991) *The Change: women, ageing and the menopause*, London: Hamish Hamilton.

Gullette, M.M. (1993) 'Creativity, ageing, gender: a study of their intersections, 1910–1935', in Wyatt-Brown, A.M. and Rossen J. (eds) *Ageing and Gender in Literature: studies in creativity*, Charlottesville, VA and London: University Press of Virginia.

Gullette, M.M. (1997) *Declining to Decline: cultural combat and the politics of the midlife*, Charlottesville, VA and London: University Press of Virginia.

Hearn, J. (1995) 'Imaging the ages of men', in Featherstone, M. and Wernick, A. (eds) *Images of Ageing: cultural representations of later life*, London and New York: Routledge.

Hepworth, M. and Featherstone, M. (1982) *Surviving Middle Age*, Oxford: Basil Blackwell.

Hill, A.M. (1993) *Viropause/Andropause: the male menopause – emotional and physical changes midlife men experience*, Far Hills, NJ: New Horizon Press.

Hughes, A. and Witz, A. (1997) 'Feminism and the matter of bodies: from de Beauvoir to Butler', *Body and Society* **3**, 1, 47–60.

Jacques, E. (1965) 'Death and the midlife crisis', *International Journal of Psychoanalysis* **46**, 502–14.

Kern, S. (1975) *Anatomy and Destiny: a cultural history of the human body*, Indianapolis, IN: Bobbs-Merrill.

Kitzinger, S. (1985) *Woman's Experience of Sex*, Harmondsworth: Penguin.

Kunzle, D. (1982) *Fashion and Fetishism: a social history of the corset, tight-lacing and other forms of body-sculpture in the west*, Totowa, NJ: Rowman and Littlefield.

Levinson, D. (1978) *The Seasons of a Man's Life*, New York: Knopf.

Lodge, D. (1995) *Therapy: a novel*, London: Secker and Warburg.

Martin, E. (1989) *The Woman in the Body: a cultural analysis of reproduction*, Milton Keynes: Open University Press.

Mills, C.W. (1959) *The Sociological Imagination*. London: Oxford University Press.

Nead, L. (1992) *The Female Nude: art, obscenity and sexuality*, London and New York: Routledge.

Neustatter, A. (1996) *Looking the Demon in the Eye: the challenge of midlife*, London: Joseph.

Pfeffer, N. (1985) 'The hidden pathology of the male reproductive system', in Homans, H. (ed.) *The Sexual Politics of Reproduction*, Aldershot: Gower.

Roberts, A. (1995) 'Secret Lodge', *Evening Standard* 4 May: 28.

Rogers, L. (1995) 'Menopausal men to get HRT patches', *Sunday Times*, 8 October.

Rothfield, P. (1997) 'Menopausal embodiment', in Komesaroff, P., Rothfield, P., Daly, J. (eds) *Reinterpreting Menopause: cultural and philosophical issues*, New York and London: Routledge.

Sheehy, G. (1976) *Passages: predictable crises of adult life*, London: Corgi.

Sheehy, G. (1993) 'The unspeakable passage: is there a male menopause?', *Vanity Fair* April: 72–5, 118–26.

Sheehy, G. (1995) *The Silent Passage*, revised edn, New York: Pocket Books.

Shildrick, M. (1997) *Leaky Bodies and Boundaries: feminism, postmodernism and (bio)ethics*, London: Routledge.

Vincent, S. (1994) 'The men in menopause', *Guardian Weekend*, 23 April: 18–23.

Vines, G. (1993) *Raging Hormones*, London: Virago.

Walker, A.E. (1997) *The Menstrual Cycle*, New York and London: Routledge.

Wei Leng, Kwok (1996) 'On menopause and cyborgs: or towards a feminist cyborg politics of menopause', *Body and Society* 2, 3, 33–52.

Wilbush, J. (1979) 'La menespausie: the birth of a syndrome', *Maturitas* 1, 145–51.

Yardley, L. (eds) (1997) 'Introducing material-discursive approaches to health and illness', in *Material Discourses of Health and Illness*, London and New York: Routledge.

Index